"When I dine at Noble [...] little detail was desig[...] the same about read[...] Beginners just getting acquainted with fine wine? Experts who know more than they need to? This book is a treat!"
KERMIT LYNCH

"What a spectacular journey Dan and Mark are taking us on: first as a magazine and a restaurant, and now in *Wine from Another Galaxy*. Serious yet never dry, knowledgeable but inclusive, I never knew wine writing could be so personal and personable."
YOTAM OTTOLENGHI

"If you're a current or aspiring *bon vivant* this is the only book you need. It takes you on a journey of pure pleasure."
KEIRA KNIGHTLEY

"It always fills me with joy to sit in the window table at Noble Rot over a long lunch, but now it is possible to have more of it. *Wine from Another Galaxy* will surely propel one well into the dinner hour – and beyond."
SIMON HOPKINSON

WINE FROM ANOTHER GALAXY

Noble Rot

Dan Keeling and Mark Andrew

QUADRILLE

CONTENTS

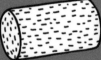

Foreword

A BLACK ASTON MARTIN pulls into The Sportsman car park and people's heads turn. Although the pub has a car park full of smart cars, and even helicopters are known to land in the field opposite, people's heads are always turned by an Aston. Someone from front-of-house comes into the kitchen and points out that the occupant of the passenger seat is my cousin Naomi. That comes as no surprise because Naomi is funny, smart and has a cool job in the music industry. She was always going to drive around in a car like that. "Wanker", we say to the male half of the golden couple as they walk past the window. It's nothing personal; it's how we deal with other people's success in England.

I was busy cooking so all I heard was, "Blah blah blah, head of Island Records, signed Coldplay", and didn't think anything more of it. A few Christmases later and my Uncle Hugh, Naomi's dad, has organised a big family gathering at the pub. It's there that I first speak to Dan Keeling, and realise that he's into wine. I meet lots of people who are into wine and once we've discussed Burgundy producers, I'm usually disappointed. It's no different to talking about bands. If you liked the New York Dolls, I would test you on Downliners Sect. If you knew them, we could be friends. But every time I threw out a name he knew who I was talking about.

"Raveneau."

"I love the way they use old oak barrels to give their Chablis a bit of richness without making it taste like high-toast young Puligny."

"Rousseau."

"Lovely – old school in a really good way. Although their 'Clos de la Roche' is overrated."

I couldn't shake him. His wine knowledge was really good and he dropped all the right restaurant names. I took him into my cellar and showed him my stash: Cathiard, Leroy, Leflaive – all the other names. The names that tell me someone thinks along the same lines as me. You see, it wasn't about the price back then – these wines were £40 a bottle at most – it was about the right producers, just as it used to be about the right bands. As the years went by, the record industry tanked and Dan found something else to do. He decided to start a wine fanzine with his friend Mark Andrew. I didn't want to be a doom-monger, but when he asked if I would contribute it felt mean to point out that I'd contributed to the first issue of another friend's food fanzine that had failed. It simply wasn't a model that could work. I expect that you've rumbled that the fanzine was *Noble Rot*, and so what do I know?

As you'll see in this book, they write about the wines they love and want to investigate further, rather than engage in some mutual back-scratching exercise with the industry. I'd become cynical about much wine writing because it seemed that many journalists were close to the producers, and much was left unsaid in exchange for continued access. I don't care if a *négociant* has made a trip financially possible; I want to know whether their wines are up to snuff. I want to read the honest, raw but poetic thoughts of a couple of very knowledgeable wine obsessives, and this is what *Noble Rot* and now *Wine from Another Galaxy* gives me.

Dan introduced me to Mark, and I had never met anyone who spoke about wine with such clarity, enthusiasm and knowledge. He has a rare ability, in the wine world, to wear his vast knowledge lightly, and it comes all wrapped up in an attractive Mancunian accent. I shouldn't have been surprised when he became a Master of Wine. Other people I knew had looked at that particular cliff face and not even attempted to climb it, but not Mark.

On regular visits to The Sportsman the two Rotters introduced me to the wines of the Jura – I'd been cooking with Vin Jaune for years but had missed the rise of this previously unfashionable region – and taught me new names such as Ganevat, Overnoy and Tissot. The magazine went from strength to strength as Dan got better writers to contribute and by issue five I was really impressed. I trusted their knowledge and was learning so much about different regions that it became a treat when the new issue turned up – a bit like waiting for the new *NME* to arrive back in the '70s. They started to win awards and I thought that was it.

Then one day the phone rang. "Hi Steve, it's Dan. We want to open a Noble Rot wine bar." I thought: Oh Jesus, why ruin everything? But instead said: "Let me know when you do and I'll help with the food 'cos you might fuck it up." I assumed a wine bar couldn't be that tricky; some good olives, ham and bread, and that should do. Then the phone rang again: "Hi Steve, it's Dan. We've found an 85-cover Parisian-style restaurant and wine bar that's perfect, but it's going to have to be proper to make it pay." This was the last thing I wanted to hear, but I couldn't have Naomi married to the owner of a failed restaurant.

I introduced Dan and Mark to Paul Weaver who would become head chef, and came up with some ideas to angle the food towards the wine. The first week was stressful, as all launches are, but all they needed from me was a bit of guidance. I was very proud of the wine list, as it didn't just concentrate on the top names. Every wine was real and carefully considered. It's easy to put together your fantasy list with endless vintages of the greats that nobody can afford, but can you come up with one that's good value? Great wines from less fashionable areas are there to be found, but few can be bothered to find them.

Every time I walk into Noble Rot I get a good feeling. They've gone from strength to strength, winning awards left, right and centre: best wine list at the National Restaurant Awards three years in a row, and even a gong at the World Restaurant Awards. They are always thinking up new ideas and I find it hard to keep up with what they want to do next. Indeed, just this week the phone rang again. "Hi Steve, it's Dan. We're writing a book – would you mind…?"

Stephen Harris, Seasalter, Kent, 2020

Above: Dan Keeling (left)
and Mark Andrew.

Introduction

I'M NOT SURE whether I believe in a single moment of revelation that sparks a fascination with wine. Such epiphanies often sound overly romanticised when, more likely, it's an ongoing series of everyday illuminations that inspires vinous thirst. Indeed, as you read these words somebody, somewhere is in the magnificent shock of a wine's perfume. Because even if you think you know that Barolo smells of roses and tar, or Chablis tastes like it has trickled through ancient oyster beds, great bottles always have an originality that begs the question: how can this be made just from grapes? But while I won't point to one moment when wine blossomed from being just another avenue of inebriation into an eye-rolling, table-thumping, multi-dimensional, holy-mother-of-Christ-I-love-this experience, I can say that one of many powerful early insights for me was the way 2005 Ridge 'Lytton Springs' combined savouriness with ultra-vivid fruit.

At the time I was working in music as Managing Director of Island Records on Kensington High Street in London, having recently been enticed away from a job as Head of A&R ('artist and repertoire') at rival label Parlophone. Things were going swimmingly, or so it seemed. I just needed to find some new multi-million-selling talent, and fast. So, I did what any under-pressure, overpaid 30-year-old in their right mind would do, and began spending more of my time in Roberson, the wine merchant next door. Although far from knowledgeable, I'd always had an inkling, as you probably do, that there is something extraordinary waiting to be discovered in wine, and I was encouraged in my explorations by my friend Nick Burton, who managed the shop and gave me the Ridge, and Mark Andrew, a young Mancunian he employed.

All wine lovers prize a fellow enthusiast with whom to explore precious bottles, and when on first meeting I asked Mark whether he preferred drinking Sauvignon Blanc from the Loire Valley or New Zealand, and he answered, "That's like asking if I prefer kissing pretty girls or ugly girls", I knew we'd become great friends. He was a little further into his vinous infatuation than I was, having fallen for a Denis Bachelet Gevrey-Chambertin a couple of years earlier, and when he began organising evening tastings of classic wines in Roberson's basement I became a regular guest. Coche-Dury Meursault, Jean-Louis Chave Hermitage, Grange des Pères, the Léovilles and more – looking back, our old tasting sheets read like a who's who of top domaines, and even when experienced luminaries such as Michael Broadbent or Jancis Robinson appeared in the audience, Mark hosted masterfully. This guy had more front than Blackpool Pleasure Beach. I was impressed.

Soon, we began drinking together after work. We'd pay corkage to open our own bottles at The Mall Tavern in Notting Hill, and educate our palates with a succession of benchmarks. Château Rayas 'Pignan', Freddie Mugnier Chambolle-Musigny 1er Cru 'Les Fuées', Lenoir Chinon 'Les Roches' – formative tastes and textures came thick and fast as we dug deeper into French wine culture. We'd devour books such as Kermit Lynch's *Adventures on the Wine Route*, Clive Coates' *The Wines of Burgundy* and Michael Broadbent's *Vintage Wine*, then plot ways to drink the bottles they celebrated. We toasted the birth of my son Arthur with Krug 1988 – the most delicious Champagne I've tasted – and marvelled over Selosse 'Substance' while watching Bayern Munich beat Borussia Dortmund in the Champions League final. Wine made us happy, inquisitive, confused, benevolent and sad (when it was out of condition), and inspired us to start *Noble Rot* to chart those feelings.

After a few years of publishing the magazine the lure of the wine life proved stronger than chasing past glories in music, and Mark and I opened Noble Rot wine bar and restaurant on Lamb's Conduit Street in Bloomsbury. While today independent publishing is a niche activity, *Noble Rot* has opened many doors that might previously have remained shut, and enabled us to tell the stories behind the wines we adore. From the renaissance of organic viticulture and the rejuvenation of abandoned vineyards everywhere from Mount Etna to Ribeira Sacra, to the legendary vintages of Bordeaux and Burgundy, *Wine from Another Galaxy* is our celebration of European wine culture. As fellow Bloomsbury-ite Virginia Woolf once wrote: "The great revelation perhaps never did come. Instead there were little daily miracles, illuminations, matches struck unexpectedly in the dark." That's exactly how we feel.

1

SHRINE TO THE VINE

GETTING ROTTEN

ARE YOU EVER really 'ready' to do anything in life? Are you ever 'ready' to push off and ride a bicycle for the first time; begin speaking a foreign language to a bemused local; launch your own business; have children and settle down? Although we all can procrastinate about starting anything, often because of the very logical reasons never to do it, now is generally as good a time as any to begin. And so it was in February 2013 when, lacking any practical experience of publishing a magazine, we launched the first issue of *Noble Rot* under the legend 'WINE MUSIC FOOD LIFE'. Nabokov, eat your heart out.

At the time Mark and I were fans of several beautifully produced indie magazines such as *The Ride* and *Fire & Knives*, which had, in true DIY spirit, inspired us to ask: "If they can do it, why can't we?" In the mid-'90s while studying art at Manchester Metropolitan University I'd written about music for *Melody Maker*, *i-D* and *Jockey Slut* magazines, while Mark, through laying out brochures for his regular tastings at Roberson, where he'd now been promoted to Head Buyer, knew how to use InDesign. What did we have to lose? Besides, we'd recently been to a *Guardian* masterclass about how to start an independent magazine and were convinced we were set to become wine's answer to News Corp.

"Do interesting things and interesting things will happen to you" is one of advertising creative – and Noble Rot regular – Sir John Hegarty's maxims that particularly chimed with us as a reason to start a magazine, although quite how interesting remained to be seen. Having read somewhere that Mike D of rap royalty the Beastie Boys was a fully paid-up wino with a passion for Raveneau Chablis, I contacted him with some interview questions which, quite surprisingly, he swiftly returned. *Noble Rot* – a wine term we liked the sound of because it juxtaposed contrasting words in a vaguely Stone Roses fashion – was on. Stephen Harris contributed his recipe for the Kentish school dinner standard Gypsy Tart, Mark wrote about the true-life attempted blackmail of Domaine de la Romanée-Conti, and I paired records with wines (try playing Kraftwerk's 'Computer World' while drinking 2007 Keller Riesling 'Kirchspiel' *Grosses Gewachs* for size).

For the cover we doctored the artwork of a long-out-of-copyright French novel that I'd found in a vintage bookshop in Beaune, and Mark laid out the text on his Flintstones-era PC, sparsely interspersed with crude black-and-white images found online. We were just about to send the files to the printers when we came to our senses: a new indie magazine without beautiful artwork? What were we thinking? And, more importantly, what did we know about magazine design? So, I asked for help from long-time family friend Mick Dean, who, as well as once being an advertising photographer and now a painter, had helped fuel my vinous infatuation. Taking simple set-up shots of wine bottles, 12-inch records and a replica blackmail note on his dining-room table, we created imagery for the first issue.

Printing 1000 copies cost us £500, which we hand-numbered in gold marker and set about distributing (yet another activity that we had absolutely no idea how to do). And if you've ever had to carry cumbersome boxes of magazines between potential stockists around London, you'll know what a thankless task it can be. But at least we had purposefully made the magazines small to take up the least amount of space possible on wine-shop counters, and gave away the first issue to an enthusiastic response. Particularly heartening was an offer from artist Louise Sheeran, who was working as a waitress at one of our earliest stockists, Brawn on Columbia Road, to illustrate the second instalment. Not only did she create beautiful images of fish in wine glasses for the cover and David Motion's article about wine and food pairing, but she also agreed to produce them as three limited-edition screen prints that we could offer as rewards for a Kickstarter crowdfunding campaign. Kickstarter fundraisers set a financial target they aim to achieve for a project, produce a video about

Left: Hand-numbering issue one.

Above: Interviewing James Murphy and tasting Jura wines, 16 December 2013. Left to right, James Murphy, Dan, Mark and James Righton.

how they'll spend it, and offer incentives for people to back it. If the campaign doesn't reach the target within a month, it doesn't receive any money; fortunately, we hit our £11,000 target within two weeks. *Noble Rot* was solvent and had a few readers, at the very least.

Issue two featured wine terrorism in southern France, German Riesling, Coldplay's Will Champion, and an article by Skint Records founder Damian Harris, chef Stephen's brother, about how the hedonistic dance-music generation had become interested in gastronomy in middle age. The piece was accompanied by a photo of Damian's friend Norman Cook cooking a paella in Ibiza. 'Replacing the Rave' could well have made an apt alternative title to *Noble Rot*, while contributor John Niven proposed the slightly less catchy 'We used to like drugs but now we're into food and wine'.

In issue three, we featured singer Lily Allen and Californian author and importer Kermit Lynch, while issue four centred on a tasting of Jura wines with James Murphy of LCD Soundsystem, and marked the first time Mark and I visited a wine region together. Maybe it was the waves of freezing sleet and oxidative yellow wine at the 2014 Percée du Vin Jaune festival that invigorated our senses, but we returned from the Jura with the ambition of opening a Noble Rot restaurant, having quickly discarded our initial idea of 'Bourguignon', a Burgundy-themed wine bar (I still want to go).

Now I was really out of my depth. But while my hospitality experience was largely confined to squandering record-company expenses on artists at Le Gavroche and Nobu around the time that Boris Becker was procreating with one of the waitresses in a store cupboard, Mark had managed a busy music-industry pub on the Harrow Road, the William IV, before taking the job at Roberson. Citing such personal claims to fame as the time Liam Gallagher leaned over the counter and licked his face while he was serving him a round of drinks, at least one of us had had a job involving customer satisfaction. We soon organised a pop-up 'Drinking Club' at Stevie Parle's Dock Kitchen in Ladbroke Grove as our first foray into hospitality. Writing a list full of mature classics from Quintarelli and Château Palmer to top natural wines by Philippe Bornard and Testalonga, we hosted a full house of *Rot* readers and friends, and even turned a small profit. The following year we continued practising for our own place with 'Big Bottles Taste Better', a magnum party at Mission in Bethnal Green, and hosting Burgundy and Bordeaux lunches at The Clove Club in Shoreditch.

By this time, I was much more excited about wine and food than working in mainstream music. Seeing portraits of *vignerons* adorning the walls of Terroirs in Covent Garden or the uber-stylish interiors and ethos of Paris's Vivant and Clown Bar reminded me of the early indie spirit of labels such as Rough Trade Records and Junior Boy's Own, an authentic culture at odds with the emerging pop-dominated middle ground. Mark and I both passed the

Previous pages: *Noble Rot* magazine has featured (left page) Yotam Ottolenghi, Mike D, Jay McInerney, Hot Chip, Hugh Johnson, Jancis Robinson, Nigella Lawson, Fergus Henderson, Richard Russell of XL Records, Victor Arguinzoniz of Etxebarri, Shaun Keaveny, James Murphy, David Shrigley; (right page) Madlib, Brian Eno, Albert Roux, Keira Knightley, Caitlin Moran, Ralph Steadman, Giorgio Locatelli, Nigel Slater, Mark Ronson, Jean-Marc Roulot and Rodolphe Péters, Simon Hopkinson, Baxter Dury and Otto Tepasse.

Overleaf: Interviewing
Brian Eno at his London
studio, 1 December 2014.

degree-like WSET Diploma in wine, which he later took to the next level
by gaining the notoriously rigorous Master of Wine qualification, but we needed
more practical hospitality experience before turning *Noble Rot* into a business.
Although a good home cook, I'd never been in a professional restaurant kitchen,
so I did two 'stages' of three days each with Stephen Harris and Head Chef
Dan Flavell at The Sportsman in Seasalter, learning to make pommes Anna
and to dispatch crabs, and took a part-time job at Handford Wines in South
Kensington to learn how retail worked. There's nothing quite like going from
running a record company to serving on a shop counter to give your ego a trim.

Back at the magazine we featured a Champagne tasting with Fergus
Henderson and Trevor Gulliver at St John in issue number five, while in
number six we interviewed artist David Shrigley, researched Parisian wine bars,
and unwittingly upped our aesthetic thanks to magCulture's Jeremy Leslie.
We'd met Jeremy at *that Guardian* masterclass and, with shared passions for
music and football, kept in contact. So when, out of the blue, he offered to help
us develop our design, we knew we were on to a very good thing. Redefining
the layout templates, fonts and logo, Jeremy helped elevate *Noble Rot*'s aesthetic
from issues six to nine, which also featured specials on Burgundy, California
and English sparkling wine, as well as interviews with Mark Ronson and one
of our all-time inspirations, Brian Eno. Soon, with Stephen Harris signed
up as executive chef, we wrote a business plan and began meeting potential
investors. Marina O'Loughlin, now *The Sunday Times'* restaurant critic,
had been an early supporter and took a consultancy role, and the remaining
shares were bought by friends and acquaintances. But were we 'ready'
to become restaurateurs? Now was as good a time as any to find out.

Feeling Hospitable

THE RESTAURANT BUSINESS is tough. René Redzepi called it "brutal", while Anthony Bourdain said it was "good for pounding humility into you permanently". Maybe that's got something to do with why eight out of ten restaurants fail within the first five years or how, post-Britain leaving the EU, good staff are now at a premium. But for some, the dream of opening their own place is hard to shake. Yes, it is all-consuming. Yes, it is difficult and stressful. But you want a tasty dinner, don't you?

From the moment we started planning Noble Rot restaurant, we were riding the proverbial emotional rollercoaster. Having raised investment in a high of enthusiasm, we were brought crashing back down to earth by London's ruthless property market. Then, just as we began to wonder if a condemned ex-kebab shop at the end of the Piccadilly Line was our only option, we found Vats, a wine bar that appeared to be stuck in a time warp *circa* 1985, on Lamb's Conduit Street in Bloomsbury. Surrounded by a florist, an undertaker, a couple of traditional pubs, some excellent independent clothes shops – and with not a Starbucks or Costa in sight – Vats was perfect: a Grade II-listed townhouse from 1701 that had been converted into a wine bar in the early 1970s by a descendant of Admiral Nelson.

After looking around the property on the pretext of needing a venue for a birthday, we found the licensee's details online, and sent a flattering letter to him via a taxi driver later that afternoon asking if he'd sell. It was a long shot, as Vats wasn't even on the market. Then the phone rang. "I've already got an offer, so if you're serious you need to move fast," said David Allcorn, the Roger Moore-esque owner. Knowing how much we loved the place, we quickly agreed a deal, and took possession of the keys in October 2015. Vats' closing party was a bittersweet, raucous affair, with Allcorn's colourful community of old-school lawyers, gangsters, advertising executives and wine merchants making merry long into the night.

We needed to transform Vats into Noble Rot wine bar and restaurant as quickly as possible to take advantage of the Christmas period, or miss a large part of our first-year turnover. This meant postponing most of our redecoration until January, and opening Noble Rot like a permanent pop-up complete with chintzy vineyard murals and nicotine stains, while interior designers Steven

Opposite: Staff outside 51 Lamb's Conduit Street, London, *circa* 2016.

Saunders and Tom Strother of Fabled Studio planned the renovation. With the brief of keeping as many period features as possible, Fabled Studio impressed us both with its sympathetic touch and willingness to work with a threadbare budget. However, we had another pressing matter at hand: staff.

Hiring and training front-of-house and kitchen teams in such a short time was a challenge. Of course, we wouldn't have had the courage to open a fully grown-up restaurant without our executive chef, Stephen Harris, through whom we hired our head chef, Paul Weaver, who had worked for him at The Sportsman and, more recently, at St John Bread & Wine. Together, Stephen and Paul are a winning combination with complementary talents and skills: Stephen, a creative genius, is in his element deconstructing why dishes work or dreaming up fresh ideas, while Paul is a master craftsman, consistently turning out plate after plate of delicious food, and enthusiastically participating in London's flourishing restaurant scene on his days off. Another friend recommended Ollie McSwiney as general manager, another great hire and still our trusted lieutenant today, and the rest of the team fell into place. We're very proud that several Rotters who were with us on our launch – Paisley Kennett, Caprice Whitford and Charlie Blightman – are all still senior managers.

We opened on 13 November 2015, and served over a thousand customers a week over the next few months. An early four-star review from Fay Maschler in the *Evening Standard* was a lovely moment, followed by glowing appraisals from Giles Coren in *The Times* ("It's dark enough to pass out here over Thursday lunch and not be found until after the weekend"), Grace Dent in *ES Magazine* and, most nerve-racking of all, the late AA Gill, who used our bread board as a metaphor to argue against the impending Brexit vote. Since then, Noble Rot

Opposite, above: Noble Rot Bloomsbury was an electrical engineers from 1946 until 1973, when it was converted into a wine bar.

Opposite, below: Vats wine bar reference photo from when we were scouting potential premises, August 2015.

Right: "Your name's not down, you're not coming in." The Veuve Clicquot chewing bulldog was the cover of issue nine, which included a tasting of English sparkling wine vs. Champagne.

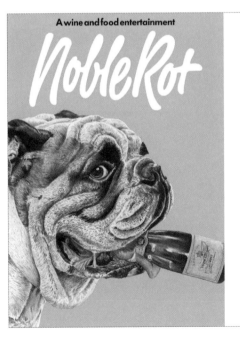

A wine and food entertainment

NobleRot

We're having a house warming and you're invited!

Join Noble Rot Magazine to celebrate the opening of Noble Rot Restaurant & Wine Bar on Thursday 12th November 2015, from 7pm on.

Chefs Stephen Harris and Paul Weaver will be in the kitchen, editors Dan Keeling, Mark Andrew and The Rotters pouring the wines...

RSVP essential:
Lisa@noblerot.co.uk

Noble Rot
51 Lamb's Conduit St
London WC1N 8NB

noblerot.co.uk
hello@noblerot.co.uk

Noble Rot Magazine is the home of exciting wine and food writing. Since 2013 it has seen chefs Fergus Henderson, Honey & Co and Stephen Harris rubbing shoulders with artists like Brian Eno, Mark Ronson and David Shrigley, blurring the boundaries between gastronomy and the creative arts.

has won 'Wine List of the Year' at the National Restaurant Awards three consecutive times (in '16, '17 and '18), and 'Red Wine Serving Restaurant' at the 2019 World Restaurant Awards. (Although we're rather partial to white, rosé and amber wine, too, of course.)

With some serendipity, 13 November was also the date in 2019 when we signed the lease of 2 Greek Street – formerly the site of the famous Gay Hussar. With its intimate Orient Express-style wood-panelled dining room, the restaurant was long a popular haunt of left-wing politicians, including Michael Foot and former Prime Ministers Gordon Brown and Clement Attlee, the latter being a regular at its pre-1956 Yugoslavian incarnation, Josef. The Gay Hussar closed its doors in summer 2018, and for us the opportunity to become the custodians of such a precious piece of Soho heritage was too good to turn down. Keeping much of the original interior, we commissioned sainted political cartoonist and Hussar devotee Martin Rowson, who drew the famous portraits of regulars who used to hang there, to create paintings for the first-floor dining room. To have the run of the atmospheric private dining room – the site of many illicit liaisons over the years – is a thrill, providing us with a perfect place for tastings and celebrations. If only its walls could speak.

Above: Mark and Dan outside pre-renovation Gay Hussar, Soho, 13 November 2019.

Opposite: Gay Hussar, *circa* 1975.

Pur Sang;

Pessac-Léognan

Vin Jaune; Jura '09

Oro; Languedoc '02

Nuits-St-Georges 1er 'Aux Bousset...

Hermitage La Chapelle; N...

Montebello; Santa Cruz Mour...

Evangile, Pomerol; Bordeaux

VDP des Bouches de

Where Everybody Knows Your Name

Marina O'Loughlin

THERE'S A WINE LIST at Noble Rot, a thing of beauty: heavy paper, thick black linen covers tooled in silver, a reproduction of one of their magazine's best covers. Inside lives an adventure – wines from everywhere in the world: classics, grand cuvées, eccentric off-piste natural producers. Grapes range from the instantly recognisable Chardonnay and Pinot Noir to the obscure Asprouda and Pignolo, to make even someone who has dedicated their life to the vine scratch her head in confusion. But despite many visits to Noble Rot – many, many visits – I've never opened it once.

Here's my schtick: every time I go I say to one of the lovely staff, "Bring me something white, cold and delicious that doesn't cost very much." This has introduced me to a new bottle of joy each and every time. Smoky Assyrtiko from Santorini, the island's volcanic rock delivering seductive minerality; Pecorino from Abruzzo, with a bouquet like an autumn fruit basket; Chablis with a fleeting back note of orange rinds, tasting as though it costs way, way more than it does. Yes, I know it has won the World Restaurant Award for serving the best reds, but we all have our predilections.

Noble Rot is one of my favourite places on the planet. Of course, there's the shallow reason: for someone who plies the peculiar trade of anonymous restaurant critic for *The Sunday Times*, it's the rarest of pleasures to walk into a restaurant and be known. It makes me understand and appreciate the very real delight of being a regular. But more than that, it always seems to be the place to be, whatever my mood. When just out to have fun, there's gluggable, affordable Vinho Verde by the bottleful and bar food: fat merguez sausages; octopus, punchy with smoked pimentón; silky *Ibérico de bellota* that floods your palate with fragrant, melting fat; and, of course, the famous bread: airy, oily focaccia with rosemary, elastic-crumbed sourdough, treacly soda bread. Or for different, more serious fun, there's the hidden restaurant at the back, perfect for losing whole afternoons, coming out blinking to discover it has somehow got dark outside while you've been ordering another glass of Simon Bize Savigny-lès-Beaune to go with thick, rosy slabs of hogget, almost gamey and slicked with a vivid salsa verde, or the luxury of the turbot in oxidised

Bâtard-Montrachet, a dish that started as an experiment in repurposing the mercurial wine and has now become a signature. I love the apparent simplicity of every menu: this is a kitchen confident in its own abilities. It never feels the need to slavishly follow trends or drone on about provenance and ingredients – even though you know that the work has very much been put in. It's food that's as timeless as it is delicious.

There was a weird serendipity to my becoming involved with Noble Rot's owners, Dan and Mark. They had launched their initial magazine Kickstarter crowdfunder at a time when I was indulging in a spot of paying it forward, and the idea of a publication designed to celebrate and demystify wine appealed enormously. From the first issue, I felt as though it spoke to me, as someone more enthusiastic about wine than knowledgeable. And it did so with wit and brio and without ever talking down. So I bunged them the huge amount of 50 quid and didn't give it much more thought. Then when they announced they were looking for investment to open a restaurant, it was at a time in my life when I was wondering what I was going to do when I grew up. So, I bunged in a little bit more and offered my services. I wanted to be part of it, even if only in the most minimal way, which, if I'm honest, has so far mostly involved dragging people down to the place and watching in glee as they fell in love with it, too.

I love that the restaurant on Lamb's Conduit Street operates almost like an insiders' secret. Sometimes you can walk into the bar mid-afternoon and it seems sleepy and quiet, but a contented, wine-fuelled rumble from the back tells you that business is being discreetly conducted over an emollient glass or two, friendships are being cemented, and romances are sparking into life in a room full of people. It's refreshingly resistant to cliques and tribes: any evening here will see groups of cashmere-clad senior legal eagles from the nearby Inns of Court; real-life rock and film stars; earnest junior doctors; cool young women from publishing; wine spods of all denominations, a gleam of sheer jubilation in their eyes. It's such a clever place, its style as organic as its menu. You can tell immediately that this is not a business that has first been incubated or plotted in a board-room.

When the odd person waxes snarky at the idea of a restaurant critic having an interest in a restaurant, it makes me laugh. I wish I could take any kind of credit for the place: for the design, for the menus, for finding the luminous Paisley who works the room like a Scottish angel, making everyone feel like they're the most important person in the place (all the staff, in fact, have a way of making us all feel uniquely welcome). For the wine; dear god, the wine. I wish I could say yep, folks, it's all mine. But I can't. I can only admire.

My association with Noble Rot may be minor, but it feels as though it was meant to be. The Sportsman in Seasalter – a "grotty run-down pub by the sea" as it styles itself way too self-deprecatingly – has always topped my list of best restaurants, its owner Stephen Harris one of the only chefs I know in real life. The involvement of Harris and that of his alumnus Paul Weaver as head chef gave me the greenest of lights. Of course, I've never been able to review Noble Rot, but since its opening I've been thrilled by those who have, by praise from hard-to-please critics such as Fay Maschler, Giles Coren and the late AA Gill. Now I'm delighted to have the opportunity to do it here, in a different way. It'll come as no surprise that it's a rave. So much so that since my first trip, I've had to ration visits like a teenager in the grips of a powerful crush.

Dan and Mark's strength as restaurateurs is that they aren't restaurateurs. They've created the kind of place they'd like to use, rather than one designed to tumesce accountants. At least, not from a spreadsheet perspective. Much of its allure seems accidental: the beautiful architectural eccentricities of the early 18th-century building; the idea to use the covers of the magazine as artworks; the relaxed, non-uniform staff uniform. When I first properly met the pair, I'd been out for a ridiculously long lunch elsewhere that had culminated in my hurtling pissedly down the Carsten Höller slide installation attached to the Tate Modern. So I found it difficult to remember which chap was which. I tried ham-fistedly to make the 'right' noises about the wine they'd chosen, discern the tasting notes, identify the grape. Kindly, they laughed at me: this sort of performative, exclusionary wine bollocks has never been what Noble Rot is about. They're as welcoming to my 'gimme something cheap and delicious' demands as they are to the deepest-pocketed, Margaux-marinated wine buffs.

Miraculously, they still allowed me to be part of it. The perks have been lavish: an automatic glass of chilled fizz in one of those exquisite Zalto glasses every time I arrive; I can always get a table; and the rare (for me) joy of being in a place where, as the *Cheers* sages said, 'everybody knows your name'. Even if I weren't on the receiving end of all this largesse, it would still be where I always want to find myself. Sorry, guys, you're stuck with me now.

FÊTE DU BEAUJOLAIS

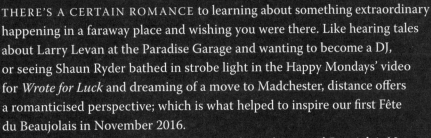

THERE'S A CERTAIN ROMANCE to learning about something extraordinary happening in a faraway place and wishing you were there. Like hearing tales about Larry Levan at the Paradise Garage and wanting to become a DJ, or seeing Shaun Ryder bathed in strobe light in the Happy Mondays' video for *Wrote for Luck* and dreaming of a move to Madchester, distance offers a romanticised perspective; which is what helped to inspire our first Fête du Beaujolais in November 2016.

A few years prior we'd been reading about the annual Beaujolais Nouveau tastings at Paris's Caves Augé on wineterroirs.com, where *vignerons* such as Jean Foillard and Marcel Lapierre would hold court outside the shop on Boulevard Haussmann, smoking cigarettes and pouring wines for customers and friends. It looked a lot of fun and we wished we could be there. So, having just opened Rotter Towers, we organised our own party instead.

Happening every third Thursday in November – the day when Beaujolais Nouveau was historically released and winos would race to deliver it to Paris and London first – our fête is a celebration of Cru Beaujolais, the region's highest-quality classification. Bona fide fine wines with terroir and vintage variations, the cru villages of Fleurie, Morgon, Moulin-à-Vent, Juliénas, Chénas, Chiroubles, Saint-Amour, Régnié, Brouilly and the Côte de Brouilly are a hotbed of organic viticulture, still offering great value when other classic French regions' prices have spiralled. But it's not just Beaujolais' delicious accessibility that we love – it's the *vignerons'* generosity of spirit. As do the roadblock of Rotters who come to drink and make merry with them long into the evening. Over the years we've been joined by many of our favourite producers, including Jean-Louis and Justin Dutraive, David Chapel and Michele Smith Chapel, Julien and Antoine Sunier, Guy Breton, Andrew and Emma Nielsen, Mee Godard and Daniel Bouland.

The fête begins early in the day when the wine-bar tables are replaced with upturned barrels, and gas heaters are stationed on the pavement outside. The restaurant opens at midday as usual, when the first customers begin arriving, followed by guests for our 'Friends & Contributors Lunch'. This is a chance for our writers and winemakers to break bread and relax before the afternoon tasting starts; others, such as Pierre Koffmann, Simon Hopkinson and Rowley Leigh, go further by providing the *menu du jour*. Pierre was our first guest on the stoves in 2016, serving up his famous *pieds de cochon Tante Claire*. Hoppy followed in 2017 and 2018, overseeing classics from his 'Cooking with Wine' column, such as fillet steak with bone marrow and Beaujolais sauce, while Rowley cooked up a Lyonnaise-inspired menu in 2019. Many, many happy calories; long may they continue.

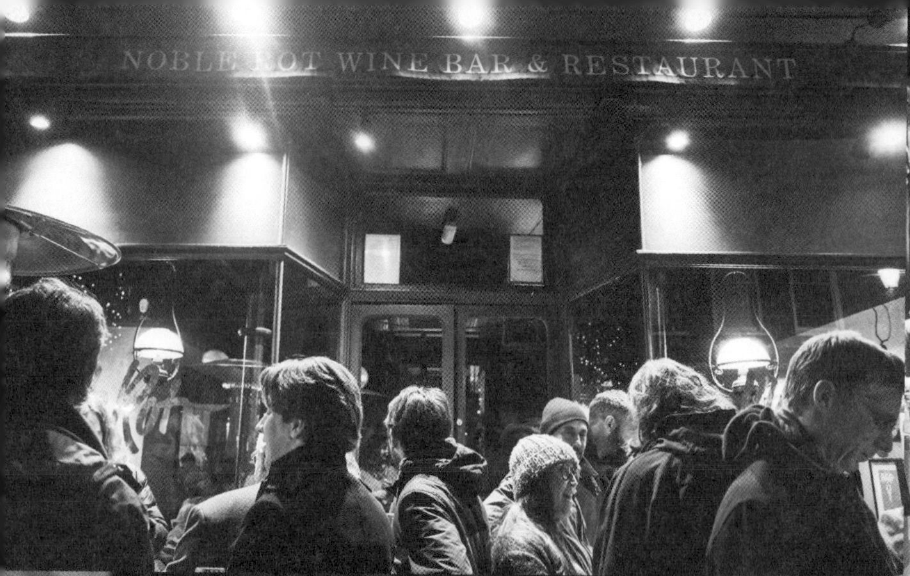
NOBLE ROT WINE BAR & RESTAURANT
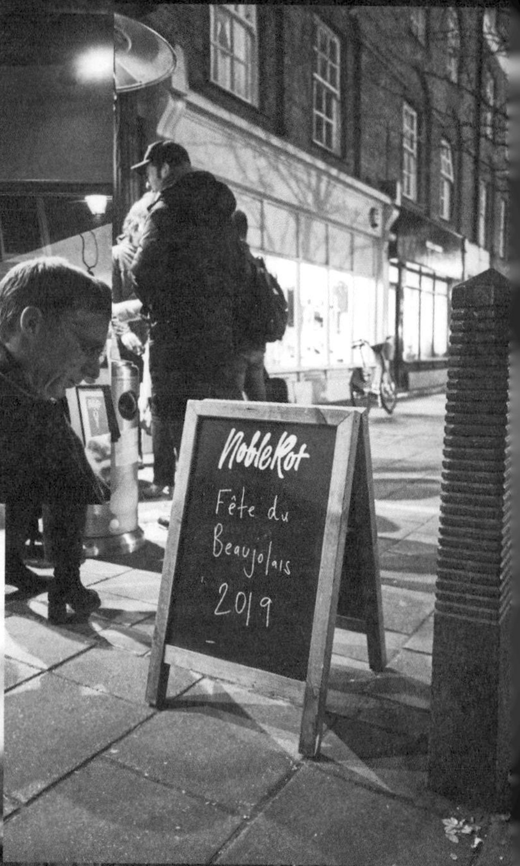
Noble Rot
Fête du
Beaujolais
2019
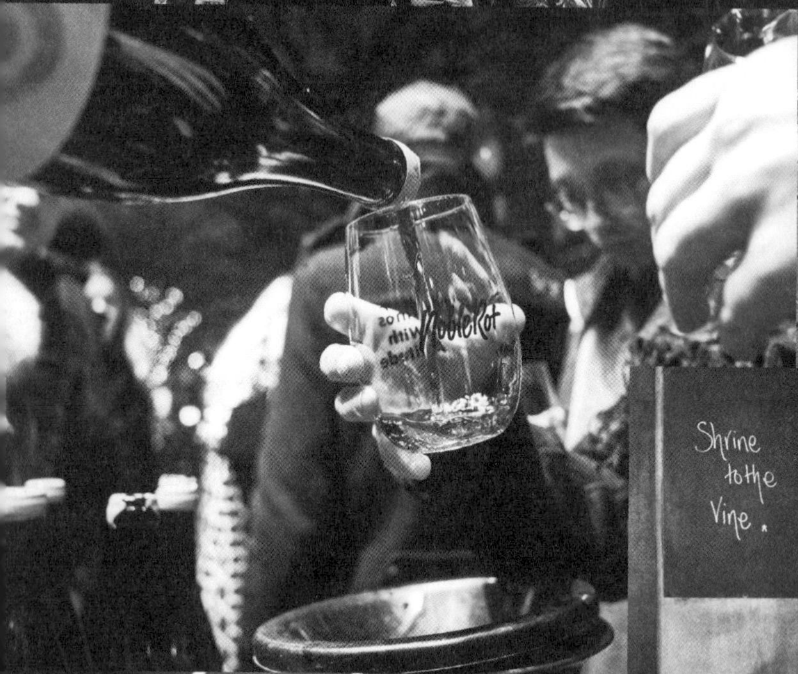
Noble Rot
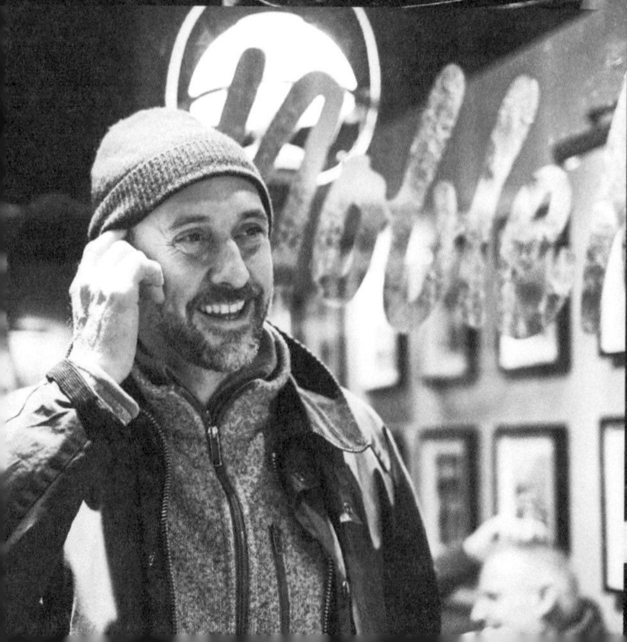
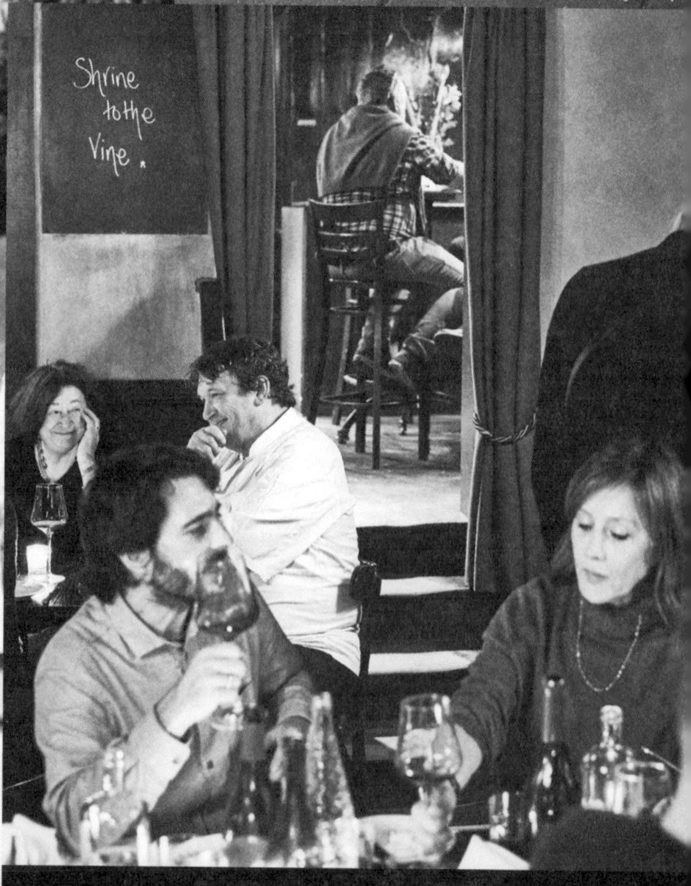
Shrine
to the
Vine

How to Order Wine in a Restaurant Without Fear

YOU'RE OUT FOR DINNER. You've been seated at a *primo* table with good friends. Menus arrive, conversation flows, and no one announces they've turned teetotal, or gluten-free. Life is good. Then someone hands you the wine list. "Here you go love, you know your vino..." The procurement of delicious wine in a restaurant seems such an innocuous task, yet for many world peace seems eminently more achievable. Of course, the sommelier is the key to unlocking the vinous treasures in the cellar: engage them in conversation, tell them how much you want to spend, and they might find you an extraordinary bottle you never knew existed, with a "If you don't like it, I'll drink it" guarantee.

It takes years of experience to order from a restaurant wine list like a lord or lady and, even then, you can often find yourself faced with a directory of unfamiliar names and places. There are, however, strategies that make you more likely to hit the sweet spot of price and deliciousness. Here are our tips, so you can rise to the challenge without regurgitating hoary old clichés such as, "I don't know anything about wine, but I know what I like". Have some self-respect, for Christ's sake.

Cru Beaujolais has become more popular over recent years but is still one of the world's most underappreciated, and thus undervalued, wines. If you're after a crowd-pleasing session red with extra layers of interest, top winemakers in crus such as Morgon, Fleurie and Moulin-à-Vent make profound, food-versatile cuvées with moderate tannins and alcohol. Look for domaines Lapierre, Jean-Paul Thévenet, Guy Breton and Jean Foillard – the 'Gang of Four' who revived artisanal winemaking in the region – and new-school stars such as Domaine de la Grand'Cour, Domaine Chapel, Jules Desjourneys and Yvon Métras.

When ordering Bordeaux you need to be savvy. Anything Robert Parker gave a big score to is routinely inflated, but there's genuine interest in mature First Growth second wines ('Pavillon du Château Margaux', 'Les Forts de Latour'), into which some of the main cuvée may have been declassified in poorer vintages. Other respected Cru Classé châteaux often offer quality and value in less heralded years, such as 1994 or 2002. Quality and value is also to be found in humble outlier AOCs such as Entre-Deux-Mers, Moulis-en-Médoc and the Côtes de Bourg (check out Galouchey, Poujeaux and Roc de Cambes).

A few hundred miles north, the Loire Valley has versatile, food-friendly options: light, thirst-quenching Cabernet Franc from Chinon, Saumur and Bourgueil (Olga Raffault, Dittière, Catherine & Pierre Breton); bracing, mineral Chenin Blanc from Anjou, Vouvray and Saumur again (Richard Leroy, Bernaudeau, Guiberteau); and mineral, refreshing Muscadet from around Nantes, the perfect accompaniment for seafood (Domaine de la Pépière, Pierre Luneau-Papin). Likewise, many Loire crémants (Huet, Vincent Carême) make a laughing stock of industrially produced Prosecco and Champagne.

Reputable non-vintage Champagne is a dependable fall-back when navigating a mediocre list. With production in the millions, it's often possible to find delicious NV Pol Roger, Louis Roederer and Billecart-Salmon. English sparkling wines such as Hambledon or Nyetimber are also worth considering. Better still, when dining somewhere progressive, choose a bottle from the expanding galaxy of Grower Champagne stars (Ulysse Collin, Bérêche, Pierre Baillette). More food-friendly than many people think, these are real fine wines perfectly suited to bookending, or even drinking throughout, a meal.

In Burgundy, humble generic Bourgogne from superstars such as Jean-Marc Roulot or Ghislaine Barthod is a formula for flavour at a fraction of the price of their top crus. Elsewhere, look to the outlier appellations where ripeness and quality have risen: Bouzeron (Ramonet, De Villaine), Hautes-Côtes (Claire Naudin, David Duband), Marsannay (Sylvain Pataille, Joseph Roty), and the Côte Chalonnaise/Mâconnais (Dureuil-Janthial, Les Héritiers du Comte Lafon). There's great value here from *vignerons* squeezing every bit of material from under-appreciated soils.

Another good strategy is to order from places with undeserved naff reputations. German Riesling, adored by legions of sommeliers, offers outstanding options. In the late 19th century, the Fatherland was home to the world's most sought-after wines, something that lakes of bad-quality imitations and a psychopath with a comedy moustache and an amphetamine habit put to an end. Today, powerhouse Rieslings from Koehler-Ruprecht in Pfalz, or light and ethereal Mosel Kabinett from Joh Jos Prüm, are among the most affordable fine wines available. And at circa 8.5% ABV for Prüm Kabinett, you might as well be drinking a health tonic. Which, of course, you are.

On Mount Etna in Sicily, high-elevation slopes and volcanic soil produce smoky, thought-provoking wines (Pietradolce, Graci, Cornelissen), just as they also do in nearby Cerasuolo di Vittoria DOCG (COS, Occhipinti). Marco De Bartoli, on the west coast, makes a dangerously moreish, fortified Marsala for

a fraction of the price of vintage Madeira. In Tuscany, top producers' cheaper
Rosso di Montalcino (Stella di Campalto, Cerbaiona) is accessible earlier
than their lofty Brunello di Montalcino siblings – exactly what you need in
a restaurant setting. Likewise, the easy Dolcetto and Barbera of Piedmontese
stars are made to be enjoyed while their tannic Barolos mellow (Roagna,
G. Rinaldi, B. Mascarello).

Further afield, Eben Sadie has been instrumental in putting new-school
South Africa on the map. His 'Columella' and 'Palladius' blends are bankers,
as are the wines of Alheit Vineyards, Craven and AA Badenhorst: value, value,
value! And if the renaissance of abandoned vineyards full of native varietals
is among the most interesting themes of recent years, so too is the way these
often well-priced wines are appearing in restaurants with increasing regularity.
Whether it's Santorini Assyrtiko (Vassaltis, Argyros), Naoussa Xinomavro
(Dalamára), Tenerife Listán Blanco (Suertes del Marqués) or Sierra de Gredos
Garnacha (Comando G), there's never been a better time to order wine in
a restaurant. Just ask the sommelier.

How Wine is Made

THE FOUNDATIONS OF WINEMAKING are simple. To produce white wines grapes are harvested, crushed and the juice (the 'must') is immediately separated from the skins; whereas for reds it is left on the skins to extract colour and tannins. Next, fermentation converts both sugar into alcohol and, in some whites and nearly all reds, sharp malic acid into yoghurt-like lactic acid. This is followed by tank or barrel ageing *(élevage)*, before the finished wine is bottled and sold. Of course, this process isn't always so simple. Winemakers make hundreds of decisions in the vineyard and winery either to cut costs, often to the detriment of quality, or to produce the best wine possible. At Noble Rot we love estates that prize terroir, tradition and conscientious viticulture. Here's how such dreamers do their thing.

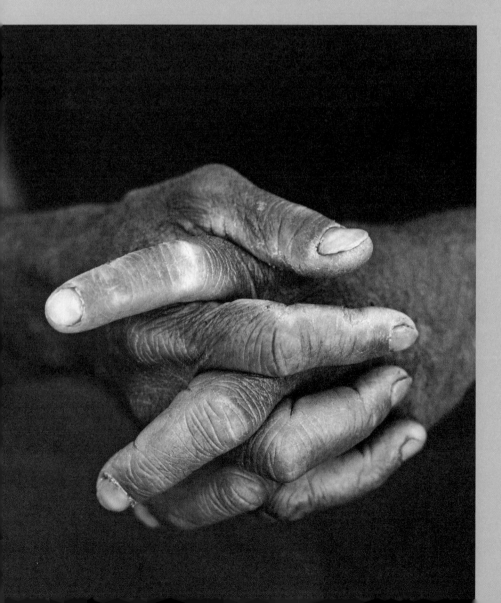

In the Vineyard

Good *vignerons* believe in 'terroir' – the combination of soil, aspect, altitude, climate, rainfall and other local elements that gives every place a distinct character. They know their vineyards intimately and are prepared for their best plots to be uneconomical, or difficult to farm, provided they give outstanding results. Syrah grown on the vertiginous terraces of Côte-Rôtie in the Northern Rhône Valley, for example, is on another-quality level to that grown on the flatlands nearby. However, farming the terraces is far, far harder.

But good wine isn't just the product of terroir – it's made from healthy grapes that have been meticulously cared for. This usually means farming without irrigation and rejecting chemical treatments for a more sympathetic approach, such as organic or biodynamic practices. Leading growers are often gardening obsessives who spend most of their lives tending their vines by hand, only applying treatments when totally necessary. Jeff Coutelou, for instance, makes some of the finest organic wines in the Languedoc, surrounded by industrially farmed vineyards destined for the local co-operative. His conscientious work shows what can be achieved on land others view as too humble to warrant proper care.

Bad decisions ruin good vintages at harvest. Many producers save resources by using machine harvesters that wrench grapes from the vine – rotten fruit, bugs and all – whereas diligent growers always pick by hand. Harvesting at the right moment is essential for achieving equilibrium between sugar ripeness – which dictates alcohol volume as all sugar needs to be converted to alcohol to make dry wine – and phenolic ripeness, the development of flavours and tannins in the skins. Picking too early makes thin and acidic wine; harvesting too late makes heavy wine that lacks freshness. Many industrial producers harvest based on when it is most convenient for them, then doctor a wine's chemistry in the cellar. However, those pursuing natural balance have only a short window to pick their grapes; the reward is harmonious wines with the potential to age.

In the Winery

As soon as the grapes are harvested they are sorted, with all rotten and under-ripe berries discarded. After the juice has been crushed from the grapes, it's a matter of time before fermentation starts. Industrial wineries add laboratory-cultivated yeasts to ensure that this begins quickly, choosing flavours and textures from a catalogue. However, the large diversity of naturally occurring local yeast populations suggests that these are a key part of terroir, and almost all of our favourite wines are fermented with uncontrollable wild yeasts (okay Haut-Brion, we make an exception for you). For most traditional winemakers, adding yeast from a packet is unnecessary when each of their vineyards has its own unique strains.

Crafting interesting wine requires an instinct for knowing when to intervene, and when to do nothing. Top *vignerons* know how to manage tannins without over-extracting, or how to build texture in white wines without excessively stirring the lees (*bâtonnage*). Sensitivity is also required during ageing (*élevage*): fresher-style wines often benefit from being stored in steel tank, while others adapt better to oak barrels to create a rounder, complex style. New oak plays an important role in softening and framing many great cuvées, but needs judicious use. Having been almost ubiquitous not too long ago, the use of new oak has declined in favour of older, used barrels that don't impart such intense flavours.

Many top producers think that filtering and fining wines to remove bitter or harsh compounds strips them of character. But there's a difference between the light filtration now advocated by low-intervention winemakers such as Mount Etna's Frank Cornelissen – whose early vintages looked like they had tiny lumps of lava floating in them – and heavy industrial filtration. Likewise, the traditional egg-white fining practised by López de Heredia in Rioja has a much lighter touch than chemicals such as carbon and PVPP.

Beyond Red and White Wine

Leaving white wine in contact with the grape skins infuses it with deeper colour and more texture, including tannins. This 'skin contact' can last days or months, with darker-hued versions becoming 'orange' or 'amber' wine. But if orange wines are whites made as if they were reds, rosés are reds made as if they were whites. 'Rosé de macération', the most common technique, involves running the juice off red grape skins after a few hours (removing it immediately produces a white wine called 'Blanc de Noirs'). Another technique is 'rosé de saignée', where the juice is bled from tank before it takes on much colour, making a rosé while concentrating the remaining red wine. The simplest method for making rosé – blending white and red wine to make pink – is prohibited by EU law for all quality wines, except rosé Champagne.

Sparkling wines require more of one crucial ingredient – carbon dioxide (CO_2) – and are most commonly made by either fermenting the wine in a sealed tank and bottling it under pressure, as in the case of commercial Prosecco, or by bottle fermentation. In 'ancestral method' bottle fermentation, used for *col fondo* Prosecco and *pétillant naturel (pét nat)* wines, the fermentation process is completed in closed bottle, trapping CO_2 and creating lightly fizzy wines packed with dead yeast cells that give a cloudy appearance. On the other hand, the most complex and age-worthy sparkling wines are made by 'traditional method', previously known as 'Champagne method', where a yeast/sugar solution is added to a finished still wine and sealed in bottle to start a 'secondary fermentation'. This produces more pressure than the ancestral method, and more of a deposit from the dead yeast cells. These 'lees' interact with the wine as it ages in the bottle, infusing it with biscuity, bready richness.

Prior to release, each bottle is 'disgorged', a process that involves removing the dead yeast cells and crystals, before a sugar 'dosage' is added to alter the dryness level and the bottle is resealed with a cork and wire crown.

Although out of fashion, fortified wines are some of the world's most historic styles. They're made by adding grape spirit brandy to the wine in order to halt fermentation – yeasts cannot work in too high an alcoholic environment – retaining any sugar that hasn't been converted. This allows the producer to make a range of styles, depending on grape sugar levels and the stage at which they are fortified – from drier Sherries and Sercial Madeira, to sweeter wines such as vintage Port and Banyuls.

'Natural' is one of the most controversial words in wine and there has long been confusion about what 'natural wine' means, or how it relates to organic and biodynamic wine. In Europe, organic wine must be made from certified organically grown grapes, but once the grapes are delivered to the winery most additives and interventions are permitted in production. Biodynamic wine must be made from certified biodynamically grown grapes, meaning the grower has gone beyond organic requirements by using preparations specified by Rudolf Steiner, the father of biodynamic agriculture, and performs tasks in accordance with the lunar calendar. As with organic wine, many winemaking additives are permitted, though to be certified biodynamic, the fermentation has to be spontaneous using wild yeasts.

Our interpretation of 'natural wine' involves using grapes that are farmed organically or biodynamically, while keeping winery interventions to an absolute minimum. That should mean spontaneous fermentations and no additions of sugar, enzymes, acid or powdered tannins. Neither should anything be taken away by de-acidification, de-alcoholisation or must concentration. The use of sulphur dioxide (SO_2) is very controversial, with most hard-line natural winemakers rejecting additions outright (referred to as *sans soufre*). Others, such as the Association des Vins Naturels, quote 30mg per litre of total sulphur for whites, and 20mg/l for reds as permissible, though these figures change depending on who you ask. For us sustainable viticulture with minimal, or preferably no, use of chemicals is the most important thing.

Most of the above parameters (including a maximum of 30mg/l total SO_2) were codified into a 2020 charter by the Syndicat de Défense des Vins Naturels, who worked with French authorities to develop a definition of 'natural wine' to be regulated by the government (initially in France but with the aim of rolling it out across the EU). It remains to be seen whether the anti-establishment ethos of many natural winemakers is compatible with an official scheme, but this definition will certainly provide clarity for consumers.

What Makes a Difference?

Below: The Côte Blonde, southern slopes of Côte-Rôtie, Northern Rhône Valley.

NUMEROUS FACTORS affect the quality and style of a finished wine. Whether world-class Northern Rhône Syrah or low-quality Sauvignon Blanc, the variability of the following is key.

1   The soil.
2   The vines.
3   The skill, philosophy and resources of the grape grower.
4   How the climate affected conditions that year, and at what times.
5   Whether or not diseases such as oidium and mildew have affected the vines.
6   The time of the harvest, the care taken over the picking, and the yield.
7   The skill, philosophy and resources of the cellar master.
8   The length and type of *élevage* before the wine is bottled.
9   The care with which the bottling is done, as well as the quality of the closures.
10   The delivery and subsequent storage conditions of the wine.
11   The care with which the wine is brought to table and served.

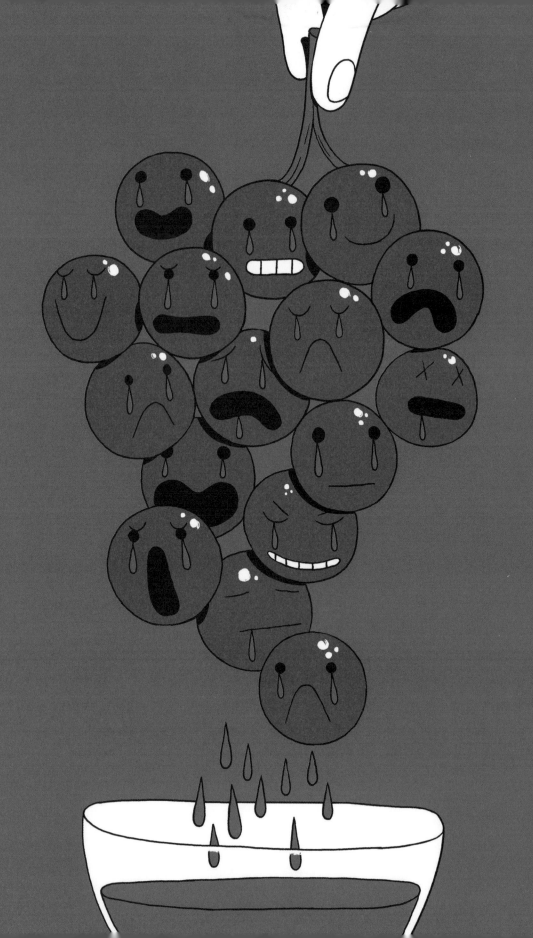

Noble Grapes

Good winemakers talk about the taste of their soil rather than any particular grape variety, but it helps to know the basics.

CHARDONNAY

Chardonnay, the king of white grapes, is a blank canvas that adapts to soils and climate. With good potential body and acidity its ultimate expression is grown in Burgundy's Le Montrachet vineyard by domaines such as Comtes Lafon and Ramonet which, according to Alexandre Dumas, should be "drunk on bended knee, with head bared". Spreading out from this holy epicentre, Puligny-Montrachet, Chassagne-Montrachet, St Aubin, Meursault, Corton-Charlemagne, Chablis, Champagne, the Côte Chalonnaise, Mâconnais and Jura also foster interstellar examples. Much abused in the '80s, when Australia flooded the UK with oceans of sickly Chardonnay, the grape still makes a multitude of anonymous wines outside of central France (Spanish Chardonnay – why?). In California producers such as Kongsgaard and Sandhi and, in New Zealand, Kumeu River make delicious examples.

RIESLING

Like Chardonnay, Riesling is moulded by terroir but is even more diverse in style, from dry Alsatian powerhouses (Trimbach, Weinbach) and ethereal, off-dry Mosels (Egon Müller, Willi Schaefer) to the sweetest *Trockenbeerenauslese* nectars known to man. With electrifying acidity and ripe-fruit characteristics, this chameleon is mostly vinified without oak, and seems to suck slaty, mineral characteristics from the ground on which it's grown. (Scientists doubt this phenomenon, but drink Klaus Peter Keller's liquid limestone *Grosses Gëwachs* if you want proof.) Outside of Germany and Alsace, excellent Rieslings can be found in Australia and Austria.

VIOGNIER

Opulent Viognier has low acidity and floral and stone-fruit aromas. It requires skill to grow, as its high potential alcohol spikes quickly at harvest, producing flabby wines. Luxuriously textured with apricot, honeysuckle and rotting passion-fruit aromas, the best Viogniers come from the tiny *monopole* Château-Grillet and surrounding appellation of Condrieu in France's Northern Rhône Valley. These vineyards were saved from abandonment in the '60s by the tireless work of *vignerons* Georges Vernay and Marcel Guigal, whose eponymous domaines still produce benchmark Condrieu. Viognier has also grown in popularity across southern France, Australia and California.

CHENIN BLANC

Loire native Chenin Blanc is versatile and often profound. From powerful, bone-dry wines in Savennières, Anjou, Saumur, Montlouis and Jasnières, through all shades of sweetness in Vouvray, Coteaux du Layon, Quarts de Chaume and Bonnezeaux, its searing acidity can balance high residual sugar levels. Domaine Huet – the quintessential Vouvray domaine of the 20th century – still makes long-lived Chenins that have been known to drink well at 100 years, while the past decade has seen a new generation of natural-leaning producers, including Stéphane Bernaudeau, Richard Leroy and Clos Rougeard, forge international reputations with the grape. Elsewhere, South Africa has adopted Chenin as its own, where it now accounts for a third of all plantings.

SAUVIGNON BLANC

Few whites are as out of fashion as Kiwi Sauvignon Blanc, whose pungent aromas contrast with the more restrained wines of the grape's Loire Valley home. There, domaines such as François Cotat and Benjamin Dagueneau make elegant wines with high-acid freshness, medium to full body, and blackcurrant, nettle and chalk aromas, the latter partly down to the fact that Sancerre vineyards are located on the same band of Kimmeridgian limestone as Chablis. Other great Sauvignons are found in South Africa and Bordeaux, where the grape is the junior partner to Sémillon in the blend of two of France's most prestigious whites, Château Haut-Brion Blanc and Château d'Yquem.

NATIVE WHITE GRAPES

Growers returning to native vines, rather than re-planting 'international' varieties, is one of the most interesting wine trends of recent years. In Muscadet, Melon de Bourgogne, and in Burgundy, Aligoté, produce affordable, refreshing whites that are perfect with seafood; in the Jura, powerful Savagnin is made in both fresh and oxidative styles, culminating in rare Vin Jaune ('yellow wine'). In Alsace, floral Gewürztraminer and Muscat are grown alongside the noble Riesling, and in the Rhône Valley, Marsanne, Roussanne and Grenache Blanc make textured 'gourmand' wines. In northern Spain and Portugal Albariño provides thirst-quenching good value; in Catalonia Xarel·lo makes saline single varietal cuvées, while Palomino is used for most styles of Sherry, as well as exciting Tenerife whites, where it is known as Listán Blanco. In Austria's Wachau Valley, Grüner Veltliner produces steely, linear wines; in Abruzzo, the oft-maligned Trebbiano is transformed into a thing of beauty by Emidio Pepe and Valentini; and on Santorini, Assyrtiko makes salty-fresh wines from volcanic soils.

PINOT NOIR

"Cabernet is for doctors, lawyers and businessmen. Pinot Noir is for artists, and people who enjoy life." So said Jean-Marie Fourrier, one of Gevrey-Chambertin's top winemakers, when hosting a tasting of wines in the late 2000s. Ironically, prices of wines from Burgundy, Pinot Noir's heartland, have rocketed over the past decade, making it more likely that only captains of industry, rather than aspiring Andy Warhols, will be able to afford it. But you can see what he was getting at with his tongue-in-cheek appraisal. Nothing compares with Burgundy's synthesis of brambles, berries and cow shit. At its best it's powerful yet weightless, rustic yet refined, as aromatic as lying under a hedge in a well-manicured garden with a bonfire close by. Early ripening with good acidity, thin skins and moderate tannins, it's nicknamed the 'heartbreak grape' because of its sensitivity to poor growing conditions. Elsewhere, Pinot Noir is grown in Champagne, for use in blends as well as single varietal Blanc de Noirs, while Sancerre, Alsace, Germany, Australia, New Zealand and the USA all produce delicious wines. But once you have revelled in a perfect Vosne-Romanée, will anything compare again?

CABERNET SAUVIGNON

Where do you start with the most-planted wine grape on the planet? At the aristocratic First Growth châteaux of Bordeaux, if you can. Rich, finessed and structured, on their day the wines of châteaux Latour, Lafite, Haut-Brion, Margaux and Mouton Rothschild are peerless, closely followed by top Crus Classés such as Lynch-Bages and the Léovilles. Late ripening and relatively easy to grow, Cabernet Sauvignon has small berries with thick skins, high tannins and good acidity. In southern France it forms part of the blend at cult domaines Trévallon and Daumas Gassac, while in Italy it spearheaded the 'Super Tuscan' category with Sassicaia in the 1980s. From California, where Ridge produces Monte Bello – one of our desert-island wines – to South Africa and Australia, there's no escaping Cabernet Sauvignon's grip on fine wine.

MERLOT

Soft, plush and early ripening, Merlot is the oft-maligned red grape of Bordeaux. Grown on clay and gravel soils, it's the power and colour of Pomerol and St Émilion, giving some of the world's greatest reds, including Pétrus and Le Pin, their signature velveteen texture. At Château Haut-Brion on Bordeaux's left bank, Merlot's gentle tannins and low acidity tempers the more structured Cabernet Sauvignon, and plays a lesser, but still vital, role in other local blends. But beware low-cost Merlots grown outside of south-west France – it is also responsible for lakes of generic, uninteresting wines.

Coteau de Vernon,
Condrieu, Northern Rhône
Valley (see Viognier, p. 57).

Jean-Paul Jamet grows some of the world's most evocative Syrah in Côte-Rôtie, Northern Rhône Valley.

CABERNET FRANC

If Merlot is Bordeaux's body, Cabernet Franc adds freshness and finesse. A highly perfumed grape with aromas of raspberry, cassis and tobacco, it has good acidity, fine tannins and light to medium body. Cabernet Franc makes up around half the blend at celebrated right-bank châteaux Lafleur and Cheval Blanc, but comes into its own as a single varietal cuvée in the Loire, where its ultimate expression is Clos Rougeard in Saumur-Champigny. However, there are many other great producers in neighbouring Chinon (Philippe Alliet) and Bourgueil (Bel Air) making more affordable Cabernet Franc to be enjoyed young, or cellared for years.

SYRAH

Northern Rhône Valley Syrah has firm tannins, good acidity and vibrant dark fruit. It is at its most smoky and floral in Côte-Rôtie (Jamet, Champet), aristocratic in Hermitage (Chave, Sorrel) and wild in Cornas (Allemand, Clape). But while such appellations increase in cost, more modestly priced wines can be found in St Joseph (Gonon, Dard & Ribo) and Crozes-Hermitage (Graillot). Many domaines ferment Syrah 'whole bunch', including the stems, resulting in wines that are sometimes less accessible initially, but become more aromatically complex with age; others remove all but the grapes, for an easy, fruit-forward style. Syrah's signatures include blackberries, black pepper, violets, graphite and game. It is widely grown in Australia where it is known as Shiraz.

NEBBIOLO

Nebbiolo is among the most noble of Italy's 350-plus grape varieties and is named after the *nebbia* (fog) that sometimes covers Piedmont vineyards. High in acid and alcohol with firm tannins, Nebbiolo can be unforgiving and hard to appreciate, even for the seasoned wino; however, drink the right bottle and you'll be hooked for life. Nebbiolo excels around the towns of Barolo and Barbaresco, producing complex wines with aromas of roses, cherries, plums and tar. With numerous communes and ideologies, the region has seen many disputes over the years: 'traditionalists', such as Bartolo Mascarello, blend all of their Nebbiolo vineyards into a single cuvée, ageing it in large old oak *botti*; 'modernists' like Angelo Gaja produce single vineyard crus using shorter macerations and new oak *barriques*. Domaines also produce Langhe Nebbiolo, a value alternative to the top cuvées, and lovely wines are also to be found in nearby Gattinara and Valtellina.

GRENACHE / GARNACHA

Garnacha Tinta has its roots in Spain where it is a vital part of many of the country's red blends, from low-quality bulk wines to the top bodegas of Rioja and Priorat. Grenache, as it is also known in France, is high in alcohol with moderate acidity, good tannins, and aromas of raspberries, strawberries, cassis and white pepper. It is grown all over southern France, and is central to the famous blends of Gigondas, Vacqueyras and Châteauneuf-du-Pape, where you can also find one of the world's singular reds, Château Rayas, made of 100% Grenache. On the Gredos

Mountains west of Madrid, and in Swartland and California, a new generation of producers has taken inspiration from Rayas and is producing high-quality single varietal fine wines.

SANGIOVESE

Sanguis Jovis, 'The blood of Jupiter' – there's a name to be proud of. Italy's most planted red grape, Sangiovese is best known in the form of Chianti – in a blend or on its own – and as aristocratic, single varietal Brunello di Montalcino. Delicate, with high natural acidity, Sangiovese's flavour spectrum runs from sour and sweet cherries to strawberries and roses, often with a delicious bitter edge. While Chianti's laws don't stipulate wines must be 100% Sangiovese (it's 70% for Chianti DOCG, 80% for Chianti Classico DOCG), winemakers increasingly seek to express the purest character of the grape. However, Brunello di Montalcino is where the ultimate expressions can be found. Look out for top producers' Rosso di Montalcino (Stella di Campalto, Cerbaiona), or 'baby Brunello', made from either the same or young vines with less time spent in barrel – offering exceptional value. And if you are ever offered the Brunello di Montalcinos of the late Gianfranco Soldera, don't hesitate; these are among the most sensual red wines on the planet, up there with the best of Burgundy.

TEMPRANILLO

Tempranillo makes up the majority of Spain's most famous wine, Rioja, where it is blended with Garnacha, Mazuelo and Graciano. An early-ripening grape with moderate acidity producing dark-coloured wines, it adapts well to being aged in oak barrels, exhibiting aromas of cherries, dried fruit, cedar, leather and tobacco. To the south-west of Rioja, the high-altitude vineyards of Ribera del Duero major heavily on Tempranillo, making higher-acidity, more muscular expressions: the region's Vega Sicilia 'Unico' is one of Spain's most iconic wines, made from 80% Tempranillo and 20% Cabernet Sauvignon. Valdepeñas, Navarra and Toro also grow significant amounts, and it is part of the blend in Port, where it's called Tinta Roriz.

LOCAL REDS

There are untold red grapes making excellent wines today. In Beaujolais, supple Gamay makes one of the world's best-value fine wines; in the Jura, Ploussard makes unusually light wines that the locals drink before whites; in Champagne, Pinot Meunier was once considered only fit for blending, but now growers make gorgeous-textured single varietal wines; while Mourvèdre and Carignan represent the soulful drinkability of southern France. In Piedmont, Barbera and Dolcetto are drunk while tannic Nebbiolos mellow, and in Sicily Nerello Mascalese is elevated to new heights. In north-west Spain, Mencía makes delicate, perfumed reds from the brutal terraces of Ribeira Sacra, as does old vine Xinomavro in Naoussa, Greece.

HOW TO JUDGE WINE

'An average human looks without seeing, listens without hearing, touches without feeling, eats without tasting, moves without physical awareness, inhales without awareness of odour or fragrance, and talks without thinking.'

Leonardo da Vinci

TASTING WINE, rather than just drinking it, requires your full focus to assess its quality, and to respect the hard work the *vigneron* put into making it. Here we look at a few things to consider.

Appearance

Hold a glass of wine in front of a white background so it is clear to see. The appearance of a wine provides several clues about it. The liquid 'legs' trickling down the inside of the glass are sugar and alcohol content – generally, the thicker they are, the higher the alcohol and/or sugar. Legs are not related to quality. Neither is how light or dark the wine is, which is down to grape variety (Aligoté makes light-coloured whites with a green tinge, for example), vinification (most modern young Bordeaux is deep purple) and/or its age – red wines tend to lighten in colour as they mature, and whites and rosés darken. If a wine is cloudy, it means it hasn't been filtered or fined. Or perhaps someone's *nonna* stored it in the airing cupboard.

Aroma

Most of what you taste is in fact what you smell, so swirl the wine to expose it to more oxygen and mobilise its aromas. Sink your nose in for a sniff and consider the perfume. What does it remind you of? Is it fresh, floral, stony and fruity, or does it smell old and musty? "I've a lot of friends who are scared to talk about wine," says Champagne grower Jérôme Prévost. "They say, 'We don't know the words', like there are authorised words to use! For me, it's a question of memories. Memories of what you smell as a child; the aromas of when your mother baked a cake, or cooked a rabbit. When you drink wine it's about relating it to your history of taste." Take time to focus on the smell of different ingredients and herbs when cooking at home, or shopping, to calibrate your senses. Also consider that your nose contains millions of olfactory receptors that act like candles being blown out by a rush of air every time you inhale – and then take ten seconds to reignite before you can have another go. Use that time to figure out whether the wine really does smell like the rancid doner kebab you ate on Saturday night after the pub, or whether you've just got garlic sauce on your clothes.

Flavour

Olfactory receptors do most of the hard work with flavour, but our taste buds detect sweetness, sourness, bitterness, saltiness and umami. Roll the wine around your mouth to coat your palate. Suck oxygen in to catalyse the aromas through puckered slurps – guaranteed to make you look as if you're on day release from a secure unit – and consider its 'structure' of acidity and tannins.

Acidity adds brightness and lift to wine, like turning up the treble dial on a stereo's EQ unit or squeezing lemon juice over fish, and relates to the climate in which the grapes are grown. In warm climates where grapes can get very ripe wines tend to have lower acidity and higher alcohol content, while in cooler regions they usually have higher acidity and lower alcohol. To judge how acidic wine is, focus on how much, or how little, your mouth waters after you've swallowed. Most wines start off with malic acid – a sharp-tasting acid akin to a Granny Smith apple – but in the majority of reds, and many whites, this is turned into softer, milkier lactic acid through a bacterial conversion called malolactic fermentation. Many white Burgundies have creamy, dairy aromas from this 'malo', while the majority of Rieslings, for example, don't.

Tannins are phenolic compounds that have leached out of grape skins, stems and pips, as well as oak barrels, and have different qualities, such as smoothness, coarseness, gentleness, bitterness, and so on. Wines from warm vintages have more tannins – grapes grow thicker skins to protect themselves from the sun's rays – and so winemakers must be especially careful not to extract too much in those years. Tannins, together with alcohol, give the sensation of body: light-bodied wines will have a watery consistency; full-bodied wines have a milk-like consistency, while medium-bodied ones are somewhere in between. Notice the shape and texture of the wine in your mouth. Is it slender, racy, oily, fat, angular? Or does it give a sensation of density and weightlessness like liquid mercury, which only the greatest achieve? By tasting lots of wines and comparing them, you develop a sense of these properties of shape and texture. "Focusing on texture is important," says Alexandre Chartogne, another respected Champagne grower. "When we judge a wine on smell, we judge a perishable part that disappears as the wine changes over time. However, texture stays more or less stable from the beginning of its life to the end."

Lastly, focus on the intensity of flavours, and their length on the 'finish' – the time that the taste stays in your mouth after the wine is swallowed. Does it build and develop? High-quality wines have an extended *période de persistance*.

Leonardo, We Are Worthy!

Now consider the wine as a whole. Is it clean? Is it simple or complex? Most importantly, is it harmonious and full of vitality? Harmoniousness is more easily identified by what a wine is not, rather than what it is. If the acidity is too shrill, the tannins too aggressive, or the alcohol burns the back of your throat, it's not harmonious. Great wine gives the feeling that everything's well in the universe. Vitality relates to tension and freshness, sometimes even manifesting itself as a visceral energy that you feel in your chest. Too little acidity, or too much alcohol, makes a wine clumsy and hinders it from fulfilling its most important role – to be enjoyed. Which brings us to our final question: do you want to drink it? Nowadays, most wines are competently made but that doesn't mean you'll like them. As Amy Winehouse remarked when asked if she would listen to her contemporary Dido's multi-million selling music: "I'd rather pour bleach in my ears."

THE LEXICON OF USEFULNESS

'Words of nuance, words of skill. And words of romance are a thrill. Words are stupid, words are fun. Words can put you on the run.'

'Wordy Rappinghood', Tom Tom Club

IN THE FIRST ISSUE of *Noble Rot* magazine we asked whether writing about wine was as futile as writing about music, something Frank Zappa once likened to "dancing about architecture". Countless bottles and adjectives later, and although putting wine into words is still frequently frustrating, we've settled on a lexicon to try to describe it without eye-rolling pomp. But let's get something straight: breaking a wine down into subjective lists of fruit, vegetable and mineral aromas that will change over minutes in the glass, let alone years in the cellar, is as insightful as awarding it a score out of 100 points. It's like describing a Francis Bacon by only referring to the different colours on the canvas, or talking about a Thom Yorke record by only identifying the individual synthesizers, guitars and effects units used in the studio. If any of your friends did that, you'd disown them. But we need the tools to do the job justice: here's our lexicon of usefulness.

Energy

Whether young Muscadet or 200-year-old Madeira, good wine has energy. The greatest, such as those from Burgundy's Romanée-Conti or Le Montrachet, often have such a lot of it that it has a visceral effect, like the feeling you get in the diaphragm from sub-bass when next to a nightclub sound system, or a chord-change in a song that makes the hairs on the back of your neck stand on end. *Other words: vitality, exuberance, life.*

Texture

Aside from its aroma and flavour, which both change over time, a wine can also be defined by its texture and shape in your mouth. French is more adept at capturing this than English, where a wine can be described as being *gras* (fat), *droit* (direct) or *carré* (blocky), having a *charpenté* (a frame), or tannins that are *sec* (dry), *dur* (hard), *fondu* (melted) or *velouté* (velvety). **Other words:** *oily, lean, plush, opulent, sinewy, svelte, linear, jagged, round – to name but a few.*

Harmony

Alongside energy and texture, harmony is wine's other most important trait. Harmoniousness means that all elements are perfectly aligned and the wine feels effortless. Rather than just the state of being balanced, think of harmony like the connectedness of musical notes in a timeless melody.

Freshness

A wine's acidity has most to do with how fresh it feels, alongside other considerations such as salinity, precision, elegance, tension and purity. Without freshness a wine is clumsy and dead. Minerality is a controversial word as it can lead drinkers to presume, incorrectly, that the vines take mineral nutrients from the soil. Rather than referring to a scientific process, we use it to describe wine's non-fruit/vegetative components, such as the aromas of hot bricks or a pavement after a rain shower, or the taste of crushed rock or slate. Such mineral-esque sensations, when allied with acidity, freshen the feeling of a wine in the mouth.

Layers

Do you have a favourite film wherein you notice something new every time you watch it? 1985 Ponsot Clos de la Roche is like that: you find something fresh in a different bandwidth each time you put your nose back in the glass. Aromatic complexity is something that usually develops with age; the most complex wines of all are famously described as having a kaleidoscopic peacock's tail of flavour on their finish. **Other words:** *nuance, detail, complexity, dimensions.*

Taste

The first time you taste a mature red Burgundy or Northern Rhône Syrah that balances the expected fresh fruit flavours with savoury and umami notes is an eye-opening moment. Think about its sweetness, bitterness, sourness and ripeness.

Originality

Great wine is so unpredictable and brilliant that it always begs the question: how can this be made just from grapes? The magnificent shock of an extraordinary perfume – just like a lyrical turn of phrase in a song, or a wonder goal – is what keeps us coming back for more. **Other words:** *chasing the dragon.*

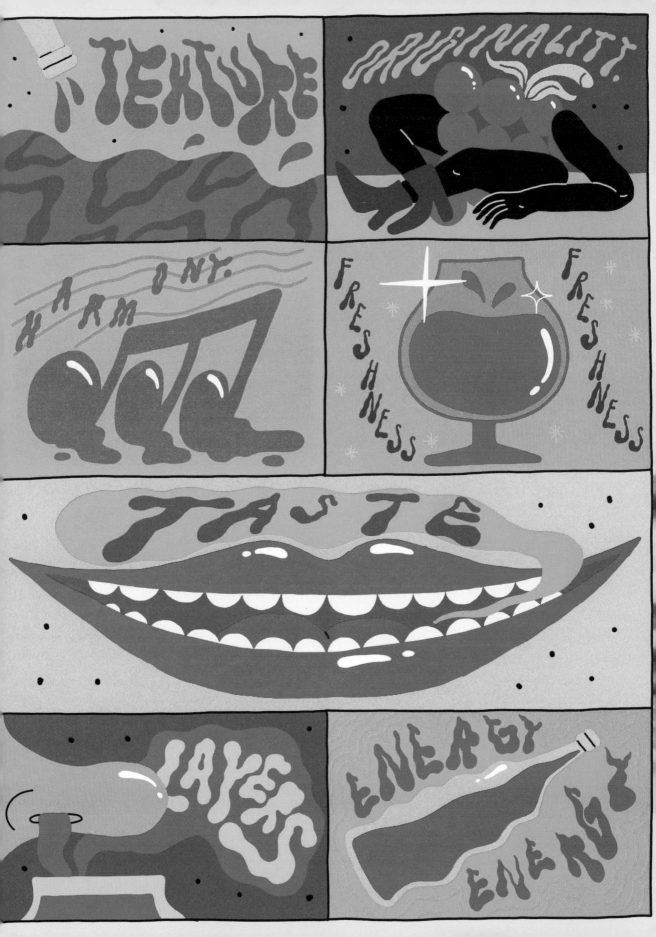

THE ALTERNATIVE WINE AROMA WHEEL

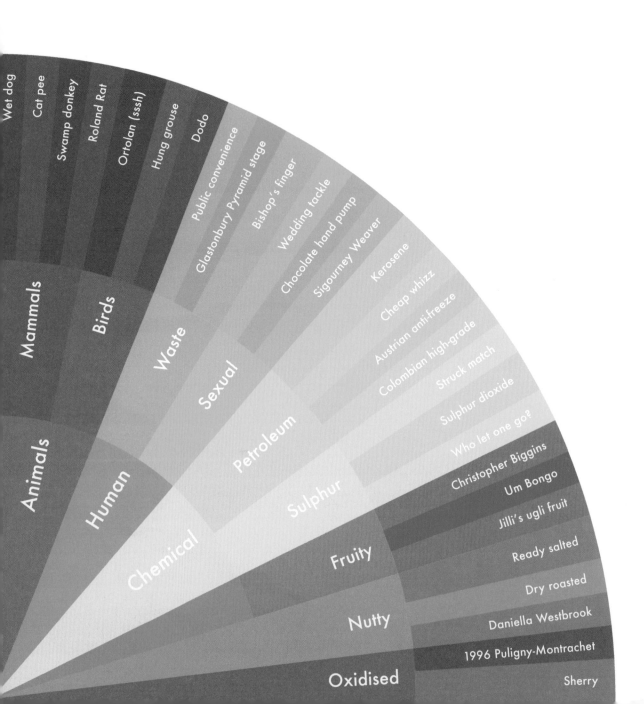

Wet dog
Cat pee
Swamp donkey
Roland Rat
Ortolan (sssh)
Hung grouse
Dodo
Public convenience
Glastonbury Pyramid stage
Bishop's finger
Wedding tackle
Chocolate hand pump
Sigourney Weaver
Kerosene
Cheap whizz
Austrian anti-freeze
Colombian high-grade
Struck match
Sulphur dioxide
Who let one go?
Christopher Biggins
Um Bongo
Jilli's ugli fruit
Ready salted
Dry roasted
Daniella Westbrook
1996 Puligny-Montrachet
Sherry

Mammals
Birds
Waste
Sexual
Petroleum
Sulphur
Fruity
Nutty
Oxidised
Animals
Human
Chemical

In the 1980s Professor Ann C. Noble of the University of California, Davis, created the *Wine Aroma Wheel*, a circular descriptor chart for helping to define wine by smell. The *Wine Aroma Wheel* was organised into categories such as 'fruity' and 'herbaceous and vegetative', then sub-divided into 'specific and analytical' smells such as 'cut green grass', 'bell pepper' and 'mint'. For the first time in history, drinkers with OCD had a standardised vocabulary with which to pull all the fun out of wine.

Today the *Wine Aroma Wheel* is still used in wine education, where the shopping list of smells to describe Pinot Noir range from 'red fruit' (strawberry, cherry) to 'oak' (cinnamon, clove, etc) and 'earth' (dried leaves, gun smoke). But if, as expert Anthony Hanson MW wrote, "great Burgundy smells of shit", surely we need to be more imaginative if we're going to capture its true essence?

Cocks, vaginas, bums and body odour – drawing parallels between sexual smells and a favourite Premier Cru might get your name on a government watchlist, but it's not so outlandish given the efforts winos go to when striving for such evocations. Indeed, the French themselves have long acknowledged the erotic side of the Côte d'Or through sayings such as *'un verre du Nuits prépare la vôtre'* ('a glass of Nuits ['nights'] paves the way for yours') and, let's face it, our libidinous Gallic chums know a thing or two about that. Like perfumers adding complexity to their elegant creations with a drop of animal odour, there's something undeniably physiological about wines that mirrors our own bodies.

So, with this in mind, please allow us to present our own chart of smell descriptors, the *Alternative Wine Aroma Wheel*. Oh, how we love the honk of mature Chambolle-Musigny in the morning!

How Wines Age

IT IS 2 A.M. on 23 February 1900, and Maurice Roger, co-owner of Pol Roger Champagne, is woken up by what he presumes to be thunder at home in Épernay, northern France. Thinking little of it, he goes back to sleep. At 4 a.m., Maurice is woken again by a second, more apocalyptic sound, "like a train crash", and gets out of bed to investigate. Downstairs, he finds that a three-storey section of his extensive wine cellars has collapsed, destroying countless bottles of Champagne and entombing others in chalk and clay. Attempts are made to rescue the undamaged stock but, at 32 metres below ground and dangerously unstable, these are soon abandoned. Nobody knows the exact quantities for sure, but more than a million bottles are lost, threatening the company with bankruptcy.

Pol Roger successfully navigated disaster, and today it has plans to build a winery extension on the site of the collapse. Used as a vegetable patch for the past 25 years, the ground has been meticulously surveyed with robotic cameras, resulting in the excavation of several dozen full bottles of Champagne, presumed to have been made between 1887 and 1898. A number of these relics are stored in a remote part of the domaine's 9 kilometres of cellars at the mouth of a rubble-filled tunnel, where we're currently standing, sinking into the sodden chalk floor as a prelude to tasting two of them. But what qualities does such ancient fizz need to have to be drinkable, let alone enjoyable, some 125 years on?

Most wines are made to be drunk within a few years of harvest, and aren't able to last anywhere near such a long period of time. However, those with good 'structure' – that is, a backbone of acidity, tannins, alcohol and sugar – can evolve for decades; firmness mellows, aromas evolve and fruit is subsumed into tertiary flavours. Acidity is the most essential ingredient for longevity, because it provides freshness and energy, followed by tannins, which bind together as sediment over time, leaving behind a rounded texture. All the greatest wines I have drunk have had a harmonious counterbalance of such opposing elements, like a perfect sphere, which enables them to gracefully withstand the erosion of time. However, judging which bottles are in their prime for drinking – whether intentionally cellared or accidentally entombed – can be determined only by opening and tasting them. Old wines are not necessarily good wines, especially if they were not harmonious in their youth.

Opposite: The entrance to the collapsed chambers at Pol Roger, Épernay.

"The idea of drinking an old wine for an old wine's sake doesn't appeal to me," says sommelier David Ridgway who, as custodian of La Tour d'Argent's cellar for 38 years, is an expert at maturing France's great growths. "If they've been aged very well they can be fantastic, but often restaurants have old wines because they haven't sold and aren't necessarily the best. We try to sell 'off' vintages first and keep the better ones for later, but the advantage of 'off' vintages is that they're often approachable earlier in their lives." Sometimes, vintages that were initially poorly received, such as Burgundy 1991s and 1993s, surpass expectations later, while celebrated years underperform. David is modest about his cellar's vinous treasures which, due to flawless provenance, increase the likelihood of diners enjoying pristine bottles. For this, however, they need to be slowly matured in sympathetic conditions.

Fine wine is susceptible to movement, bright light and fluctuations in temperature, but most of La Tour d'Argent's stocks have lain in darkness there since release. Air-conditioning was installed in 1975 due to an increase in the soil temperature, with the labyrinth of chambers varying slightly from 11°C in winter to 12.5°C in summer. This range is ideal for long-term ageing, with humidity close to 75 per cent, and bottles stacked on their side so the liquid covers the corks to prevent them drying out.

Back in Épernay, the fact that Pol Roger's excavated bottles had been buried in clay and chalk is potentially good for their evolution and, having never left

Above: Recently excavated Pol Roger bottles with new wax tops.

the domaine, their provenance is perfect. Like the consignment of 1907 Heidsieck Champagne salvaged in 1998 from the wreck of a ship torpedoed in the First World War, which went on to be auctioned for up to $275,000 a bottle, these wines are liquid history. Besides, very old Pol Roger has real quality, such as the celebrated 1914, heralded by Maurice Pol-Roger as "harvested to the sound of gunfire but to be drunk to the sound of trumpets". With marketing like that, no wonder Champagne went on to become the gangster rapper's drink of choice.

Our two 19th-century bottles might only have been buried to what sounded like a rail crash, but judging by their generous fills, we have high hopes. Both have lain here, undisturbed, through decades of turbulence, from the Battle of the Marne ten miles to the north in September 1914, to the Second World War when Pol Roger built fake cellar walls to stop celebrated vintages falling into Nazi hands. However, Champagne-making techniques were still relatively unevolved when these wines were produced in the late 1800s, based on low yields of under-ripe grapes harvested as early as August from pre-phylloxera vines, then chaptalised and fortified. Indeed, up until the 1950s, Pol Roger bought large quantities of Hine Cognac to strengthen its Champagnes which, allied to dosage levels of 12–14g of sugar per litre – compared with 9g/l for Pol Roger Brut reserve today – make the odds of these wines still being alive better than otherwise.

Right: Opening time.

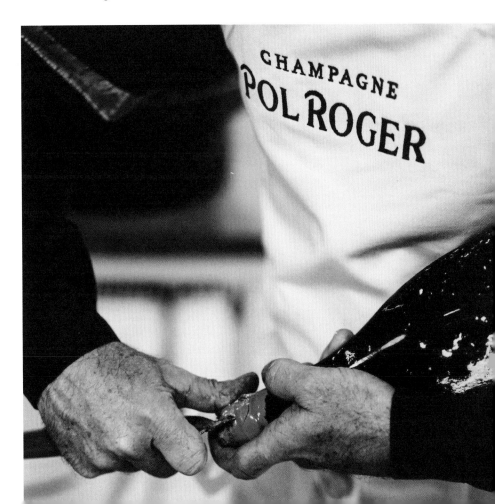

A Pol Roger cellar hand begins scraping away the first bottle's seal, surrounded by a huddle of photographers jostling for a better view. Camera flashes illuminate the congregation of journalists and employees until, minutes later, a stream of Champagne finally dribbles out and merges with the constellation of wax and dirt on the winery floor. The cellar hand smells the wine and pours a taste for the cellar master, Damien Cambres, before repeating the process with the second bottle. Both are made of heavy-duty green glass, with blackened corks held in place by a single wire rather than a modern cage. Finally, someone asks Cambres if he'd like them to serve the current Blanc de Blancs vintage to calibrate palates, but the anticipation is too much. What does a man have to do to get a glass of 125-year-old fizz around here?

The first Champagne is poured, and although, predictably, it has no mousse or fizz, its mid-golden colour is lighter than I expected. This can be a good sign for the condition of white wines, which darken as they age, whereas reds lighten. Gradually, decrepit aromas of grandpa's musty old wardrobe unfurl; this wine is not so much over the hill as six feet under the mountain. Dang, the story of the cellar collapse is intriguing, but have we come all the way to Épernay for a taste of long-dead Champagne? The first requirement of all wine is to be alive, to be drunk and, above all, to be enjoyed.

Below: 125-year-old Pol Roger is served.

Above: Dan Keeling.

The second bottle is served, similar in colour to the first and again without bubbles. However, this time the wine has tiny brown specks and, more importantly, faint aromas of roasted hazelnuts and waxed oak floors. I roll it around my mouth, and am impressed by its slightly oily texture: it tastes of dried-out caramel and leaves vague umami flavours on the tongue. Then the freshness kicks in, one of the sensations I love most about drinking great wine, and, lo and behold, this time traveller is alive! Who could fail to be impressed by the ability of fermented grape must, ripened by sunbeams that shone before their grandparents were born, to have outlived everyone on the planet, and still be enjoyable 125 years later? Maurice's descendants have a few fascinating bottles back on the books.

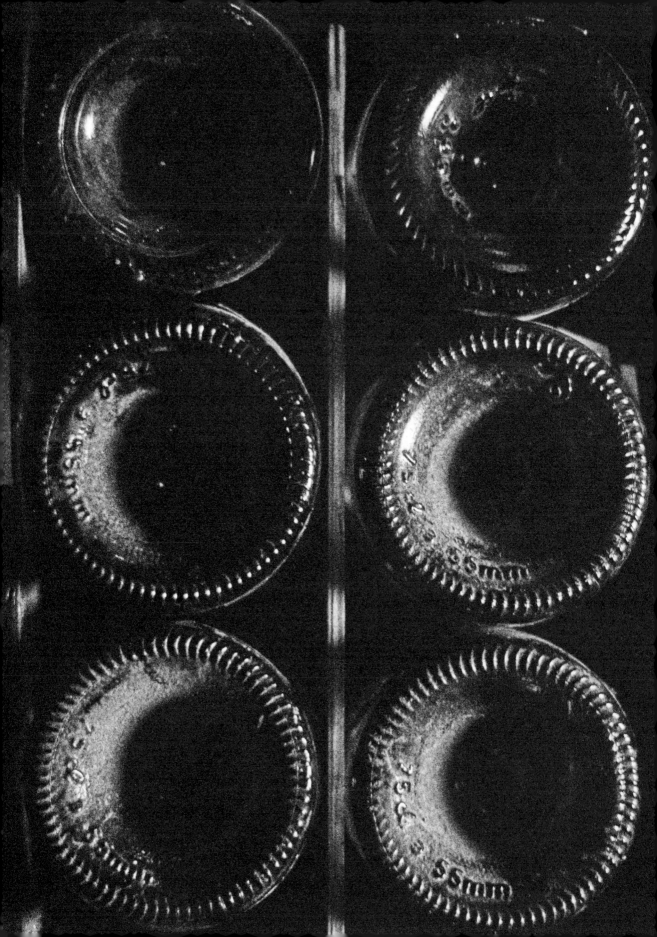

The 21st Century Wine Cellar

"THE QUICKEST ROUTE to paradise is the stairs to the wine cellar" is a fabulous old Gallic expression that still rings true today, even if many people's wine cellars are now more likely to be a cupboard or improvised space. At a time when many people have been priced out of buying their own property and city rents are hugely inflated, the idea of a room dedicated to maturing fine wine seems like a throwback to a more benevolent age. But we all can dream, and having graduated from keeping a handful of bottles under the stairs, to a Eurocave refrigeration unit, an account at a bonded warehouse, and an early 18th-century restaurant cellar, I can attest to the benefits of collecting wine – even if the word 'collecting' isn't totally apt for a pursuit based on regular depletion. Sure, fine wine is an excellent investment – if not always financially, then in future happiness – but unlike, say, collectors of stamps or antique watches, whose acquisitions are emotional endeavours, I'm as cold-hearted as an oligarch chairman of a Premier League club. Some wines are for keeping, some are for drinking, and some are for selling; and when one doesn't live up to expectations, onto the transfer list it goes.

Price

"Is it worth the money?" is one of the most frequently asked questions about fine wine – unsurprisingly, given many of the prodigious prices. Around the time of the widely heralded 2009 and 2010 vintages' *en primeur* campaigns, Cru Classé Bordeaux was regarded as the world's most prestigious, cellar-worthy wine. But since then prices of the much more limited Burgundy crus have risen to levels that make the former almost look like a bargain. Take two of the region's top domaines, Bordeaux's Château Lafite and Burgundy's Domaine de la Romanée-Conti, in the rated 2015 vintage: the former produced over 300,000 bottles, which now sell for around £450 each on the secondary market, while the latter produced just 5500 bottles from its eponymous top vineyard, which today trade for around £15,000 a piece. Does that mean that the quality of Romanée-Conti is 30 times better than that of Lafite? While the 2015 DRC is no doubt majestic, £15,000 is a distorted reflection of reputation, scarcity and demand rather than innate quality, however good it is. But while such bottles may be disproportionately expensive, now is still the best time

ever to start collecting wine. Almost everywhere the general standards of winemaking, and climate temperature, have risen to such an extent that under-ripe, bad wines are hard to find, and the diversity of styles, grapes and regions on offer is simply mind-boggling. Who just 20 years ago could have foreseen that Garnachas from the Gredos Mountains in Spain, or Xinomavros from Naoussa in northern Greece, would become bona fide age-worthy fine wines?

Even in Burgundy there are still bargains to be had, such as Claire Naudin's aromatic Pinot Noirs 'Myosotis Arvensis' and 'Orchis Mascula' – grown on the high slopes of the Hautes-Côtes and stylistically reminiscent of the wines of her superstar husband Jean-Yves Bizot at a fraction of the price. Then there are the Mâconnais Chardonnays of Jean-Marie Guffens-Heynen and Jules Desjourneys, again more delicious than many expensive Côte de Beaune Premier Crus. In Chablis, young domaines Eleni et Edouard Vocoret and Pattes Loup are making wonderful wines that, judging by the demand for their long-established neighbours Raveneau and Dauvissat, will cost considerably more in years to come, while just a few miles further north, Grower Champagne is in its heyday. World-class domaines such as Ulysse Collin, Agrapart and La Closerie are making the wine of their lives, and prices remain relatively affordable. Why not lay down a few cases now and reap the benefits later?

Elsewhere, cellaring Jura overlaps with what makes neighbouring Burgundy so desirable: terroir-expressive cuvées with tiny productions.

Above: La Tour d'Argent, Paris.

Although uber-cult natural wine icon Houillon-Overnoy's Ploussards and Chardonnays have risen from around £25 to over £450 per bottle in a few years, cuvées from Jean-François Ganevat, Stéphane Tissot and the now-retired Jacques Puffeney are still good value, and will provide years of superb drinking. Top Loire Valley Chenin Blanc from Thibaud Boudignon and Richard Leroy, or Cabernet Franc from Philippe Alliet, will also repay long maturation, as will top Beaujolais Cru and Northern Rhône St Joseph (we've been hoarding Pierre Gonon's wines for several years). Spain's artisanal renaissance of abandoned vineyards is exciting and accessible – I'd bet on Telmo Rodríguez Rioja 'Las Beatas' and Comando G 'Rumbo Al Norte' making elegant old bones – while in Italy, the Brunello di Montalcino of Stella di Campalto and Il Paradiso di Manfredi, as well as the Barbarescos of Luca Roagna, are perfect for laying down. The fun is not only in spotting the style of wine you like drinking, but the names of tomorrow: like our sometime mature wine supplier, Simon Stoye, who built a cellar full of superstars such as Armand Rousseau and Nöel Verset when they were still nobodies. Quite some taste.

Where to Store Wine

Custom spiral cellars are costly but space effective to install at home, but if you have no available room to store wines, your best option may be to open an account at one of the several bonded warehouses around the UK, where they can be kept in optimal conditions for an annual fee. Nexus Wine Collections offers an excellent service, sub-contracting part of Octavian Vaults in Wiltshire – previously Britain's second-biggest munitions store during the Second World War – while The Wine Society in Stevenage offers members a similar service for bottles bought from its stocks. Another benefit of buying 'in bond' is that VAT and duty are only payable once a wine is taken out of the warehouse, which, due to inflation, will be cheaper to pay in ten or 20 years' time. Lastly, whether you're starting a collection to sell a proportion to fund drinking the remainder, or purely to build a cache of beautiful bottles to open over the coming years, make sure to buy them from a reputable merchant, and be wary that prestigious vintages from sought-after producers are often faked. While it has traditionally been Bordeaux, Burgundy and Northern Rhône that collectors have cellared, and that have seen the most substantial price increases, other regions and producers are now steadily rising towards the top tier. Ultimately, a well-chosen wine collection is a source of superlative pleasures. We all have a finite number of bottles in our life; be kind to yourself, and generous with your friends, and make every one of them count.

La Tour d'Argent, Paris.

Desert Island
Wine Lists

A WORD OF ADVICE for any serious wine lover contemplating treating a not-so-wine-loving spouse to a meal at La Tour d'Argent in Paris: don't. Not if you want to stay married. Sure, the views from the sixth-floor dining room over the Seine are among the city's most romantic, and its historic pedigree and antique duck press famed the world over. No, this advice is based on La Tour d'Argent's *Le Grand Livre du Vin* – a wine list of such dimensions it wouldn't look out of place propping up a prehistoric stone circle – and the blazing domestic that neglecting your husband, wife or lover will incite while reading it.

For a Francophile, *Le Grand Livre du Vin* is the mother lode of vinous delights and, without doubt, the wine list that I'd most like to take to the proverbial desert island. Even describing it as a 'wine list' is an understatement of epic proportions – like calling the Mongol conquests 'anti-social behaviour'. But while it offers more vintages of France's best wines in pristine condition than nearly any other restaurant, many gems are a fraction of their market value. Having time to find them with an enthusiastic co-imbiber is one of life's great pleasures, guaranteed to make you feel like children at Christmas (on our last visit, a mind-bending 1996 Coche-Dury Meursault 'Les Rougeots' – perhaps the most delicious white Burgundy I've drunk – and a 1990 Chinon 'Clos de la Dioterie' from retired Loire genius Charles Joguet).

Today, when anyone can instantly access a bottle's average retail cost via websites such as wine-searcher.com, sharp pricing is what elevates a wine list from the serviceable to the get-your-drinking-boots-on fantastic. Aside from the very rich or generous-expenses endowed, why would anyone accept many restaurants' unscrupulous profit margins of more than 75% across all price points – typically, a bottle that costs the restaurant £50 exc VAT is sold for £240 inc VAT – even if the place does have starched-white tablecloths and a nice selection of mature Barolo?

"The best lists not only have a comprehensive list of rare and collectable wines, but are loaded with value," says Californian winemaker and sommelier Raj Parr, a man with magnums of experience in both building and demolishing restaurant cellars. "La Tour d'Argent is among the world's best, but there are other restaurants that have all the collectable wines priced well, and many other 'under-the-radar' bottles. My favourites include Rekondo in San Sebastián, which has to be the greatest Spanish selection in the world, Bern's Steak House in Florida and Maison Troisgros in Roanne, just outside of Lyon, you can still drink Henri Jayer for a relatively good price." However, says Parr, a wine list doesn't need to be big to be great, citing New York's Pasquale Jones as an example of a smaller list "loaded with value while being focused on the best producers".

When we set about building the wine list at Noble Rot restaurant, there were several non-negotiable factors. Aside from benevolent margins on more prestigious fine wines, it was just as important to offer a delicious selection of £20 to £30 bottles for non-wine geeks, something that's easier now than ever given the upturn in quality across the board. Diversity in style and ethos gives a list more character, while prejudices and generalisations about things such as sulphur additions and certified organics should be ignored for the merits of specific domaines. Other essentials include regular updates to ensure all bottles are available to buy (sadly, often not the case in many places across France); knowledgeable and helpful wine service (ditto); and ready-to-drink mature vintages – not just recent releases of *Grands Vins* that warrant decades of slumber to fulfil their potential. Obviously, satisfying all those requirements takes considerable resources on the part of the restaurateur – unless, like La Tour d'Argent, he or she has been buying direct-from-domaine allocations to squirrel away for the past few centuries. Sourcing from a reputable merchant or auction house is another way to offer these wines; purchasing from private cellars – where you can see the conditions they have been stored in – is by far our preferred route.

So what other restaurant lists would we recommend? In New York, as well as Pasquale Jones and sister restaurants Charlie Bird and Legacy Records, The Modern has a diverse and extensive cellar, from mature Ridge Zinfandels to Maximin Grünhaus Mosel Rieslings, while The Four Horsemen is the place to go for great natural wine. In Paris, Marco Pelletier's Vantre offers many interesting choices, while in London, Andrew Edmunds, whose eponymous Lexington Street establishment has long been a Soho favourite, and Nigel Platts-Martin, who co-owns the estimable Chez Bruce and La Trompette, exemplify the time-honoured tradition of buying wines on release and cellaring until à point before adding kindly margins. For Burgundy fans, Platts-Martin's lists offer copious vintages of Domaine François Raveneau's coveted Chablis, while Edmunds has unadvertised stocks of Jean-François Coche-Dury Meursault sometimes available on polite request.

Above, left and right: A sommelier uses red-hot Port tongues to open 1964 Viña Tondonia, 'the vintage of the century', at Rekondo, San Sebastián.

Below, left to right: Marco Pelletier of Vantre, Paris. Carlos Orta Cimas of Villa Más, Catalonia.

Further afield, in the ancient Sicilian town of Ragusa, the Michelin-starred Duomo is worth a special journey for the wine alone, featuring cult natural wine stars such as Emidio Pepe and Marcel Lapierre next to even-harder-to-find rarities such as 100-year-old Marco De Bartoli Marsala. Northwards, high among the Dolomites, Hotel Ciasa Salares has both breathtaking views and verticals of some of Italy's leading estates (including Quintarelli, Gaja, and pre-amphora Gravner) alongside an impressive selection of mature German and French classics. This is the place to get snowed in among the mountains.

Over in northern Spain, Elkano and Kaia-Kaipe in the fishing port of Getaria have a fabulous shared cellar of 40,000-plus bottles, while in San Sebastián, along with Rekondo's peerless stash of Rioja, Ganbara is an outstanding *pintxos* bar for wine lovers. Reserve a table in its basement restaurant-cum-drinking-den to feast on Basque delicacies such as *percebes* (goose barnacles) and *angulas* (baby eels), accompanied by a who's who of cult artisanal wines. In Sant Feliu de Guíxols in Catalonia, Villa Más is our dream beachside restaurant, combining the simple cooking of outstanding local ingredients such as Palamós prawns with a sublime list of Burgundies and Rhônes. Restaurant co-owner, and ex-Limelight NYC DJ, Carlos Orta Cimas recently brought in chef Roger Co and sommelier Agathe Arnaud as partners to afford him more time out of the kitchen to focus on his passion for gardening. As well as growing many of the restaurant's fruits and vegetables, he has put together an outstanding collection featuring many of the Côte d'Or's great domaines.

Au Fil du Zinc in Chablis is another favourite, although, like many places with extraordinary-value wines, prices have risen as its popularity has grown. Indeed, it sometimes seems like there's a parallel universe of obscure restaurants in rural France owned by geriatric couples whose cellars burst with iconic wines at historic prices, their locations kept as closely guarded secrets until hordes of thirsty tourists cotton on and plunder them.

When first visiting Au Fil du Zinc in 2016 we were fortunate to enjoy a sublime 2009 Coche-Dury Corton-Charlemagne – as good as white Burgundy gets – for €400 a bottle. When we returned a few months later, the price had risen to €1200. You might think this is preposterous – and you might be right – but considering the same bottle now retails worldwide on wine-searcher.com for over £4000 it could also be described as a bargain (and, yes, it lived up to the hype). In Lyon, La Cave des Voyageurs is an old-fashioned bar with a great selection of Rhône and Beaujolais, while Bordeaux's L'Univerre – once co-owned by Beaune-based merchant Fabrice Moisan – was the place to discover wines that you never imagined existed, let alone could hope to find again.

Opposite: Dinner at
Ganbara, San Sebastián.

"Having mature vintages of great wine is very important," says Fabrice when asked what sets apart his favourite lists. "People may appreciate drinking young Armand Rousseau Chambertin for half the market price, but it's not really my wish. What I appreciate is finding something that you can't find elsewhere, and not only prestigious wines." On our last visit to L'Univerre – during which Fabrice was packing up a van with possessions for his move to Burgundy – we enjoyed a sainted selection including a 1970 Clos Joliette Jurançon, and 1990 Charles Joguet Chinon 'Les Varennes du Grand Clos' Franc de Pied, a humble but impossibly rare Cabernet Franc from very old ungrafted vines close to the La Dioterie drunk at La Tour d'Argent. "La Tour d'Argent has a great choice of mature wines at fair prices that have been kept in perfect conditions," agrees Fabrice. "Everything's there, and although the legendary bottles are still expensive, there are so many other great wines for very fair prices. I don't go there to drink a Domaine de la Romanée-Conti, but for an old Robert Chevillon Nuits-St-Georges, a Pousse d'Or Volnay, or a Chablis with 20 years' age. And, of course, why not a mature Joguet?" So many treasures, but so little time – oh, for the delights of desert island wine.

Bumping into Geniuses

AHMET ERTEGUN, the co-founder of Atlantic Records, was once asked how he found such great artists, and gave a simple answer: "Keep walking around until you bump into a genius – and when you do, hold on and don't let go."

While in my first career, also as a record company A&R man, I thought this sound advice, it wasn't until reading Kermit Lynch's *Adventures on the Wine Route* that I learned wine had similar mavericks, too. Sure, many writers were informative, but here was a voice I could really relate to: insightful, irreverent, witty and opinionated, Kermit may have done his own bumping into geniuses in the cellars of provincial France rather than Manhattan music halls, but his was another métier based on the thrill of discovery. Epiphany time! Unearthing then little-known winemakers such as Jean-François Coche, Henri Jayer and François Raveneau for his fledgling Californian import business, Kermit's roster 30 years later reads like a *vignerons'* hall of fame. Ahmet was no slouch either, signing Led Zeppelin, Aretha Franklin and The Rolling Stones, among many others, but as one of the most successful A&R men in history, he also knew something about hits.

Today there is a vibrant global market for the traditional wines that Kermit championed in *Adventures on the Wine Route*, but this was far from a foregone conclusion in the 1970s and '80s when he was writing it. Back then trends such as new winery technologies replacing centuries-old methods, the mass replanting of native vines with 'international' varieties, and the rise of powerful critics were all contributing to homogenisation, when wines of place seemed increasingly surplus to requirements. But it wasn't just that Kermit championed underappreciated classics; he also enthralled generations of readers with his talent for telling the stories of the people who made them, as well as for describing his interactions with aroma and flavour as he educated his own palate. More than any other book, *Adventures on the Wine Route* was the impetus for us to start *Noble Rot* in early 2013.

So, here we are, several years on, with Kermit, his photographer wife Gail Skoff, and English sommelier David Ridgway in the cellars of La Tour d'Argent in Paris, about to revisit one of his seminal discoveries. These days Kermit and Gail split their time between California and Le Beausset, near Bandol in Provence, with a few weeks in the French capital in between. So, with over 15,000 different wine listings here at benevolent prices, we've met for a leisurely lunch. "What I imported was maybe a corner of a region compared to the scale of La Tour d'Argent's list," says Kermit, browsing shelves stacked with the great and the good of French wine.

"I remember visiting a lot of winemakers on buying trips and seeing barrels with 'Reserved for Kermit Lynch' written on them," says David Ridgway. "It was always interesting to see if you'd chosen a wine, as then we knew we didn't have to do any work." We've already drunk 1983 Ponsot Morey-St-Denis 1er Cru 'Clos des Monts Luisants' and 1979 Pierre Morey Meursault 1er Cru 'Charmes' upstairs in the sixth-floor dining room over lunch, marvelling at the

Opposite: Kermit Lynch,
La Tour d'Argent, Paris.

time-defying effects of impeccable provenance. However, as a finale, Kermit has chosen a red with a personal meaning: 1978 Domaine de Montille Volnay 1er Cru 'Les Taillepieds'. David decants the wine over candlelight as cold spiders of anticipation crawl up our spines.

"Hubert de Montille changed my life," Kermit says, of the Volnay's late producer. "He was my first discovery, as nobody had heard of him outside France when I took my first consignment of wines from the 1971 and 1972 vintages. At the time I didn't speak French, so Hubert and I had to go to Beaune tourist office to translate payment terms and seal the deal."

"He divided a lot of people," says David, passing around fish bowl-shaped glasses containing the wine. "I remember recommending a De Montille wine to a customer once and them saying, 'Never!' It turned out that Hubert had represented the man's ex-wife in his second career as a divorce lawyer."

"You can understand that! Look at this – 1978 'Les Taillepieds'! This really is something. This was the last vintage I bought, because when the 1979s appeared I said to Hubert, 'This doesn't taste like your wine'. I shouldn't have said that, because he really didn't like it."

"It was his mother who was making the wines up until 1979, when she passed away," says Ridgway.

"Oh no, really? I never bought again." Puzzle solved.

The cellar falls silent, save for gentle slurping and the rattle of an air-conditioning unit. In *Adventures on the Wine Route*, Kermit wrote about the challenges of transporting highly perishable fine wines from France to the west coast of America, doing his best to preserve their condition by hiring expensive refrigerated containers ('reefers') to maintain constant temperature. Having drunk his last bottle of the 1978 'Les Taillepieds' some four years earlier, when it seemed at the end of its life, he seems astonished by the wine in his glass.

"Wow! Forty years old!" he says, laughing. "The youth in this cellar is beyond anything we could replicate in California. I'm surprised by how much lively acidity there is in the wine. Even after the reefers and the careful transportation there's still a difference. But how can anyone ever replicate this in Cali when this wine has only had to travel a few hundred kilometres? Long live the cellars of La Tour d'Argent!" Now on a plateau of perfection, the delicate 1978 'Les Taillepieds' drinks as if it were made of liquid silk, a core of pure dark fruit enmeshed in layers of undergrowth and umami flavours. Will today's richer, lower-acidity styles evolve into something so ethereal and elegant? Nobody knows, but they stand the best chance in France's greatest restaurant cellar.

Opposite, clockwise from top left: Kermit Lynch and Dan Keeling; sommelier David Ridgeway prepares the wine; 1978 Domaine de Montille Volnay 1er Cru 'Les Taillepieds'.

£5 BOTTLE

Cost of wine: £0.30
(6% of total price)

Packaging: £0.35

Logistics: £0.15

Duty: £2.23

Retailer margin: £1.14

VAT: £0.83

£10 BOTTLE

Cost of wine: £2.24
(22% of total price)

Packaging: £0.70

Logistics: £0.25

Duty: £2.23

Retailer margin: £2.91

VAT: £1.67

£50 BOTTLE

Cost of wine: £20.53
(42% of total price)

Packaging: £2.00

Logistics: £0.25

Duty: £2.23

Retailer margin: £16.66

VAT: £8.33

Finding a Good Sauce

DRINKING GOOD WINE begins with a good source. While supermarkets are the most popular retailers, their shelves are mostly full of competent yet bland, industrially made bottles, so buy from an independent merchant instead. These specialists are usually passionate and knowledgeable, and will deliver a more personable service. Besides Keeling Andrew & Co, our own wine merchant and import company, some of our favourites include Noble Fine Liquor, Handford, The Winery and Berry Brothers & Rudd in London; Parcelle, Verve and Chambers Street in New York, and Maison Malleval and Antic Wine in Lyon, to name but a few.

Buying mail-order has potential pitfalls (how hot does the delivery van get in July?), although companies such as Blast Vintners and The Wine Society offer excellent service. Established in 1874, The Wine Society is the world's oldest wine club with a house range bottled exclusively for it by top domaines, and a strong quality-to-price ratio. Wine-searcher.com is useful for searching the databases of trusted wholesalers such as Farr Vintners, which despite not having a retail space, trades thousands of bottles of rare fine wines from its own bonded warehouse. Beware some other companies that operate as brokers, and often don't have the wines they are selling in stock.

Buying Bordeaux and Burgundy *en primeur*, where wines are usually purchased before they are shipped into British bonded warehouses such as London City Bond and Octavian, can be cost effective (excise duty and VAT are only payable on 'in bond' wine when it is taken out of bond). Cru Classé Bordeaux châteaux thrived on *en primeur* sales for decades, back when the offer of an allocation of a new vintage at its lowest release price was considered a win, but excessive increases have diminished their appeal. Meanwhile, Burgundy *en primeur* has become increasingly important, as the chance to buy some of the tiny productions of top crus at opening prices will be most people's only hope of acquiring them without having to sell a kidney. Although you might find you can't buy a bottle of Richebourg without taking a few cases of Château Old Farty, too.

Buying wine at auction can be canny, but you should know market prices, vintage ratings and domaine histories inside out, and have factored in the auctioneer's premium. We've bought many great bottles under the hammer, but are prepared to write off a small percentage of out-of-condition wines. Lastly, consider basic wine economics. Despite being shipped in bulk and sold in the cheapest packaging, approximately £0.30 of a £5 UK supermarket bottle is spent on the actual wine, just 6% of the total price. That proportion increases significantly when spending a little more – for example £2.24 of a £10 bottle, 22% of the total – as many costs are fixed, or increase only a relatively small extent, such as excise duty, packaging and logistics.

HOW TO SERVE WINE

Nothing is more essential to enjoying wine than serving it correctly.

Temperature

The ideal serving temperature for sparkling and white wines is between 7°C and 14°C, with sparkling at the cooler end, and high-quality whites, such as Premier Cru Burgundy, at the warmer end. Temperature accentuates or suppresses a wine's characteristics: too cold, and it is less flavoursome and expressive, with emphasised acidity and tannin; too warm and it will lack definition and interest. "Many people drink white wine too cold, so they'll only perceive its edges," says Paul Grieco, sommelier-owner of New York's Terroir.

Red wines should be served between 12°C and 18°C, with lighter-bodied ones and rosé at the cooler end. No wine benefits from being served at room temperature – an idea formulated long before central heating was invented. However, a cellar temperature of 13/14°C is good for high-quality examples. "Reds that are served too warm are unbalanced, as alcohol jumps out and fruit becomes muted," says leading American sommelier Daniel Johnnes. "You might be surprised how much fresher the fruit in a red wine tastes when it's slightly chilled." Indeed, few things in life are more hateful than warm red wine, and 15 minutes in the fridge before serving it will often be enough to make your world a happier place.

If you need a wine cold quickly, put it in a bucket of ice mixed with water so it chills fast and evenly. If time really is of the essence, and you have especially thirsty guests, wrap the bottle in a damp kitchen towel and put it in the freezer for ten minutes, but be warned, sparkling wines can explode if left in there too long! Warming a wine up is more difficult, but you can use a heat jacket, or submerge the bottle in hot water for two minutes. Be careful not to overheat and re-chill it too much, as fluctuating temperatures can cause damage. Better to pour a glass and let it naturally reach the desired serving temperature.

Opening Bottles

Many mature red wines throw a sediment and need to be stood upright for several hours for it to settle in the punt before opening. Use foil cutters to neatly remove the top of the foil capsule and expose the cork, preventing wine from dripping off any jagged edges, and wipe away cellar detritus with a cloth. Winos usually have a preferred corkscrew; ours is a 'waiter's friend', with a foil knife at one end, a corkscrew down the middle, and a single or double lever at the other, which makes for easy cork extraction.

Specialist tools are sometimes required for very old bottles. A 'butler's friend' corkscrew has two flat prongs for inserting either side of the cork, which is then extracted by twisting and pulling up the handle. Some somms swear by the Durand, a corkscrew combined with a butler's friend, which provides leverage and support along the sides of the cork to extract it. If a cork breaks, try to remove the remainder with a corkscrew by pushing it against the inside of the neck and delicately pulling upwards. Or push what's left down into the bottle and use a cork retriever, a group of steel rods, to catch floating debris. Tiny fragments of cork can be removed by decanting the wine through fine cheese cloth or a sieve.

Some *vignerons* seal their bottles with wax, to help protect the wine from oxidation, but many people are unsure about how to open them. The best method is to confidently screw straight down into the wax top and pull out the cork, sweeping up the broken seal with a cloth. Sparkling wines are usually sealed with a protruding cork held in place by a wire cage. Once this has been removed, the bottle becomes a lethal weapon, so make sure to firmly clasp the top of the cork between forefinger and thumb with one hand and use the other to grip the bottom of the bottle and twist. This avoids the cork snapping and allows the cork-holding hand to exert downward pressure, thus preventing it from shooting out and killing one of your in-laws. Another, more eccentric technique for opening Champagne is the Napoleonic tradition of 'sabrage', or running a sword along the neck of a bottle to break the top of the neck away, creating plenty of spray. Just as hazardous is the use of red-hot Port tongs to melt the neck of a wine bottle, and then snap it off (see page 87). Both techniques are best filed under 'Don't try this at home'.

Opposite: Although produced some 250 years apart, this Zalto 'Bordeaux' glass and Georgian taper decanter have a beautiful simplicity in common.

To Decant, or Not to Decant?

That is often the question with fine wines. I can tell you from experience that a decanter can be responsible for both epiphany and tragedy, either bringing out latent magic or hastening a rapid demise. The first reason for using one, aside from a love of the ritual, is to remove sediment from old wines, although I'm quite partial to chewing on the ripe grape skins sometimes found at the bottom of Paolo Bea's Sagrantinos. The second is to maximise younger wines' exposure to oxygen in the hope of making them more expressive; tannins soften, edges round out, and hidden nuances are revealed. Extended aeration – anything from a couple of hours to a few days – also gives a glimpse of how a wine will develop in the future.

Your sommelier should always ask whether or not you would like a wine decanted, but they don't, as we found at a restaurant with a famous and well-priced cellar in Baden, Germany. Ordering 1981 Domaine de la Romanée-Conti Romanée-St-Vivant at a fraction of the market value, this sainted Pinot slowly met God in an unrequested decanter for over an hour while we finished our whites, and was fit only for seasoning chips by the time it arrived in our glasses. Had it shone brightly for ten minutes before turning into vinegar, as many delicate old wines do? We'll never know, but little wonder many top producers – especially Italians such as Barolo's Maria Teresa Mascarello – consider decanting their wines as sacrilege.

By contrast, one of my greatest epiphanies came from decanting a mighty 2000 Raveneau Chablis Grand Cru 'Les Clos'. Finding it devoid of all flavour or aroma at the beginning of a meal, I returned the remaining wine to the fridge and opened a couple of other bottles, re-pouring it five hours later to see if it had improved. The kitchen filled with aroma-clouds of chalk and seaweed so dense you could almost see them: the Chablis had transformed into one of the most evocatively perfumed whites I've drunk. How many special bottles, I wonder, have been dispatched too swiftly in social situations, before oxygen has had a chance to unlock their potential? Indeed, many other white Burgundies are more delicious the day after they've been opened. Similar was a recent un-decanted 1982 Chave Hermitage rouge, which blossomed from muteness to magnificence at the end of the last glass – another domaine whose wines I must remember to decant.

Although my two favourite decanters were made some 250 years apart they have a beguiling simplicity in common, and are both entirely unadorned. For everyday use, I like a narrow Zalto Wine Carafe No. 75 (pictured left),

Opposite: Top Chablis often improves with aeration in a decanter.

which can easily be stood in a fridge door, while for special occasions I love my Georgian taper from *circa* 1770, whose clean, flowing lines make it one of the most elegant of all decanter shapes. I bought it from antique glass specialist David Glick, whose shop Still Too Few, on Westbourne Grove, I walked past for over two decades before I saw it open. Since chancing upon him there one Saturday morning, we have commissioned him to source a variety of decanters for our restaurants. However, one thing's for sure: whether paradise or vinegar, we'll always ask before decanting your wine.

Glassware

As a wine's aromas account for most of what is tasted, wine should be poured no more than halfway into a proper wine glass. Some people insist that tiny ISO tasting glasses or, worse still, stout bistro glasses are as good as any others but they're mistaken. We've been saddened by rare and special wines that have been blunted by inappropriate glassware on several occasions. Romanée-St-Vivant in a tumbler? Go the fuck away!

Noble Rot's Non-Negotiable Wine Glass Requirements

1. The glass should be plain without bothersome etchings to obscure the wine's appearance.
2. The glass should be as thin as possible, minimising its presence.
3. The glass must have a stem – cupping it in your hands warms the wine, and besides, you're not on a camping holiday.
4. The glass should have a tulip-shaped bowl, with a mouth narrower than the widest point to prevent aromas from escaping.
5. It must expose a wide surface area of wine to oxygen.

Our favourites include the Zalto Universal glass, which we use across all types of wine, along with the Zalto Bordeaux, the Gabriel-Glas, and Richard Brendon's Jancis Robinson range. There are other specialist glasses intended to enhance particular styles, such as the unique designs made by Italian winemakers Joško Gravner, Gianfranco Soldera and Giacomo Conterno, and the common Champagne flute. However, we always serve Champagne in the same glasses we use for white wine so it becomes more expressive.

Leftover Wine (As If...)

Keeping wine chilled with as little exposure to oxygen as possible is essential for its preservation, so store bottles with corks in the fridge. Young wines can sometimes improve over several days (again, young white Burgundy is often better on the second day of being open), but delicate old wines should be drunk relatively swiftly. A Coravin is a useful device if you don't want to drink a whole bottle, or, if like us, you own a restaurant serving fine wines by the glass. You don't even need to pull the cork as it extracts wine through a hypodermic needle and replaces it with inert gas.

Opposite, left to right:
Zalto 'Bordeaux' and
'Universal', Gabriel-Glas,
Richard Brendon's
Jancis Robinson glass.

Out of Order

IT'S AN INCONVENIENT fact of life that not every wine will be in good
condition by the time it reaches your glass. So, the next time you smell
wet dog or damp cardboard, or a white Burgundy that whiffs of Fino Sherry,
use this guide to know why. Yuck.

Brettanomyces

Is *Brettanomyces* a fault, or does it add complexity? That depends on your tolerance to it, but the yeast *Brettanomyces bruxellensis*, also known as 'brett', certainly provides strong flavours. The chemical compounds it produces smell like medical plasters, cloves, sweaty leather saddles and barnyards. Some highly regarded estates, such as Château de Beaucastel and Château Musar, often have high levels of brett, and while many drinkers hate it, others feel it adds complexity at low levels. Grapes such as Carignan, Mourvèdre and Syrah are more susceptible to brett than others, and keeping it at bay requires cool temperatures and rigorous hygiene, with judicious levels of sulphur dioxide in the winery.

Cork Taint

Corked wines smell a bit like a damp cardboard box, or a flooded basement. It's a distinctive aroma, although some old Clarets have a similar musty aroma when opened, and need time to open up and breathe. On the palate, corked wines are dull, and their fruit muted. Taint is caused by individual corks being infected with 2,4,6-trichloroanisole (TCA), and has nothing to do with broken cork floating in a wine.

Oxidation

Oxygen is essential for turning grape must into wine, but too much of it, or exposure at the wrong point, causes irreparable damage, ultimately resulting in vinegar. Certain styles, including some Sherries, traditional Rioja and Barolo, are deliberately exposed to some oxygen to give 'oxidative' characteristics, such as dried fruit, roasted nuts and leather. But many wines are exposed to too much oxygen through incorrect handling, resulting in whites that taste of bruised apples and mouldy nuts, and reds that smack of dried blood, prunes and Bovril cubes.

Premature Oxidation

Tiny amounts of oxygen gradually penetrating the cork are fundamental to wine maturation, but it sometimes goes wrong. Premature oxidation, a.k.a. 'premox', has blighted white Burgundy since the mid-1990s, resulting in many bottles becoming undrinkable long before usual. Premoxed Chardonnays lose all vitality and develop Sherry-type aromas with a honeyed, yoghurt texture. There's still no consensus on the cause, with many potential reasons cited: a reduction in sulphur dioxide levels, changes in corks, and aggressive stirring of the lees in barrel incorporating too much oxygen. Much remains unexplained, including how premox has continued for so long without being eradicated.

Heat damage

Portuguese merchants sailing to the New World hundreds of years ago accidentally discovered that leaving casks of wine on the sun-baked decks fundamentally changed their contents' character. Extreme temperature fluctuations between night and day temperatures gave Madeira its distinctive flavour, but when other wines become 'maderised', or 'cooked', it's a problem. Heat damage is caused by excessive or large swings in temperature, usually during transportation or storage. Such swings make corks expand and contract, breaking a bottle's airtight seal and making oxidation more likely. Another reason why provenance is so important when buying mature wines.

Mouse Taint

Mouse taint, also known as 'mousiness' or 'puppy breath', is a bacterial infection that results in feral flavours and aromas reminiscent of the inside of a mouse cage that's been doused in sour milk (a beautiful mental image). It is usually detected on a wine's finish, as it requires the taster's saliva to raise the pH and activate the aromas 'retro-nasally'. Although the science behind it is still being studied, mouse taint is believed to originate in rotten grapes and is exacerbated by the absence of sulphur dioxide during winemaking. It is a common fault in badly made natural wines.

Volatile Acidity

Wine contains multiple acids: tartaric and malic are key to body, texture and mouthfeel, while others are 'volatile' and produce other aromas. Chief among these is acetic acid, a.k.a. vinegar, and the level of this volatile acidity (VA) needs careful managing so it doesn't become a fault. VA is produced by certain yeasts during fermentation, so producers using wild fermentations need to be scrupulous about cellar hygiene, and protect their wine against oxygen. At low levels, VA can add florality to a bouquet, but over a certain threshold tastes of vinegar. In extreme cases acetic acid leads to ethyl acetate, which has nail-polish aromas. Some winos become accustomed to VA, and there can be big variation between detection levels, so it's not uncommon for people to disagree about its presence.

Reduction

Reductive winemaking is the opposite of oxidative winemaking, and is typically done by producers minimising exposure to oxygen using temperature-controlled steel tanks and inert gas. Most wine is made this way nowadays, but the risk is that it becomes so starved of oxygen and nutrients that it develops volatile sulphur compounds. There's a fine line between 'good' and 'bad' reduction, and some reductive characteristics are not faulty. Indeed, many drinkers refer to 'struck-match' reduction as a positive aroma that increases the sense of minerality (try Stéphane Tissot's 'En Barberon' Chardonnay to experience it for yourself). Some fruit aromas, such as the passion fruit in Sauvignon Blanc, are also by-products of reduction. As a wine becomes increasingly reduced, it may develop stinky barnyard or burnt-rubber aromas. While some of this will blow off after aeration – either by 'racking' the wine during production, or decanting it from the bottle – more extreme reduction smells, such as cabbage, rotten eggs and blocked drains, can be *awful*.

Other Faults

There are many other wine faults, some of which aren't really faults at all. Tartrate crystals precipitate in some chilled white wines; these are harmless and not, as many a panicked Pinot Grigio aficionado has supposed, tiny shards of broken glass. The pristine technological wines of the 1990s resulted in cloudiness in wines becoming a taboo, but the popularity of natural wine has brought back some perspective. Elsewhere, there are taints that, due to environmental circumstances, have impacted specific vintages. Smoke taint from forest fires has affected Australia and California vineyards in recent years, contaminating wines with the aroma of dirty barbecues. The under-ripe, 'green' characteristics of 2004 red Burgundy was alleged by some to have been caused by an infestation of ladybirds in the vines. Once crushed, the bugs release a chemical that tasted like bitter green vegetables – or so the theory goes.

Wine Loving Food

Left: Pierre Koffmann.

PIERRE KOFFMANN, a master chef who once held three Michelin stars, understands that his cookery can never reach the heights of the world's greatest wines. "La Tâche is a one-off of nature," he has told me on several occasions. "I can cook well, but how could I ever match that?" Anyone who has drunk such sainted juice would surely agree, but not all chefs yield to the supremacy of fine wine when planning a menu, even if deciding what should take the lead is an important decision. An ethereal Burgundy such as La Tâche is better alongside a simple dish that won't obscure its complexity; on the other hand, if a recipe involves elaborate techniques, the wine is often better kept in the background to provide a refreshing counterbalance. As any film director worthy of their Academy Award can tell you, it's hard keeping two stars happy at the same time.

Of course, wine itself is often used as a cooking ingredient. 'Turbot braised in oxidised Bâtard-Montrachet' – Stephen Harris's sublime riff on Jura's Vin Jaune sauce, and an ingenious use for prematurely oxidised Burgundy – regularly appears on Rotter Towers' menu, while The Clove Club's duck consommé with 1911 Boal Madeira is one of the most life-affirming amalgamations of umami ever devised. But what of actual wine and food pairing – the dark art of sommeliers, and a cause of anxiety for anyone who has ever invited friends over for a meal? Are there sureties for gastronomic glory? Or is it all nonsense, devised long before the invention of avocado toast?

Let's start with some certainties. Our ancestors didn't have the option of buying imported food very often, so most was made or raised locally. Indeed, we can testify that 'what grows together goes together' is as true today as it ever was, as we've tasted many times on our travels in wine regions. At Domaine Weinbach in Alsace, Catherine Faller introduced us to the traditional pairing of floral Gewürztraminer and stinky Munster cheese which, although neither of them are individually our favourite things, proved a heavenly combination, while at Paolo Bea in Umbria, Giampiero Bea's mum's fig tart was an exquisite foil for his *passito* Sagrantino. Elsewhere, classic combinations such as Muscadet and oysters, or Sauternes and foie gras, stake a claim for being proof of the existence of God. However, most of the time it's enough that what's in our glass and on our plate are broadly complementary. Not every combination can be Zen.

A moist roast chicken is happy with so many different wines, does it matter what you drink alongside it as long as you love both? Domaine de la Romanée-Conti's Aubert de Villaine, custodian of Koffmann's beloved La Tâche, cites a magnum of 1966 Tempier Bandol served by writer Richard Olney with a roast chicken as one of the greatest pairings he's tasted. For us, a Guffens-Heynen Mâcon-Pierreclos or a Freddie Mugnier Chambolle-Musigny would be a beautiful match, depending on whether the chicken was served with a light, citrusy gravy, or a dark, reduced sauce. But aside from such classics, gastronauts should also consider the way natural wine's galaxy of tastes, allied to the proliferation of diverse world cuisines, is making it such an exciting time for fresh ideas. Ganevat Savagnin *sous voile* and chicken tikka, or Gravner

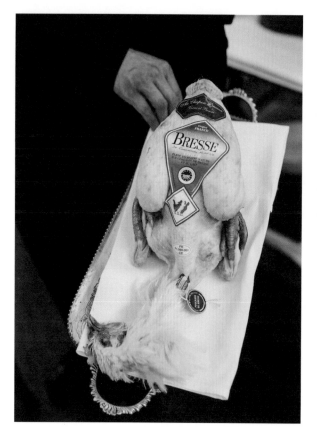

amber Ribolla Gialla with miso cod? Yes please! Whatever – here are five suggestions to make mealtimes a harmonious experience.

1   Think about whether the weight, colour, temperature, intensity, sweetness, bitterness and umami components of the dish complement or contrast with the wine. The only way to know the characteristics of many wines is to drink a wide range – but, hey, it took Picasso years of practice before he painted *Guernica*.

2   Consider the weather, environment and occasion. Don't drink your rarest bottles at a family celebration where they won't be the focus – or with garrulous friends who won't pay them due attention. The lunar cycle and weather pressure affect wines and our perceptions of them, which you may, or may not, think important. Rosés and chilled light reds are perfect on a hot summer's day, while mature Bordeaux and Northern Rhône reds come into their own in the autumn. It's all about context.

Above, left: Poulet de Bresse are famed as France's best chickens, with a rich depth of flavour.

Above, right: Fig tart and Parmigiano-Reggiano with Paolo Bea passito.

3   When in doubt, open a Grower Champagne. We love bookending a meal with one, providing a refreshing high to begin, and a lift to proceedings after the food coma of a substantial main course. Champagne is a superlative

Below: Being introduced
to the traditional Alsace
pairing of Gewürztraminer
and Munster cheese
by Catherine Faller,
Domaine Weinbach.

all-rounder that works with everything from sushi and fried chicken to a strawberry tart or cheese. Go for a Pinot-based Blanc de Noirs for body and richness, or an 100% Chardonnay Blanc de Blancs for a racier, more linear style. Likewise, mature white Burgundy with earthy Brie, or nutty Comté, can make for a magical pairing at the end of a meal.

4   Strict rules like 'only drink red wine with meat' or 'white wine with fish' are fallacies. Light reds from Tenerife, Beaujolais crus and the Jura can be delicious with smoky chargrilled fish, while in Santorini the traditional pairing for roasted lamb is saline local white Assyrtiko. Many lightly tannic skin-contact whites also have the weight to work with red meat. One of the most important considerations is not to let a powerful wine overwhelm a delicate dish, and vice versa.

5   Keep it simple. No matter how good a home cook you are, none of your friends will appreciate smears and vertical stacking of ingredients on their plate. Above all, never admit you've messed anything up in the kitchen – there's much to be said for positive projection.

THE RESTAURATEURS' GUIDE TO EATING IN

Cooking for friends at home can be a fraught experience. Does Anna eat gluten? Has Nick enrolled at AA? And why didn't he tell us his girlfriend is a militant vegan who runs an animal sanctuary before we made foie gras parfait? As home cooks as well as restaurateurs we have many trusted recipes that complement wine but don't require a professional kitchen brigade to produce. Here are our favourites, to go with a few special bottles.

All recipes feed six jolly imbibers

Crab & Tarragon Salad

*Sweet white crab meat in a creamy tarragon dressing is a luxurious beginning
to a meal, and sets high-acidity whites such as Champagne, Burgundy and
Chenin Blanc in a favourable light. An adaptation of one of Yotam Ottolenghi's
genius recipes, the mixture is served in a slightly bitter chicory leaf to contrast
with its richness. If you have the time and inclination, buy a live crab to cook.
If not, use the best-quality crab meat possible, not the bland pasteurised variety
now available in supermarkets.*

Lightly flake 350g of white crab meat into a bowl and check for shell fragments.
Combine with approximately three heaped tablespoons of mayonnaise, three
heaped tablespoons of crème fraîche, 30g of baby capers, and a small handful
of finely chopped tarragon. Season perfectly with salt and pepper and balance
with a large squeeze of lemon juice. It must be creamy and rich but fresh
and slightly piquant. Add a pinch of cayenne pepper if you like. Cut the ends
off approximately ten medium green or red chicories and divide out the best,
uniform-sized leaves. Add a spoonful of crab mixture to the centre of each
leaf and let everyone help themselves using their fingers.

Quails & Peas

This Simon Hopkinson adaptation of the classic French recipe for pigeon and peas from his book Week In, Week Out *is a lighter main course that is also perfect with red Burgundy. Wait until early summer to buy the best peas possible as they make a big difference, but if not, the frozen garden variety also give a good result. If your guests are greedy, double the quantities so everyone has two birds each.*

Preheat the oven to 180°C/350°F/Gas Mark 4. Cut a thick slice of pancetta or streaky bacon into lardons. In a large, deep frying pan or sauté pan for which you have a lid, melt a knob of butter over a medium heat. Add the lardons and fry until crisp. Remove to a plate with a slotted spoon. Next, brown 6 seasoned quails in two batches in the remaining fat. Once brown on all sides, remove and set aside with the pancetta. Add 18 small peeled whole shallots and 8 peeled cloves of garlic to the pan; cook until gently coloured but not brown, being careful not to burn them. Next, add 450ml white wine, turn up the heat and boil until reduced by one third. Add 200ml of good chicken stock, then reintroduce the quails and pancetta along with 1.5kg (unpodded weight) fresh podded peas and 3 sprigs of sage, and season well. Bring to a simmer, cover and cook in the oven for 35 minutes. Remove the lid for the final 10 minutes to give the quails a brown. Serve with a bottle of Sylvain Cathiard Vosne-Romanée 1er Cru 'Aux Malconsorts' and pinch yourself to check you're not dreaming.

Onglet Braised in Pinot Noir

We've dined out on this Bourguignon-esque beauty on many occasions.
The recipe is from Henry Harris's wonderful Harvey Nichols: The Fifth Floor
Cookbook *and uses a flavoursome and cheaper cut of beef called onglet*
– a.k.a. thick skirt steak – which can be ordered from good butchers.
Don't skimp on the quality of the wine used to braise the meat – bad wine
tastes like bad wine, whether in a glass or a sauce. If you are drinking
Bordeaux or Northern Rhône with this, feel free to vary what you are
braising it in and use Cabernet Sauvignon or Syrah accordingly.

Preheat the oven to 170°C/340°F/Gas Mark 3. Trim 2kg of onglet, reserving the
fat. Cut the trimmed meat into 4cm cubes, roll them lightly in seasoned flour
and brown them in batches in a hot frying pan on a medium-high heat with
a little groundnut oil. Make sure you don't overcrowd the pan as they won't
colour properly. Transfer the browned meat to a casserole dish with a slotted
spoon and deglaze the frying pan with a glass of ruby Port. Tip this into the
casserole dish, too. Gently fry 200g of pancetta lardons in the frying pan until
lightly coloured and transfer to the casserole containing the meat, then do the
same with 500g whole peeled shallots and 500g trimmed button mushrooms,
browning them in the residual fat. This takes time but is worth the effort.
Pour off the remaining fat and add 1 teaspoon of tomato purée to the empty
frying pan. Gently cook for 5 minutes until brown, then add 4 finely minced
garlic cloves and, 30 seconds later, one bottle of red Bourgogne Pinot Noir;
simmer to reduce for 5 minutes. Add this lot to the casserole, along with
1 teaspoon of redcurrant jelly, 1 litre of beef stock, 1 fresh bay leaf and the beef
fat trimmings tied up in a piece of muslin. Bring to the boil, skimming off any
scum, and place in the oven with the lid tightly on for roughly 2½ hours until
tender. Remove the trimmings and discard. Check the seasoning. If, like us,
you prefer a thicker sauce, remove the beef, shallots and mushrooms with
a slotted spoon and reduce the remaining liquid over a high heat to the desired
consistency. Return the ingredients and allow to cool before leaving to mature
in the fridge for a couple of days. The taste will only improve over time. Reheat
and serve with *pomme purée*, green beans and a bottle of Gevrey-Chambertin.
Relax and bask in the glow of the plaudits that will inevitably come your way.

Rose-Scented Strawberries

Being English, for us nothing beats crap football, Monty Python, and ripe strawberries and cream. Again, make sure the strawberries are the very best you can find, and that you serve them at room temperature rather than straight from the fridge.

Once you have washed, dried and removed the cores of 2kg strawberries, cut them into attractive shapes and discard any damaged berries. Put these in a bowl, and when you are ready to serve, lightly dress them with 2–3 teaspoons of rose syrup, a drop of kirsch, and a light dusting of caster sugar. Serve with a bowl of crème fraîche to pick up on the lactic tones of Vouette et Sorbée 'Blanc d'Argile' Champagne for an invigorating end to a meal. Well, we did say keep it simple.

The Last Unicorn

WHAT'S A UNICORN WINE? It's a rare-as-rare-can-be bottle that people might hear about, but never see. It could be a legendary, tiny-production vintage from a prestigious château, or an under-the-counter cuvée from a *vigneron* in a so-un-cool-it's-cool appellation. Sometimes, like a celebrated artist whose fanbase grows more feverish after their death, when a winemaker retires with no heir to take over, the remaining bottles on the market gallop off into the ether. But whether delicious or not, one thing's for sure – when you open a unicorn the likelihood is you'll never see it again. Damn!

Wine geeks and trainspotters: locate five or more of the unicorns opposite to enter into a draw for a chance to win a lifetime's supply of blush Zinfandel. Send your answers, including GPRS co-ordinates, on the back of a Coravin instruction manual to sellyoursoulforadropofjayer@nobrot.com.

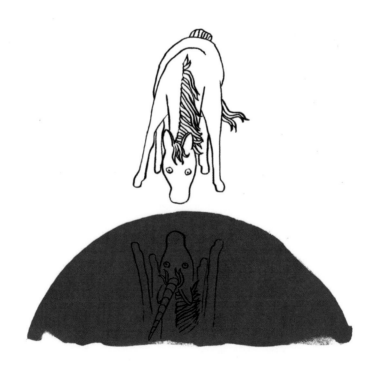

Auguste Clape 'Roussanne VV' 2010
Only two cases made.*

René Engel Grands-Échezeaux 1993
Dreaming.

Raymond Trollat St Joseph 1992
Rare shizzle.

Petrus 1991
Rudy, are you sure this is real?*

Coche-Dury Montrachet 1990
Hen's teeth.*

Edmond Vatan 'Clos la Néore' 1989
You wish.

Gentaz-Dervieux Côte-Rôtie 'Côte Brune' 1985
Proper unicorn.

Charles Noellat Richebourg 1978
Yeah, right.

Clos Joliette Jurançon 1970
Never going to get it.

Pol Roger 1928
Was your great-grandfather in the SS?

Okay, we made these wines up.

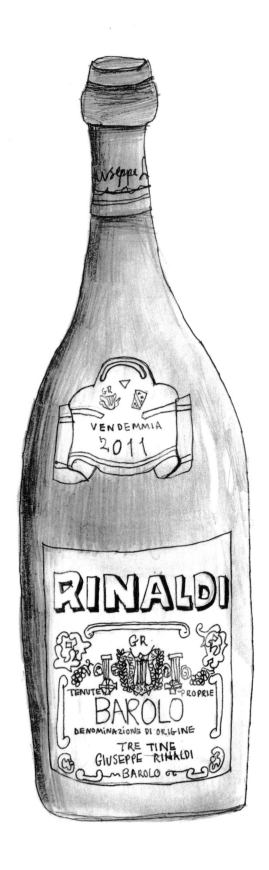

BOTTLE ART

FACTORY RECORDS' Tony Wilson was such a master at turning legend into fact that it wouldn't be surprising if the rumours surrounding New Order's *Blue Monday* (1983) were exaggerated. The biggest-selling 12-inch in history, its Peter Saville-designed sleeve, featuring die-cut holes and special inks, was said to have been so expensive to make that the label lost money with every copy sold. Whether embellished or not, the story has gone down in pop folklore as both a promotional tour de force and a cautionary tale.

The latter might well resonate with design agency Kellenberger-White, and its client Tillingham Wines. Still a young domaine, not only has East Sussex-based Tillingham quickly garnered attention as the first English winery to use amphorae and low-intervention techniques, but also for its striking bottle designs – several of which it has learnt how to manufacture the hard way, including minimalist screen-printed debut 'PN17'.

"As we were just starting out making natural wine we didn't know how many bottles we'd need, so could only send them to be printed once full," says Ben Walgate, Tillingham's winemaker and owner. "The trouble was that screen-printed glass usually has to be finished in a furnace, which wouldn't work for us, and meant that we had to develop inks that were hardy enough to stick." Using Kellenberger-White, an innovative agency more used to working with art galleries and publishing houses, was a neat fit for Walgate and his love of experimenting with varietals and techniques. Whether referencing the Bauhaus or rosé winemaking during the Middle Ages, the pair's nascent collaborations typify the fresh perspective natural wine has brought to bottle art.

Beginning with the Parisian 'Bistrologie' movement of the mid-'90s, when limited-edition cuvées with homemade labels contravening strict appellation laws were sometimes sold under the counter, wine bottles started to reflect the do-it-yourself approach to sleeve design that had been pioneered by punk bands and dance music DJs two decades earlier. Fast-forward to the present, and young winemakers are now more comfortable creating visual identities than ever before. If 'Who are you to tell us how to make our wines?' defines the zeitgeist, so too does the lack of affinity with corporate branding agencies.

Opposite: Giuseppe Rinaldi Barolo 'Tre Tine', by Nancy Keeling, age 10.

Left: Tillingham Wine PN18 and COL17, '4Kilos'.

Right: 'Terrain Vague', 'You Fuck My Wine'.

Clockwise from top left: 'No Barrique, No Berlusconi', old and young Viña Tondonia, Noble Rot house white 'Chin Chin', Armand Rousseau Chambertin with Timo Mayer homage.

From the elegant (Mallorca's 4Kilos' Man Ray-esque imagery and 'Terrain Vague', a project illustrated by celebrated graphic artist Malika Favre) to the irreverent ('Inherently good but has an evil streak / Not to be sold to assholes' by ex-Fat Duck head sommelier Isa Bal), wine merchants' shelves are full of exuberant titles and designs.

    Humour isn't synonymous with traditional labels, where generic château scenes are still ubiquitous, but some new-wave producers use it effectively to draw attention to themselves. I'm not sure I fully appreciate Fabien Jouves' crude 'You Fuck My Wine?', featuring a shot of Robert De Niro in *Taxi Driver*, but it's an honest reaction to the Cahors appellation forbidding Jurançon Noir grapes in his blends. Similarly, another cuvée, 'Omar m'a Abuser', references a cellar master he didn't get along with, as well as a notorious Marseille murder trial. Jouves is obviously a man not to cross. However, celebrated late Barolo producer Bartolo Mascarello's hand-drawn 'No Barrique, No Berlusconi' labels are most amusing. On release, a consignment of these now rare cuvées were confiscated by the *Carabinieri* from a wine shop in Alba for "displaying political propaganda in an unauthorised space" but later returned. A staunch traditionalist, Mascarello commented: "No Barrique, because I'm against the use of *barriques* in Barolo. No Berlusconi because I don't like his type of politics." Each label featured a photograph of Berlusconi behind a small paper flap. "When you're sick of looking at him, pull down the shade," he said.

    Elsewhere in Barolo, the label of Mascarello's cousin Giuseppe Rinaldi is a personal favourite because of its utterly Italian combination of simplicity and flair. Before I learned about wine I made choices simply because such designs appealed to me – the same as I did with records, which, pre-internet, were also difficult to sample before buying. As a teenager, the Jackson Pollock-esque

splatters of the Stone Roses' debut album earned my adoration before I'd heard a note, as did the Vaughan Oliver-designed cover of *Doolittle* by the Pixies. Happily, an affinity between sleeve art and music meant I struck gold. However, when I later worked signing and developing artists for record companies, excellent sleeve design was far from a foregone conclusion. While some acts, such as The Beta Band, featured a member capable of creating superb imagery, others struggled, often due to the tendency of labels to work by committee. The cover of Coldplay's debut album *Parachutes* looked like a cross between a pregnancy test and a box of Terry's All Gold until Chris Martin intervened at the last minute, using a disposable camera to take a photo of the illuminated globe that sat on his piano during gigs.

"There's a lot to be said about transferring the values of music into wine," says award-winning designer Tom Hingston, who has created standout imagery for Massive Attack and The Chemical Brothers, as well as for wineries. "Our ethos is born out of music – not only to try to create something iconic, but also disruptive." Having recently developed a pop-up hotel with art installations for Ruinart Champagne, and in the process of redesigning bottle labels for another French domaine, Hingston relishes working with clients willing to try something new. "Because of Instagram, audiences are more visually aware than ever before, so you have to go a little further to stand out," he says. Today, of course, a bottle of wine or album sleeve not only has to look captivating in real life but also in miniature on tablet and smartphone screens. And therein lies an opportunity for small producers to build engaged audiences with exceptional design. "That Tillingham wines are so visual makes people want to post them on Instagram," agrees Ben Walgate. "It's almost like they're saying, 'We've drunk them too, and now we're part of the club.'"

2

ROTTERS' ROAD TRIP

The people and places behind
our favourite wines

ALL ABOARD THE NOBLE ROT EXPRESS

There shall be no fighting, biting or aggressive pours • No *barriques*, no Berlusconi, or tutti-frutti tasting notes • Numerical scores are for wine accountants • Welcome early ravers on biodynamic Beaujolais • Revelling in unfettered bacchanalian excess until kicking-out time • Tannins like stardust found under the sofa • Tweezing micro-ingredients expressly forbidden by management • Monologues about sulphur additions surplus to requirements • No frills, no fuss, just to drink honest, authentic wine with people you love

Noah et JP Robinot

L'Ange Vin

Ctx du loir

La Dive Bouteille

Loire Valley, France

I HAVE ALWAYS hated wine fairs. Trying to gain a useful insight around a trellis table, while being jostled by a crowd of drinkers with spatial awareness issues, for the teensiest pour of warm Sauvignon Blanc from a *vigneron* who no more wants to be there than at a family funeral isn't my idea of fun. And don't get me started on how difficult it is to tease aromas from such meagre measures. Or how long-term assessments of wines only just out of barrel are pure speculation; or why tasting hundreds of bottles with only Carr's water biscuits to eat, in a venue whose atmosphere makes Watford Gap services feel like The Wolseley, is a dubious context. If wine appreciation has as much to do with mood, surroundings and company as with what's in your glass, wine fairs are a fail. All of which makes La Dive Bouteille an atypical and uplifting affair.

Taking place in the Loire Valley every February, La Dive Bouteille is the world's greatest natural wine happening, and a mecca for those looking to discover new growers, grapes and flavours. What makes it different from other wine fairs isn't that it has radically reinvented the format – although the setting is remarkable – but that it has a unifying spirit and lack of preachiness, something that blights both the orthodox and natural wine scenes. At 2019's event in Caves Ackerman's sprawling warren of cellars on the outskirts of Saumur, the atmosphere was euphoric. Recalling the rave parties of the late 1980s, it is an annual knees-up for a sub-culture with a clear sense of purpose, even if until very recently 'natural wine' was never clearly defined at all.

Indeed, who could have imagined the word 'natural' would become so contentious? The dictionary definition is 'as found in nature and not involving anything made or done by people', which rules out planting vineyards, tending vines, or putting grapes into fermentation vessels. But not to be pedantic, everyone at La Dive Bouteille produces only organic, non-filtered, non-fined, and generally non-fucked-around-with wines, with no chemical additions and as little sulphur as possible. Although at some point we've probably all been traumatised by a natural wine that tasted like rancid dog water, made by

Opposite: Jean-Pierre Robinot, La Dive Bouteille, Caves Ackerman, Saumur.

an ideologue who began making wine before grasping the fundamentals, today the general standard has been raised by a better understanding of farming, hygiene, fermentation and *élevage*. As Vouette & Sorbée's Bertrand Gautherot, who has been showing his superb Aube Champagnes at La Dive since its early years, says: "Ten years ago people thought everything here was good, even if it was vinegar. Today, people have better palates and don't accept badly made wines." Natural wine – for want of a better definition – has come of age.

La Dive Bouteille was founded in 1999 by Bourgueil winemakers Catherine and Pierre Breton, before they grew tired of the organisational workload and passed it on to journalist Sylvie Augereau to run. Although it has moved to towns in Normandy, such as Le Havre and Deauville, its spiritual home is the Loire Valley, where until recently it was held in Saumur's magnificent – and in early February, icy cold – Château de Brézé, surrounded by some of France's most venerable Chenin Blanc vines. This whole region has long been a breeding ground of traditional, low-intervention winemaking, from the iconic dons of Cabernet Franc, Clos Rougeard, to new-wave stars such as Romain Guiberteau (search out and drink his wines while they are still somewhat available). At 2019's La Dive another notable local winemaker, the larger-than-life Jean-Pierre Robinot, held court, pouring bottles and making merry with an entourage of fans. Before he returned to his childhood home in the northern Loire in 2001 to begin life as a *vigneron*, his Paris bistro L'Ange Vin was among the first to promote natural wine, counting pioneers such as Pierre Overnoy and the late Marcel Lapierre as customers.

Few natural winemakers have been as influential as Lapierre (whose son Mathieu and daughter Camille still show the domaine's wines at La Dive). He popularised the philosophies of Jules Chauvet, the founding father of the natural wine movement, who prized living vineyard soils – just as they had been for millennia prior to the development of agricultural chemical treatments in the 1950s – and insisted that fermentations be carried out by wild yeasts with no sulphur additions. Along with a group of his *vigneron* friends around the town of Villié-Morgon in Beaujolais, Lapierre embraced traditional viticulture, sharing his outsider ideals during the '90s through Paris's 'Bistrologie' movement in raucous tastings at places such as Robinot's L'Ange Vin, Le Baratin, and latterly Le Verre Volé and Racines, and inspiring the large community of *vignerons* who now show wines at La Dive Bouteille and the natural fairs that have followed, including RAW, The Real Wine Fair and ViniVeri.

At 2019's 20th edition of La Dive Bouteille, navigating the labyrinth of tuffeau caves containing over 250 small domaines showing multiple wines on upturned barrels, as well as the thousands of winos who'd come to taste them, required an ingenious strategy. Condensing it down to one day of intense action, we arrive on Monday at 10 a.m. and pay the €10 fee for entrance and a tasting glass. At each stand part of the skill of the *vigneron* is to remember who in the crowd around them has tasted which

Above and previous page: La Dive Bouteille, Caves Ackerman, Saumur.

cuvées, in what sequence, while fielding technical questions, like a kind of farmer-cum-artisan-cum-bartender-cum-*Mastermind* contestant. "You like it?" asks Burgundy's Philippe Pacalet about his 2017 Meursault, the first bottle we taste. "We make the wines we like to drink!" As Marcel Lapierre's nephew, and one of few winemakers here who worked with Jules Chauvet, Pacalet is – like Jean-Pierre Robinot – La Dive royalty. By 10.30 a.m., half of the winemakers have yet to even make it to their barrels, possibly still lying comatose in bed after one of the many parties in Saumur the previous night (or maybe it's to do with France's 35-hour working week?). At 11.20 a.m., it's four winos deep in front of Adrien Berlioz's stall in the Savoie section, while a few feet away Jura superstar Jean-François Ganevat holds court with a roadblock of drinkers. Moving on, we drink funky Gewürztraminer and Pinot Gris amphora blends from one of the leaders of the Alsace new school, Mathieu Deiss; soulful, southern Grenache from Luberon newbie, Laura Aillaud; elegant, smoky Listán Blanco from Tenerife's Suertes del Marqués; and many, many cuvées from Marsannay's Sylvain Pataille. All brilliant wines, but in this environment there is only so long I can keep concentration.

And therein lies the rub. After so many interesting bottles, I feel guilty that my waning application doesn't do them justice, that my senses are now not as finely attuned. I'm continually amazed by the garrulous tutti-frutti tasting notes many critics pull from a thimble of wine, but what do they mean? Ideally, you need to watch a wine develop over a few hours, with one or two interested friends, simple food, and no other distractions. La Dive doesn't offer that, but what it does offer is a window on to what some of the planet's best *vignerons* are making. "People don't come here who want a palace to taste in," says Bertrand Gautherot. "But there's no distance between wine lovers and producers: you see the reality, and for us it's a great moment." See you next year.

Above: Jean-François Ganevat holds court, La Dive Bouteille.

Savennières & Anjou

Loire Valley, France

A CAR PULLS UP next to an overgrown patch of dirt on the outskirts of Savennières, Loire Valley, on a bright morning in early 2011. "I can't tell you why, but I had the feeling that I was meant to be here," recalls the driver, Thibaud Boudignon, a 30-something Borderlais man who, having made wine locally and in Burgundy, was searching for vineyards to start his own estate. "Sometimes you choose the place, but sometimes it chooses you." The semi-forested plot is 'Clos de la Hutte', a site that had produced award-winning Chenin Blanc at the beginning of the 20th century, but had fallen into neglect. Having researched old books about historic Savennières terroirs, Thibaud is sure he's found what he's been looking for; after all, nearby Coulée de Serrant was rated alongside Le Montrachet as one of the five greatest white wines in the world by the famous gastronome Curnonsky in the 1930s. "I had nothing, but I knew this was the one," says Boudignon. Perhaps it was fate, because his timing was impeccable. The vineyard owner had just had an application to build 70 homes on it rejected, and was ready to sell.

Nearly a decade on, Boudignon has reinstated 'Clos de la Hutte' as the source of one of the Loire's great white wines. Direct and forthright, just like the Chenin Blanc he produces (only Chenin, here in its heartland), this ex-judo champion is one of several wine-obsessed outsiders who have been drawn to Savennières and Anjou over the past couple of decades, creating a hotbed of cutting-edge French viticulture. Like his new-school contemporaries, Boudignon farms organically, often using biodynamic treatments, eschewing the industrial farming of the majority of growers in the area. While others cut their costs to the detriment of taste, these visionary outliers excel.

The first time I drank a Boudignon Savennières, 2016 'Les Fougeraies', I was taken aback by its power and precision; it's a thrilling, austere Chenin that demands to be paid attention. Similarly, 'Clos de la Hutte' gives a visceral feeling of controlled power, but with dialled-up finesse. Besides exceptional terroir and farming, Thibaud puts much of these wines' streamlined purity

Opposite: Coulée de Serrant, the Loire Valley's most famous wine estate.

down to never following a recipe and always improvising *élevage* with an array
of different tanks and oak barrels. Stylistically, they remind me of Jean-Marc
Roulot's superlative white Burgundies – chiselled wines without an ounce of
superfluous fat, as elegantly economical as Orwellian prose. But whereas Roulot
reinterpreted Meursault in a different way to the one broad, buttery style it was
long known for, Thibaud's wines are just one of numerous styles and sweetness
levels in Savennières and Anjou. Sometimes it's difficult to see what links the
various Chenin Blancs in this part of the world.

Close to the limits where grapes ripen in the northern hemisphere,
Anjou gained fame for its off-dry to sweet Sauternes-esque wines, created
by the combination of Chenin's long growing season and *Botrytis cinerea*
infection (a.k.a. noble rot), brought on by the humid climate around the
Layon river. With honeyed, opulent flavours and high natural glycerin levels,
Coteaux-du-Layon appellations such as Quarts de Chaume and Bonnezeaux
were once highly prized as liquid desserts, while *Coulée de Serrant* was also
sweet when Curnonsky lauded it before the Second World War. Today, most
Savennières are dry wines, ranging from sinewy and svelte to fat-bottomed
and alcoholic. If anything, their common denominator is the rich textures
they develop from the area's dominant schist soil.

"I think sweet wines are very attractive, but how many bottles do I drink
a year? Probably two," says Nicolas Joly, an ex-banker, and leader of French
biodynamic winemaking, who returned to Coulée de Serrant, his family's
estate, in 1976. "Unfortunately it's a tiny market, so many people have returned
to making dry wines." Having witnessed several vintages of Coulée de Serrant
polarise a dinner table of winos a few years ago, I can safely say Marmite is not
a patch on these wines. But like many unique tastes, in the right context they

are a decadent pleasure, in their element alongside a chicken liver paté or slab of foie gras. The only producer in the appellation to still use ancient *tri* selection to include botrytised grapes, Coulée de Serrant produces a very ripe, full-bodied, golden-coloured wine, often with the aromas of candied exotic fruit, slaty minerals, and a long bitter finish.

Who knows what vinous juju connects Loire Chenin Blanc with the financial services, but Richard Leroy is another *amateur de vin* who swapped a career as a Parisian banker for the life of a *vigneron* after he was mesmerised by a Coteaux-du-Layon. Intrigued, he began driving down to explore Anjou's wine villages in the early '90s. "When I arrived it was like the Wild West," Leroy says, "a place with a great history that'd lost its way." When 'Noëls de Montbenault', another historic vineyard whose neighbour Château Montbenault once sold its wines for the same price as Château d'Yquem, came on the market in 1996, he picked it up cheaply. After three years as a weekend farmer, he moved to beautiful Rablay-sur-Layon just before the turn of the millennium.

But although high-quality dry white wine hadn't been commercially produced in Coteaux-du-Layon for decades, Leroy really wanted to make Chenins without sugar or sulphur masking their sense of place. After discussing his ideas with his friend and fellow *vigneron* Mark Angéli, who was the first in the area to make beautiful dry whites in 1998, he felt sure he also had terroir capable of doing so and set out in a new direction, releasing his final

Right: Richard Leroy,
Rablay-sur-Layon, Anjou.

sweet wines in 2005. Having been successful in his previous career, Leroy isn't primarily motivated by money – an important distinction for someone who wants to make wines without compromise. His idea of being a *vigneron* involves spending as much time as possible in his vines, and he has no plans for expansion. Owning a relatively small amount of land means he can oversee every part of production – which is inherently more risky in his case because he doesn't use sulphur.

"My greatest pleasure is that I don't make wine at all," says Leroy of the simplicity of his work, using long fermentations and *élevages* to give his wines their equilibrium and signature smoky, reductive aromas. Having never studied winemaking he was initially encouraged by Burgundians including Dominique Lafon who told him "If you can grow good grapes, you can make good wines". Leroy's elegant and long 2015 'Montbenault' is a streamlined giant, while the 2014, one of my favourite whites of the last few years, is so packed full of life and smoky bacon aromas that, if you put it under a microscope, you'd surely find a universe of merrily vibrating atoms. But with just 2ha of the volcanic 'Noëls de Montbenault', and 0.7ha of the earlier accessible schist-dominated 'Les Rouliers', these wines are difficult to find. Undoubtedly the rarest of all is a Savennières from a steep 0.2ha vineyard near Coulée de Serrant, which he bottles in magnum and saves to drink with his friends. Unicorns are more common.

Eric Morgat is another outsider making dream wines in Savennières, whose self-planted 'Clos Serteaux' vineyard is just 200m from Coulée de Serrant. Like Thibaud Boudignon, the self-made Morgat was drawn to the village from his native Layon by a strong sense of belonging. Again, what's particularly impressive is that he's built his domaine completely from scratch

Below: Eric Morgat, Savennières.

over the past 25 years – an exceptional endeavour considering Savennières is not an internationally recognised brand name, or an easy-to-define style of wine. "Chenin Blanc is difficult to get right because it has vegetal aromas when under-ripe, but also explosive maturity," says Morgat. "You don't find average wines in Savennières, like you would somewhere like Chablis – it's either terrible or exceptional." Unusually for whites, Morgat's two Savennières, 'Clos Serteaux' and 'Fidès', are defined by their delicious tannins and pithy bitterness, and at their best have a weightless density comparable to Grand Cru Burgundy. But what is it that makes them taste so different to Leroy's, Joly's or Boudignon's? "Matisse would paint a landscape one way, but another artist would interpret it completely differently," says Leroy. "Which is just like how *vignerons* interpret their vines."

Above: Noëls de Montbenault vineyard, Anjou.

Champagne

France

CHAMPAGNE IS SO UNDERRATED. I'm not thinking of the nasty novichok-grade bubbly gathering dust on the top shelf of your local corner shop; or the prestige cuvées wheeled out in business class to mitigate the nightmare of a £5000 air fare; or even the rapper-endorsed bottles in full Barbie-doll packaging – as classy as a Trump election pledge, and just as hard to swallow. No, what I mean is, even though everyone regards Champagne as the ultimate aperitif and signifier for celebration, few consider it a 'serious' wine.

For most people, there's wine and then there's Champagne. Even today, many of the region's *Grandes Marques* ('big brands') repudiate the fact that Champagne is categorically a wine, pontificating about 'pleasure' and 'special moments' in place of growers, grapes and vineyards. But while Champagne may always be dominated by these large houses, which traditionally don't own vineyards and buy in grapes from among 19,000 local farmers, a niche movement of *vignerons* who have decided to make wines from their own crop has ushered in huge changes over the past two decades. Today a return to organic farming, indigenous yeasts, fully mature grapes, no chaptalisation, oak barrel *élevage* and minimal dosage have become more commonplace. However, it's not as simple as saying that big companies are bad and small ones are beautiful, as first- and second-rate wines are made by both. It's a matter of valuing terroir; of capturing the taste of a place, not of a brand.

One of the things that strikes you about travelling around Champagne is how long it is. And how wide. At 25,000km², the region is almost as big as Belgium, and it takes more than an hour-and-a-half to drive from Reims, the commercial hub in the north, to Troyes, the pre-French Revolution capital in the south, near where our journey begins.

A vast open landscape of big skies and small villages, the Aube (a.k.a. La Côte des Bar) has historically had a tempestuous relationship with its northern neighbours, who in the 1908 tried to exclude it from the Champagne appellation, resulting in its classification as a secondary zone. Geographically

Opposite: Anselme & Guillaume Selosse, Domaine Jacques Selosse, Avize.

Left: Aurélien Gerbais,
Domaine Pierre Gerbais,
Celles-sur-Ource.

closer to Chablis than Reims – and with a Burgundian approach to terroir –
no wonder many in this exciting region don't feel very Champenois:
'Les Champundians' might be a better fit.

"I definitely feel more Burgundian than Champenois," says Aurélien
Gerbais, shivering in the frozen vineyards of Celles-sur-Ource. One of
an incoming generation of young winemakers, Gerbais spent five years
studying in Beaune in Burgundy, rather than Avize in Champagne, which is
reflected in his preference for oak barrels and the low sugar dosages common
in a region capable of consistently growing ripe fruit. "My spiritual father
is Olivier Lamy in St Aubin, which is where I worked my first harvest and
made my first wine. All my best friends are in the Côte d'Or." Like taut white
Burgundy with bubbles, Aube Champagnes from the domaines Pierre Gerbais
(Aurélien's grandfather), Roses de Jeanne, Marie Courtin, Ruppert-Leroy, Olivier
Horiot and Vouette et Sorbée similarly reflect the place where they are grown.

"We're in a new period for Champagne – before it was all about image,
now it's all about wine," says Vouette et Sorbée's Bertrand Gautherot in the
nearby village of Buxières-sur-Arce. "Very early on, my friends and I realised
we could buy marvellous barrels, bottles and corks, and learn every technique
for making wine. We could go to the moon. But nobody knows how to create
a kilogram of soil. That's the only thing that's permanent, and that's what gives
taste to the wine." If any *vigneron* would prefer to be considered a custodian
of soil rather than a winemaker, it's Gautherot. That he christened his domaine
after the hillside vineyards at the rear of his winery – Vouette et Sorbée –
rather than himself, encapsulates his humble philosophy, growing bone-dry,
ripe wines crackling with energy from the Aube's ancient soil (part of the
same Kimmeridgian limestone chain as Chablis and Sancerre).

Following a career as a product designer for cosmetics houses in Geneva ("Brands always use high-quality materials to manufacture luxury goods, except for Champagne"), Bertrand returned home to become not only the fifth-generation Gautherot to make wine but, in 2001, the first to produce Champagne. Up until then, the family had only made red wine as fuel for 40 thirsty workers on their 240ha farm ("We didn't sell it as we'd get through a barrel every five days") and, unlike most other growers, had never offered grapes to *négociants*, bar a sole unpaid crop in 1933.

A thoughtful man – quietly spoken and quick to smile – Bertrand's devotion to biodynamics is reflected in the harmony of his wine. From *Noble Rot* favourites 'Blanc d'Argile' Blanc de Blancs and 'Saignée de Sorbée' rosé to 'Textures', an amphora-made Pinot Blanc, and 'Fidèle' Blanc de Noirs, these are delicious, unadulterated Champagnes whose terroir characteristics aren't

Right: Bertrand Gautherot,
Vouette et Sorbée,
Buxières-sur-Arce.

obscured by dosage or commercial yeast. One of several second-wave growers encouraged to begin making wine by Anselme Selosse – widely regarded as the godfather of the Grower movement – today Bertrand is himself an influential figure, mentoring other up-and-coming winemakers such as Bénédicte Leroy and Gérard Ruppert of Ruppert-Leroy in Essoyes. "Anselme helped us to choose our own way, but he didn't give us a recipe for making wine," says Bertrand. "Instead, he asked many questions, which is more interesting than solutions."

We drive 60 miles north to Champagne Ulysse Collin in Congy, another A-list grower initially encouraged by a short internship with Selosse at the beginning of his career. "I was surprised by the simplicity of the work and natural winegrowing," says owner and *vigneron* Olivier Collin. "I'd imagined you had to do lots of technical things to make good wine, but in reality, when you work the vineyards regularly and grow good grapes, it's easy." Now many vintages on, Olivier's Champagnes have a rare precision that is very different from Selosse's oxidative style. But what's particularly impressive is how, by following his own creative instincts and ideas, he has almost single-handedly elevated the humble Coteaux du Petit Morin and Côte de Sézanne, areas that historically aren't highly regarded, to the top table of French wine. "The Sézannais is still quite unknown, but I like being able to open the door for other local growers to say, 'This is possible'," says Olivier.

From a bloodline of grape farmers dating back to 1812, after studying law in Nancy and Salamanca, Olivier took back the lease to his family's vineyards from Pommery after a 2003 court case. With no customers or stock to offer, he continued selling grapes while beginning to make his own Champagne, gradually growing production from 5,400 bottles in 2004 to 50,000 in 2018. "I've never produced a non-vintage brut blend, only single-vineyard cuvées under oak," says Olivier, a whirlwind of energy, whose rapid-fire sentences are frequently punctuated with laughter. "Why? Because I like Burgundy! Once I'd tried site-specific wines from 'Mersault-Perrières' and different growers in Vosne-Romanée, I found lots of emotion in Burgundy and asked myself, 'Is it possible to do this in Champagne? I don't know, but I'm going to try'." Like *vignerons* in the Aube, Olivier benefits from consistently mature fruit, balancing weight with a signature style as sharply cut as a Savile Row suit. From the linear 'Les Pierrières' (100% Chardonnay from Vert-Toulon in the Coteaux du Petit Morin) to sumptuous 'Les Maillons' Blanc de Noirs – (100% Pinot Noir from 50-year-old vines grown on chalk and clay in Barbonne-Fayel, Coteaux du Sézannais), Ulysse Collin has long been one of our favourite 'buy-on-sight' selections, including two other rare single-vineyard Blanc de Blancs: 'Les Enfers' and old-vine 'Les Roises'. (Disclaimer: even though we now import the wines into the UK we still can't drink them enough.)

We bid farewell to Congy the next morning and head ten miles north-east to Le Mesnil-sur-Oger. One of four famous Grand Cru villages on the Côte des Blancs slope, along with Oger, Cramant and Avize, Le Mesnil is home to stark white chalk soils that are among the planet's most acclaimed Chardonnay terroirs, epitomised by three distinguished Champagnes: Salon 'Le Mesnil', Krug 'Clos du Mesnil' and Pierre Péters' 'Les Chétillons'. "Our philosophy is that Le Mesnil doesn't need oak," says Rodolphe Péters of Domaine Pierre Péters, one of the few growers we meet who only uses steel tanks. "The Chardonnay here is so transparent it would be a mistake to put another influence between the terroir and the wine. Barrel winemaking is very fashionable and romantic, but you have to understand your raw material." A powerful laser beam of pure Chardonnay, 'Les Chétillons' is a vinous force of nature that requires years in the cellar to fulfil its potential.

Just as Mesnil-sur-Oger produces Chardonnay characterised by austere, stony minerality, so nearby Avize produces richer wines due to more clay in the soil, especially in the hands of Anselme and Guillaume Selosse, the father-and-son team at Domaine Jacques Selosse. A pioneer of oak barrel *élevage* who lowered yields and converted to organics in an era when high production was the prime objective of most houses, Selosse's full-bodied Champagnes are in some ways the opposite of Pierre Péters', although both make superior examples of contrasting styles. "It was a really important moment for me when I saw long Reserva and Gran Reserva maturation in oak barrels at Rioja's López de Heredia in 1972," Anselme says. "I prefer older, traditional styles of winemaking; in Barolo, I prefer Conterno 'Monfortino' to Roberto Voerzio; in Brunello di Montalcino, I like Soldera. But that's just my taste."

A big fan of Sherry ("If they put bubbles in Manzanilla, it'd be great!" he half-jokes), Selosse's idiosyncratic wines contrast layers of oxidative nuance with fresh citrus and salty minerality. The best are a mind-trip of epic dimension that divide opinion, none more so than the inspired 'Substance'. Cited by detractors as an example of the house style's excessive oaky and oxidative nature, 'Substance' is a blend of successive vintages combined in a Sherry-style *solera* with the aim of averaging out vintage characteristics and intensifying the effects of terroir. "When I set up the *solera* in 1986, I didn't want it to be just one *lieu-dit*," remembers Anselme. "Gérard Chave [of Domaine Jean-Louis Chave, Northern Rhône] once told me that the ideal model of Hermitage is a blend of wines from its different soils. Likewise, 'Substance' is a blend of two Chardonnay plots in Avize: 'Les Chantereines', which is at the foot of an east-facing slope with poor clay soils, and 'Le Mont de Cramant', a south-facing slope with chalky soils." Luxurious yet fresh, with a kaleidoscope of flavours (exotic spices, nuts, baked bread, rum, grapefruit... the list goes on), 'Substance' is a wine from another galaxy with the power to make you reconsider everything you think you know about Champagne.

Working alongside his father, Guillaume Selosse also produces two of his own cuvées using similar techniques under the name Guillaume S: 'Au Dessus du Gros Mont', a 100% Chardonnay from vines in Cramant given to him by his grandmother, and 'Largillier', a 100% Pinot Noir made with fruit bought from

Above: Anselme Selosse, Avize.

Jérôme Coessens in Ville-sur-Arce in the Aube. A graduate of the Bordeaux wine school, Guillaume rents a small separate winery in Avize to produce his wines (French law stipulates that at least one road separates a domaine from a *négociant*), which Anselme proudly acclaims are "getting better and better every year". As influential in Champagne as the late Henri Jayer was in Burgundy, Selosse has done more than anyone else to encourage successive generations of growers, as well as crafted some sublime wines.

"The most successful growers have become houses," says Jean-Baptiste Lécaillon, cellar master at Louis Roederer, as we drive through the hillside vineyards of Aÿ. "I once said to Anselme Selosse that Louis Roederer could've been him 200 years ago." If any *Grande Marque* exemplifies how big can be progressive, it's Louis Roederer and its reconversion to pre-chemical-era farming. Owning a market-leading 240ha of organic vineyards – 110ha of which are also biodynamic – it's not just its attention to detail, but the scale on which it is doing it, that is impressive for a big brand. "Everybody in Champagne used to plough their land until herbicides became popular in the 1960s," says Jean-Baptiste. "For a few years it worked well, because the soils were still very strong, and the herbicide allowed the growers to do less work, but after 30 years something changed. The wines were not the same; some became more dilute and aged faster, a little like premox in Burgundy. For me, the turning point was the 1996 vintage; it should have been something rare that we see only every 30 years, but in the end it was good but not outstanding."

To counteract the under-ripeness and excess acidity that held back the vintage, Roederer opted to reduce yields by dropping herbicides and gradually beginning to plough its vineyards – to the annoyance of some of its neighbours. "The first time we ploughed one plot, we accidentally left some earth on the road. Two days later, I received a letter from the mayor saying that it wasn't acceptable to leave dirt on the road. They'd forgotten that 60 years ago it was a dirt road! We are growers. That's the essence of this place, but they'd lost the memory, and now we're back to it. Look at what you see here. Green, green, green! Twenty years ago, it would have been black. No weeds, nothing; lifeless."

The 10.27 a.m. train from Strasbourg to Paris thunders past Jérôme Prévost's 'Les Béguines' vineyard, shattering the calm. We're six miles west of Reims in Gueux – our final stop – a handsome village featuring a derelict 1950s grandstand on its approach, a relic from when it used to host the French Grand Prix. Jérôme is another cult grower originally encouraged by Selosse – as well as fellow former apprentice Alexandre Chartogne of Chartogne-Taillet in the nearby village of Merfy – to challenge Champagne's established practices. They embraced old techniques as new, with ideas gradually passing through a pyramid of today's most successful *vignerons*. "On the first day in his winery, Anselme taught me a lesson I'll always remember," says Prévost, handing Alexandre Chartogne and us glasses of his rosé, 'Fac-Simile'. "I had to pump wine out of a barrel to a tank, and as he started to explain, he stopped and said,

Opposite: Derelict 1950s Grand Prix grandstand near Gueux, Champagne.

'Jérôme, when you do something to a wine, you have to think what the reasons are that you're doing it.' For me, that was an incredible lesson. The question is always 'Why?'"

Prévost produces just two cuvées, both from Pinot Meunier – 'Fac-Simile' and 'Les Béguines'. They far surpass the traditional Champenois view of the grape as a simple blending ingredient, acting both as terroir transmitter and metaphor for the Grower revolution's celebration of the humble. Likewise, Chartogne produces a sumptuous 100% Pinot Meunier from 60-year-old vines alongside a range of single-vineyard Pinot Noir and Chardonnay, using oak barrels, steel tanks and concrete eggs to experiment with the boundaries of Champagne production. If billions of bottles of generic bubbly have tasted much the same as each other for generations, under such imaginative *vignerons* Champagne begins to crystallise into an intricate mosaic of terroir expression like Burgundy or Alsace. Add discernible vintage variation, organic vineyard management and buoyant demand, and from the Aube to here on the Montagne de Reims, you have all the hallmarks of a 'serious' wine. "For the past 20 years I've learned to do nothing to the wine – there's no recipe as it all takes place in the vineyard," says Prévost. "The taste of our Champagne is the taste of the place, rather than winemaking," Chartogne agrees. "It's not better or worse."

Chablis

Burgundy, France

A NORTHERN BURGUNDY outpost on the border with Champagne, Chablis is better known for its steely Chardonnay than gender equality – something that's not lost on its next generation of *vigneronnes*. "Bad luck for the men, they had a lot of daughters," says Isabelle Raveneau, inspecting a green-tinged Grand Cru 'Valmur' in her cellar's artificial light. Now at the helm of Domaine François Raveneau, which, along with nearby Domaine Vincent Dauvissat, is Chablis' most revered winery, she is one of a number of young women, who also include Eleni Vocoret, Alice De Moor and Nathalie Oudin, involved in a tradition that until recently was an exclusively male bastion. "If my grandfather François were still alive, I'm not sure I'd even be allowed in here. My aunt wanted to work at the domaine, but he told her that it was no place for a woman."

Although chauvinism may be rife in rural France, there's no doubting the fine value-to-quality ratio offered in Burgundy's most northerly vineyards. Dominated by the same Kimmeridgian clay soil found in Sancerre and parts of Champagne, the landscape around Chablis is vast and open, with its seven Grand Cru vineyards on oscillating, wave-shaped hillsides overlooking the north of town. Chablis is one of the white wines we drink most of at Rotter Towers, as much for another hit of briney deliciousness as to wonder: how can grapes taste so oceanic? Although scientists say that Chardonnay can't take on flavour characteristics from soil, it surely can't be a coincidence that a wine that tastes like ancient fossilised oyster beds is *actually grown on ancient fossilised oyster beds.* Ten to 15 years from vintage is the prime window to drink top bottles, while the acidity is still strong, although the best can evolve graciously for decades, developing layers of honey, mushrooms and dairy (a heavenly match with Brie de Meaux). Because of its fame some people might dismiss Chablis as an overrated brand name, lacking the excitement and integrity of more fashionable regions, but they miss the point. It is a French classic whose next chapter is being written by a compelling new generation.

Opposite: Domaine Vincent Dauvissat barrel cellar, Chablis.

"When I moved to Chablis in 2010 I wasn't a fan of Chardonnay," Eleni Vocoret shouts over the sounds of French hip hop group Suprême NTM (short for 'Nique Ta Mere', or 'Fuck Your Mother') while husband Édouard drives us to their vineyards. "After about a week we were invited out for a dinner where a friend gave me a glass of 2005 Dauvissat Chablis Grand Cru 'Les Clos' without telling me what it was. As soon as I tried it, I said, 'I want to make wine like this!'" Having been given 5ha of vines from Vocoret et Fils – Édouard's family's domaine – by Édouard's father at the end of 2012, the couple now make excellent wines that belie the fact that their eponymous estate, Domaine Eleni et Édouard Vocoret, is still a relative newcomer. "My dad never told us what to do. He said: 'Here's your vines, you make the wine the way you want,'" says Édouard. With his grandfather lending them the use of a garage for their first vintages, and local legend Vincent Dauvissat (for whom Eleni used to work part-time) on hand for advice, the couple began using techniques such as natural yeast fermentations and ploughing with the aim of expressing terroir.

"I trained with Daniel Barraud in the Mâconnais and fell in love with how he made wine – that's when I chose to work in a different way to how my family work," Édouard says of the time before he met his wife while travelling in New Zealand. "Most Chablis is only made in steel tanks, but that's not what we're looking for," says Eleni as the Audi ascends a hill on the outskirts of the village. "We want stoniness, saltiness and acidity, but use old oak barrels to help smooth the wines out." Although the traditional style of Chablis was pioneered centuries ago by Cistercian monks using oak, the use of old barrels versus steel tanks has become a stylistic division between *vignerons* today. Later, we meet Eleni's friend, Nathalie Oudin. "I make wines only in steel tank because that's my taste: I love Chablis that's pure, clean and straight," she says. On the evidence of her crystalline 2010 Chablis 1er Cru 'Vaucoupins', it's easy to see Oudin's point of view, even if my preference is for the rounded style of Vocoret Jnr, Raveneau, Dauvissat et al.

Our car stops at 'Bas de Chapelot', a village vineyard where the Vocorets own the majority of their vines, just under Premier Cru 'Chapelot'. Although the two sites are adjacent, the vines on the lower-lying 'Bas de Chapelot' have red leaves where frost has been, while the higher Premier Cru is less affected, with only bright green. Historically Chablis is renowned for its susceptibility to hail and frost: crops on the steepest slopes were destroyed every two to three years before the introduction of smudge pots and sprinklers in the 1960s. Although frost isn't so much of a problem if it comes early or late in the year, if it strikes in April or May, when vines are budding, it can be devastating – as many winemakers have been reminded.

Domaine Alice et Olivier De Moor is one such estate that has suffered in recent years, losing 95% of their crop to frost and hail in 2016. "The weather has changed a lot," Alice says. "A friend's grandfather started writing the date of the harvest on his winery wall at the beginning of the 20th century. From 1900 to

Opposite, from top:
Édouard and Eleni Vocoret,
Isabelle Raveneau,
Vincent Dauvissat.

Overleaf: Grand Cru
'Valmur' from Grand
Cru 'Les Clos', Chablis.

1980 the date was nearly the same, but after that it started getting earlier. We have vineyards in three different villages, so we thought that if we had a problem in one, it would be okay in the other two. But this year every village was destroyed." As well as the actual town of Chablis, the Chablis appellation contains satellite villages, including Fyé, Fleys, Milly, Chichée and Courgis, where the De Moors' winery is based. Respected growers in the 'natural' wine world, the couple studied oenology in Dijon before planting vines on a relative's field – something that was much easier to do in 1989 when there weren't so many government restrictions. "Olivier used to work for a big local domaine and saw that although they produced good grapes, they manipulated them so much in the cellar that the wine wasn't as good as it could be," Alice says. "When I studied oenology I realised that the best way to make good wine is to grow good grapes. For us it's better to own a small domaine and to be able to decide everything ourselves."

When, back in 2016, they lost most of their crop, they improvised by filling their empty barrels with Clairette, Viognier, Roussanne, Bourboulenc and Grenache Blanc from like-minded growers as far south as Tavel, Ardèche and Tournon. "We bought grapes from Eric Pfifferling, and Michèle and Maxime-François at Domaine Gramenon in the Southern Rhône," she explains. "They're great friends – when we met Gramenon we felt like we'd known them since we were children." Solidarity in the face of disaster is gratifying, and it's intriguing to imagine what kind of wines these southern-grown, Chablis-vinified abnormalities will become. A chalky-textured Viognier, or oyster-shell Châteauneuf-du-Pape-alike, perhaps? Like women in the barrel cellar, even the most conservative places can be surprising.

Opposite: Alice De Moor, Courgis.

The Côte d'Or

Burgundy, France

DRIVING PAST the superstar vineyards on Burgundy's D974 is thirsty work. Puligny-Montrachet, Meursault, Vosne-Romanée, Chambolle-Musigny, Gevrey-Chambertin: these are names that have launched a thousand lunchtimes; names that, once wedded to the correct combination of producer and vintage, provide some of the most pleasurable vinous experiences known to humankind. Today, winemaking in such sainted communes has never been better: improved organic viticulture, rising temperatures eradicating anaemic vintages, and better prevention of the premature oxidation of Chardonnay that has blighted the region since the mid '90s make it easy to drink well here, if you know where to look. However, with the price of land quadrupling over the past decade, making it hard for family-owned domaines to expand or afford crippling inheritance taxes, Burgundy faces existential questions. Will its identity as a region of smallholder *paysans* be replaced by luxury brands and financial foundations? That remains to be seen, but as well as producing sublime wines, it's the Burgundians who safeguard this place as the home of the most venerable vineyards on the planet.

We begin our journey in northern Burgundy, in the city of Dijon. Having visited Chablis in the region's uppermost reaches, we'll now travel through the prime villages of the Côte d'Or in its middle section, passing the medieval town of Beaune on the way to the Côte Chalonnaise in the south. The Côte d'Or itself is split into two sections: the Côte de Beaune, which specialises in Chardonnay (with notable exceptions in places such as Volnay and Pommard), and the Côte de Nuits to its north, where Pinot Noir hits its heights. As our hire car leaves Dijon train station, passing the industrial units and historic vineyards of Chenôve on the way to Marsannay, a rush of blood courses through our veins. We're in Burgundy again.

No one has done more for the reputation of Marsannay than Sylvain Pataille. A trained oenologist who consults for other elite Burgundian domaines, Pataille has accumulated 15ha of organic and biodynamic vines

Opposite: Jean-Marc Roulot in 'Les Luchets', Meursault, where he played as a child.

since starting out with a single hectare in 1999, producing delicious, accessible Pinot Noir, Chardonnay and Aligoté using indigenous yeasts and minimal added sulphur. His Marsannay village wines represent some of Burgundy's best-value reds, while his 'L'Ancestrale' cuvée, from vines planted between 1930 and 1945, is an intense, layered beauty. However, it's when Sylvain starts talking about his four single-vineyard Aligotés – Burgundy's often misunderstood third grape – that the conversation gets animated.

"Aligoté is one of the best grape varieties but has almost completely been forgotten, like a northern Carignan," he says. "We have rediscovered our roots, our history, because Aligoté and Chardonnay were classified at the same level as each other in the past, and were good when blended together." Farming plots of old vine Aligoté Doré – rather than the modern, high-yielding clone Aligoté Vert – he creates wines that are on another level compared with those from the often poorly located young vines that have given the grape a bad name. "Famous 19th-century books described Aligoté as a variety that has to be planted on the top slopes in gravel soils, pruned very short and picked late. Today, it's completely the opposite: it's planted on very strong soils on the planes, with long pruning, and is harvested early. How can it be good? A Pinot Noir from the bottom of Vosne-Romanée will never be Richebourg." Fresh, linear white wines with green tinges, whose moderate alcohol makes them a traditional lunchtime favourite, Aligoté typically combines stony minerality with citrus and herbaceous, tarragon-esque flavours. Other top domaines growing old-vine Aligoté Doré include Roulot, Coche-Dury,

Left: Sylvain Pataille, Marsannay.

Right: Grand Cru
vineyards, Vosne-Romanée.
La Romanée and
La Romanée-Conti are
in the middle section
on the right.

De Villaine, Lafarge, Naudin, and perhaps most famously, Domaine Ponsot, where it historically accounted for most of their Premier Cru 'Clos des Monts Luisants' as part of a field blend. A recently drunk 1983 'Monts Luisants' was full of verve at over 35 years old: "Aligoté has incredible potential for ageing," says Sylvain.

We leave Marsannay, passing the hamlets of Couchey, Fixin (pronounced Fees-Anne) and Brochon, and arrive at one of the most famous wine names in France: Gevrey-Chambertin. Just off the main road, an anonymous building that was once a post office during the reign of Louis XV now houses the winery of Denis Bachelet – the king of Charmes-Chambertin, which is the least prestigious of Gevrey's nine Grand Cru vineyards. In Bachelet's hands Charmes-Chambertin is a rich, elegant wine with a slight animal edge that can stand toe-to-toe with the best in the village, such as Armand Rousseau's now stratospherically priced Chambertin. Elsewhere, talented *vignerons* such as David Duband, Denis Mortet and Jean-Marie Fourrier are making beautiful Pinot Noir from sites around the village, but for a taste of a favourite Premier Cru, 'Aux Combottes', we travel a few miles south to 'The Domaine of Jacques'.

Nestled on Rue de la Bussière in Morey-St-Denis, Domaine Dujac makes the quintessential wines of the commune, as well as of surrounding appellations – a remarkable feat considering that the estate is a relative newcomer in Burgundy terms. While it is common for domaines to be passed through families for generations (although divided up because of Napoleonic inheritance law), Jacques Seysses was a Parisian outsider who, having caught the wine bug from his father Louis, worked two harvests with legendary *vigneron* Gérard Potel before buying Domaine Graillet in 1967 and renaming it Domaine Dujac. "One day Gérard called me and said 'What you are looking

for is for sale', and a week later I signed the freehold," says Jacques. "People don't realise that Burgundy was not a great way to make money in the '60s. When a winery came up for sale it could have stayed unsold for a year or more. It's not like today, where they never even make it on to the market. Then, there was no competition."

Enlisting the help of top local winemakers, including Pierre Ramonet and Aubert de Villaine, as well as reading all that he could about viticulture, Jacques set about defining a style. "I pinpointed the wines that I loved, met their producers, and talked with them about how they made them," he says. "My number one reference was 1938 Domaine de la Romanée-Conti La Tâche in magnum. I drank that wine several times with my dad. It was dark pink, but the complexity and the length were fantastic. It was exactly what I wanted to create. The job is to make the wine that you want to drink, and you hope that customers will enjoy it."

Following in the footsteps of their now retired parents, the next generation of Seysses – Alec, Jeremy, and his wife Diana – are continuing Dujac's standards. One of a number of domaines that include stems during fermentation – a once widespread technique that adds silken viscosity and savoury perfume – Dujac makes wines relatively light in colour, focusing on finesse rather than concentration. Beginning with village Morey-St-Denis, its portfolio moves through well-positioned sites in Gevrey-Chambertin, Chambolle-Musigny and Vosne-Romanée, peaking with Grand Crus including Clos St-Denis and Clos de la Roche. "Clos de la Roche is the wine that most defines Morey for me," says Jeremy. "It has the spicy warmth that you get in the Morey village wine, but with a stony minerality you'd expect from the thinner soils in the Grand Crus, and another level of elegance to its tannins."

Indeed, identifying the aroma characteristics of Côte de Nuits communes during a blind tasting with Jeremy is a fascinating endeavour. "For me, the dominant elements of Gevrey-Chambertin are fruit and stone; Morey-St-Denis is more fruit and spice; Chambolle-Musigny is fruit and flowers, and Vosne-Romanée is exotic spices – cardamom and turmeric, rather than nutmeg in Morey," he says. The next two communes south of Morey-St-Denis, Chambolle-Musigny and Vosne-Romanée, are candidates for being home to the finest red wines in the world, bar none. In Chambolle-Musigny, next door to the iconic Château du Clos de Vougeot, Grand Cru Musigny and Premier Cru 'Les Amoureuses' produce silken, multidimensional, transcendent Pinot Noir, especially from Frédéric Mugnier and Christophe Roumier, master winemakers at the top of their game. However, it's in Vosne-Romanée, at the domaine many consider to be the best in the world, where we stop next.

Roald Dahl once wrote: "To drink a Romanée-Conti is like having an orgasm in the mouth and the nose both at the same time." Who are we to disagree? One of few Burgundian estates to exclusively own only Grand Cru

Opposite: Jeremy, Diana, Alec and Jacques Seysses, Domaine Dujac, Morey-St-Denis.

vineyards, Domaine de la Romanée-Conti is named after its Romanée-Conti *monopole*, the pinnacle of the region's hierarchy of vineyards. Drinking this wine, as well as those from surrounding crus farmed by Comte Liger-Belair (which owns neighbouring La Romanée) and Sylvain Cathiard, it is easy to be wowed by their harmony and naturalness, typically showing aromas of rose petals and exotic spices. Indeed, it's these wines' completeness, rather than anything extra that they offer per se, that makes them so special. We've been fortunate to drink the spherical 2002 Comte Liger-Belair 'La Romanée' on a couple of occasions – a wine you savour as slowly as possible because you're delighted just to be in its presence.

"Pinot Noir doesn't have a very strong character by itself, so it needs good terroir to really speak," says Aubert de Villaine, who runs Domaine de la Romanée-Conti with nephew Bertrand. Like Dujac, Domaine de la Romanée-Conti uses whole bunch fermentations (vintages with good ripeness such as '15, '09 and '05 include all stems), believing that "they bring a finesse that is not immediate, but comes with age." Tasting its unrivalled portfolio (Richebourg, Romanée-St-Vivant, Échezeaux, Grands Échezeaux, La Tâche, Romanée-Conti, Corton and Montrachet) from barrel while Aubert talks about his quest for simplicity in winemaking is an intoxicating privilege. Just as it is a few hundred yards away, across the Place de l'Eglise, at Comte Liger-Belair, whose red wines are some of the most sensual we've drunk.

Descended from a long military background ("My family is quite simple – either you're in the army or you're in the vineyards,"), Louis-Michel Liger-Belair prefers to de-stem his grapes, resulting in early accessible yet long-lived wines. "A good bottle is an empty bottle," he says. "I'm not a fan of big extraction – I like delicacy, elegance, freshness and vibrancy. Wine is meant to be drunk, not to be tasted, so my question always is: are you enjoying it? Do you want to finish the bottle? It could be a simple, cheap wine, or it could be a very expensive one, but my approach is the same."

For many wine lovers who can't afford the lofty premiums of Vosne-Romanée, the good news is that elegant Pinot Noir is now being made on the humble high slopes of the nearby Hautes-Côtes. "Climate change means that we get good maturity here now," says David Duband, who produces delicious Hautes-Côtes de Nuits among a portfolio of more prestigious appellations. Likewise, Claire Naudin in little-known Magny-lès-Villers makes a Hautes-Côtes de Beaune called 'Orchis Mascula' that has Vosne-esque aromas of rose petals and coriander, and drinks better than many other producers' Premier Crus. Who says quality is hidebound to hierarchy?

We leave Vosne-Romanée and pass through the town of Nuits-St-Georges on the way to Beaune. Here, Domaines Henri Gouges, Robert Chevillon and Freddie Mugnier's *monopole* 'Clos de la Maréchale' make savoury, full-bodied wines, and as we leave the Côte de Nuits and enter the Côte de Beaune the sweeping vista of the hill of Corton (home to Coche-Dury

Opposite: Louis-Michel Liger-Belair, Comte Liger-Belair, Vosne-Romanée.

Corton-Charlemagne – a true desert island wine), with Savigny-lès-Beaune behind it, comes into view. Like the Hautes-Côtes, the vineyards surrounding Beaune (Savigny-lès-Beaune, Chorey-lès-Beaune, Pernand-Vergelesses and Beaune itself) are a source of more affordable Burgundy: favourites include Savigny's Domaine Simon Bize, where Chisa Bize is continuing a long tradition of fine, supple Pinot, and Domaine des Croix, where David Croix is on a mission to prove what long out-of-fashion Beaune Premier Crus are capable of.

Driving around Beaune's medieval centre on its ring road, we see the Hotel-Dieu's famous spire, and turn south toward Pommard and Volnay. While Pommard's heavy, iron-rich soils are sometimes considered second class, they can produce wines of great finesse (an otherworldly 1978 De Montille Pommard 1er 'Les Pézerolles' will live long in the memory), but it's the Volnay of Domaine Lafarge and Domaine Marquis d'Angerville that set the standards for Pinot Noir in the Côte de Beaune. Silky, floral wines, Lafarge's 'Clos des Chênes' and d'Angerville's 'Clos des Ducs' have been compared to top Chambolle-Musigny, although the latter has more power. Interestingly, Volnay, like its neighbour Meursault, and Nuits-St-Georges, doesn't have any Grand Cru vineyards – something that Guillaume d'Angerville attributes to when his grandfather Sem and Henri Gouges were tasked with writing Burgundy's appellation classifications in 1935. Before starting work, the pair agreed they would not put a Grand Cru in their home villages, so other people would see that they were working for the common good, rather than for themselves. Since then, there have been few changes to the classifications, with prices of Premier Cru vineyards of Grand Cru quality ('Les Amoureuses' in Chambolle, 'Les Perrières' in Meursault, etc.) corrected by the market. The 'Clos des Ducs' *monopole* is another contender for elevation to Grand Cru status, but is it worth provoking communal disputes, as happened in St Émilion? Guillaume d'Angerville thinks not.

Consult oenological textbooks about the white wines of neighbouring village Meursault, and you'll invariably find them described as big, fat and buttery. But if you tried to identify such characteristics in the wines of Jean-Marc Roulot, you'd be forgiven for assuming their chalky minerality and pitch-perfect acidity had more in common with Chablis than the Côte de Beaune. Taut, precise and rippling with tension, Roulot's Chardonnays are magnificent interpretations of wines from this top appellation. "There is a specificity for Meursault that I would define as more fleshy than a Puligny-Montrachet," says Jean-Marc when asked what differentiates the village from those around it. "But, just like sheet music, everybody is free to interpret it as they like. In the past, the wines here have often been interpreted as fat and powerful, which with time has become like a brand image for the appellation. Thankfully, different styles have appeared, and it's great that today we can express them all in the same appellation."

In the late 1970s, Jean-Marc left his family domaine to train as an actor at the Conservatoire de Paris, but returned full-time in 1989, a few years after his father Guy's death. Even today, Jean-Marc splits his time between his two enduring passions and his CV boasts a string of screen and stage appearances, including the role of a winemaker in the 2017 film *Ce Qui Nous Lie* (a.k.a. Back to Burgundy). He cites 2007 Meursault 'Les Luchets' – a vineyard he used to play in as a child – as the wine he is most proud of producing "because it's a good illustration of what I wanted to make and drink, and all from a simple village appellation". He also continually trials new methods to improve viticulture and winemaking, including hiring Professor Denis Dubourdieu with his close friend Dominique Lafon in 2009 to help eliminate premox. Premature oxidation, where Chardonnay turns flat and Sherry-like when in its prime, has been a big problem for Burgundian white winemakers since the mid-'90s, but thankfully is now more under control (it was also a big problem in white Bordeaux, but you hear much less about that).

"When I started winemaking there was a big emphasis on work in the winery and ageing wines," says Dominique Lafon, who alongside Roulot, and locals Jean-François Coche and Arnaud Ente, is among the world's greatest white winemakers. "The wines my father made were more Comtes Lafon in style than 'Genevrières', 'Perrières' or 'Charmes' [Meursault Premier Cru vineyards].

He was using a lot of new oak barrels and doing very long ageing." Indeed, if the early vintages Dominique produced after taking over in 1986 fit with the fatter old-school Meursault profile, his wines have gradually evolved, keeping the weight but eking out more minerality, moving towards the racy Roulot style. Outside of Meursault, Lafon also owns a third of a hectare of Burgundy's most regal Chardonnay vineyard – 'Le Montrachet' – which produces an extremely dense and persistent wine with breathtaking energy, as well as much humbler vineyards in the Côte de Mâconnais, where he makes cheaper, but still very delicious wines. "I liked the challenge of buying vineyards in the Mâconnais, as I was frightened about doing exactly the same thing all my life," Dominique recalls. "In Meursault, if you need a new tractor, you buy a new tractor. In Mâcon, if you have a problem with your tractor, you fix the old tractor. I wanted to feel like a normal *vigneron*, rather than a spoilt one; to balance my mind and keep my feet on the ground."

Close by, the famous villages of Chassagne-Montrachet and Puligny-Montrachet – with Grand Cru 'Le Montrachet' straddled between them – rival Meursault as the epicentre of mind-blowing Chardonnay. Although there are few actual wineries located in Puligny due to its high-water table, which renders digging deep cellars almost impossible, classic domaines such as Leflaive and Jacques Carillon and excellent new micro-domaine Thomas-Collardot make taut, mineral wines. Back in 1988 Domaine Chavy-Chouet was tipped as Puligny-Montrachet's 'domaine to watch' by Jasper Morris in *The White Wines of Burgundy*, an early promise that its hell-raising owner *vigneron* Hubert Chavy never delivered on. Since he passed away in 2014, his son Romaric Chavy has been staking a claim as one of the region's next stars, producing wines from sites in Puligny, as well as Meursault and St Aubin. Over in Chassagne-Montrachet, Domaines Ramonet and Bernard Moreau set the blistering standard, their roster of wines always expressing site characteristics – not something that every Burgundy domaine achieves. Likewise, the 1.2ha Domaine Lamy-Caillat, run by Sébastien Caillat and Florence Lamy, employs meticulous organic farming and long *élevages* to make some of the Côte de Beaune's most exciting new wines. And that's not forgetting all the talent in surrounding communes Auxey-Duresses, St Aubin and St Romain.

As we leave the Côte de Beaune, our Burgundy journey draws to a close driving south into the Côte Chalonnaise past Bouzeron (a great Aligoté village) and stopping at Domaine Dureuil-Janthial in bucolic Rully. *Vigneron* Vincent Dureuil-Janthial is a classic overachiever, crafting gorgeous wines from humble Rully terroir (and a Puligny-Montrachet Premier Cru), exemplifying what makes this region, and the Côte Mâconnais further south, such rich hunting grounds for savvy winos. Yes, Burgundy makes some of the world's rarest and most expensive bottles. Yes, it makes its most transcendent wines, too. But if you know where to look, there is also an abundance of humble-yet-beautifully crafted wines to be found.

Opposite, clockwise from top right: Dominique Lafon, Romaric Chavy, Sébastien Caillat, Jean-Marc Roulot, and Vincent Dureuil-Janthial.

La Paulée de Meursault

Château de Meursault, Burgundy, France

FORGET *WEDDING CRASHERS* – any Burgundy lover going to La Paulée de Meursault for the first time feels like they're infiltrating the jackpot of all celebrations. Held in the grand Château de Meursault as the third part of the Côte d'Or's annual 'Trois Glorieuses' extended weekend (the other two are the Hospices de Beaune wine auction and a stuffy black-tie dinner in the Château du Clos de Vougeot), like any wedding party, it features rambling speeches, funny dancing and intense hand-wringing conversations between ruddy-faced men who dress like it's 1985, not to mention hours of everyone singing the region's twee drinking anthem, 'Le Ban Bourguignon' (imagine Widow Twankey belting out 'Hey Jude' while doing 'The Birdie Song' routine). But where La Paulée happily deviates – besides the fact that it's a traditional lunch put on to thank local vineyard workers after harvest and nothing whatsoever to do with holy matrimony – is by requiring every guest to bring at least one magnum of eyeball-rolling, table-thumping, foot-stomping, hairs-on-the-back-of-the-neck brilliant Burgundy to aid the collective goal of getting well and truly plastered. It's the BYO bash to end all BYO bashes, and you don't even have to make uncomfortable small talk with the bride's weird uncle.

The lunch begins at midday, as expectant as a Catholic maternity ward. Tickets are only available to the winemakers of the village, so La Paulée de Meursault has become one of the most-talked-about-but-exclusive events in wine – a kind of bacchanalian Glastonbury or Super Bowl of Chardonnay – only much more fun. By 12.15 p.m. the queue for the unisex toilets is snaking out of the château (whoever coined the expression "couldn't organise a piss-up in a brewery" may have been French), and thirsty revellers fervently scan table plans like combat troops locating their stations. As guests of Romaric Chavy – a rising star who is making great improvements in quality at Domaine Chavy-Chouet – we're at table 'Genevrières' (sections are named after local vineyards) where a man sporting a magnum of Champagne-god Jacques Selosse's awesome 2003 Blanc de Blancs kicks off festivities by sloshing some bubbly in our glasses. A whiff is all it takes

for affirmation that the world's top *vignerons* make extraordinary wines in even the most challenging vintages (we could say it had a bouquet of roasted hazelnuts, biscuit and savoury consommé with a Madeira-esque edge but that, of course, would be to miss the point – no one comes to La Paulée to pull the legs off wine). From here on in, the afternoon accelerates through a cinematic time-lapse sequence of large-format bottles (jeroboams, methuselahs and nebuchawhatchamacallits), relentlessly served by random benefactors to friend and stranger alike.

The Champagne continues with a friend's lovely 1999 Egly-Ouriet before Romaric's godfather, winemaker François Mikulski, and a grey-haired Englishman arrive toting magnums of 2002 Meursault 1er Cru 'Charmes' and 2002 Raveneau Chablis 1er 'Montée de Tonnerre'. Down the hatch. Next up, an extraordinary 2008 Coche-Dury Meursault 'Les Rougeots' is passed along the table by our neighbours – all typical Jean-François gun-smoke reduction and grapefruit attack – followed in quick succession by 2002 Jacques Carillon Puligny-Montrachet 1er 'Les Perrières' and 1989 Chavy-Chouet Meursault 1er 'Les Charmes'. When leading winemaker Jean-Marc Roulot greets us with a magnum of 1996 Meursault 1er Cru 'Perrières' we waste no time making room in one of the several glasses we have on the go. From Meursault's greatest vineyard in an outstanding year, 1996 Roulot 'Perrières' tastes like a repressed memory of the way aged white Burgundy ought to taste in fairytales, a mind-bogglingly complex concoction of honey, nuts, citrus and mushroom that grips the palate like buttered velcro.

By 3.30 p.m. the toilet queue is out of control, and copious guests are silhouetted in the grounds siphoning gallons of wine back out on to the terroir whence it came. Serving hundreds of consecutive courses of lobster ballotine, scallops with *beurre blanc*, *poularde de Bresse rôtie*, fillet of Charolais beef, cheeses and chocolate mousse, head chefs Cédric Burtin and Dominique Dansard have done a respectable job, although no one is here for the food. Anne-France Ramonet, scion of Chassagne's venerable Domaine Ramonet, struggles to hold aloft a methuselah of 2002 Ramonet Bâtard-Montrachet for a crowd of onlookers to take photos of on their iPhones, while three weary journeymen chefs in traditional garb struggle past hordes of well-oiled diners waving white serviettes or merrily hiccupping into glasses of Mugneret-Gibourg 'Clos de Vougeot' and DRC La Tâche that have begun to do the rounds. For these chaps, the concept of 'celebrity' chefdom must be an aberration.

By 6 p.m., renditions of 'Le Ban Bourguignon' have reached fever pitch and everyone is standing on chairs doing 'The Birdie Song' routine. The château is buzzing with a profound sense of fellowship – a reminder that the best thing about Burgundy isn't its investment potential or bragging rights, but its magical ability to bring people close together when shared. As the lunch slowly winds down and guests begin departing for after-parties held in various cellars around the village, we bid *au revoir* to our château full of friends, some old, some new. La Paulée de Meursault is a no-holds-barred celebration of the world's greatest wine region, and one hell of a good party to crash.

Opposite: Primetime Paulée.

Jean-Marie Guffens

Mâconnais, France

"I'm a very awful man because I say what I think, and what I think is mostly right," Jean-Marie Guffens tells me, leaning across the table to emphasise the point. Producing scintillating interview copy and scintillating white Burgundy are two entirely different things, but this self-proclaimed 'crazy Belgian' – or maverick master-*vigneron* of the Mâconnais, in the south of the region – does a commendable job of both. Now in his mid-sixties, the loquacious Guffens is in many ways my ideal interviewee, relishing putting the world to rights on the eve of a retrospective of his wines in London – not that I agree with all he says. Try a few of his quotes on for size.

"Biodynamics is just a way to sell wine," says Guffens. "Do you know that Rudolf Steiner, the guy who wrote the book, never even had a garden? And he was pro-Nazi." Or: "You generally don't find great wines made by estates that are passed from father to son. Some of them go so far back I call them 15 de-generations." And how about: "I hate it when a young wine doesn't taste good and people say that means it'll improve. Do you think your children have to be stupid and ugly to grow into beautiful adults?" Although such nuggets are invariably followed up with a gravelly, 20-a-day chuckle, Guffens' penchant for plain-speaking has cost him dearly in the past. Many people want him to shut up; some, such as the fraud-squad officer he once threatened to sue, have even tried to send him to prison without evidence of wrongdoing (more about this anon). But although Guffens' story is a roller-coaster ride of epic highs and lows most people can only imagine, it is among the most remarkable of any winemaking great.

Newlyweds Jean-Marie Guffens and Maine Heynen moved from Belgium to the Mâconnais to learn winemaking and French in 1976. Having been discharged from national service for reporting to the army administration hall in the nude, complaining of a problem with authority, Jean-Marie was full of optimism for their new life in a foreign country when he enrolled on a course at Davayé wine school. Here, Guffens learnt about herbicides, machine harvesting and, as he says now, "every stupid thing that you don't have to know about making wine". Although you wouldn't know from his wine labels, or the vitriol that he lavishes on organic and biodynamic certification, Guffens has never used industrial chemicals, employing a pragmatic, traditionalist approach to farming.

Mâcon-Pierreclos, his flagship vineyard, and contender for the best-value fine wine in France, was the first that he bought; no other grower wanted it because it didn't have a track record and was, ironically, considered too steep. "It's more pleasurable to make great wines from something that doesn't already exist," says Guffens. "My Pierreclos are the wines from somewhere that didn't previously exist." His first vintage was 1980, a terrible year in the Mâconnais, but by 1982 he'd already begun to make a name when his wines were reviewed by ascendant American critic Robert Parker.

"Parker wrote 'There's a crazy Belgian who makes Mâcon as good as Puligny-Montrachet, and a Pouilly-Fuissé as good as Grand Crus from the Côte d'Or,'" Guffens says. "I wrote him a letter and said 'I read what you wrote about my wine. I'm very worried.' Why would a writer want to write like Victor Hugo, or a painter to paint like Picasso? I make Guffens wines in Mâconnais and I don't want to be compared. Anyone who makes great things in life has to be original." Indeed, one of the worst things you can say about Guffens' Mâconnais wines in his presence is that they are only 'as good' as the Côte d'Or, even if he far over-performs on what's considered humbler terroir. His point is simple: tour the affluent villages of the Côte de Beaune, and for every *vigneron* who has elevated a family domaine to greater heights, you'll find numerous others complacently living off an appellation's reputation. "For years Avis was the biggest hire car company in the USA, and their competitor Hertz's marketing slogan was 'We try harder,'" says Guffens. "The Mâconnais is like Hertz."

Having quickly sold out of his early vintages, in large part due to Parker's early praise, the two became friends, not that it saved him, or other critics, from Guffens' mischievous nature. Presented with a glass of a mysterious wine by Guffens as a 'blind tasting', Parker was angered after mistaking 1986 Mouton Rothschild – a First Growth he'd recently awarded a '100-point' score – for a generic $10 Californian Cabernet, while Burgundy expert Clive Coates mixed up unidentified samples of Coche-Dury Meursault 1er Cru 'Les Perrières' and Guffens-Heynen Pouilly-Fuissé 'La Roche'. Guffens may have a peculiar way of making friends and influencing people, but tests like this proved just how good his wines had become.

The following decade was to be his heyday, making "the wines of my life" in 1985, 1989, 1990 and 1992. The beginning of the '90s also saw him team up with Jean Rijckaert to co-found Verget, a ground-breaking micro-*négociant* winery buying in fruit from the Mâconnais and the Côte d'Or (at the time a *négociant* being hands-on in the vineyards was unheard of).

Opposite: Jean-Marie Guffens.

With easy-to-obtain bank loans and access to fruit from some of the most prestigious terroirs in Burgundy – something very difficult to get now – Verget grew quickly. In 1992 it made 18 barrels of Bâtard-Montrachet and bought eight barrels of Chevalier-Montrachet from Beaune *négociant* Bouchard Pères et Fils. The only trouble was they were in the red for 3.8 million francs with no buyers for the new wines. Until the Parker effect took hold once again.

"Why does a young Belgian make better wines than the guy who owns the land? What's wrong in Burgundy?" Parker asked in his influential newsletter, awarding Verget's 1992 Bâtard-Montrachet a 97-point score. Guffens' fax machine whirred into action, and soon became inundated with enquiries from around the world. "I wrote back, 'We're very pleased about your interest in our wines, but the only thing we know about you is that you can read English and count to 100,'" Guffens says, laughing. "That made me a lot of enemies! But we sold all the wines in two weeks and I paid the bank back and had 2 million francs in the account from pre-sales." Sure, Guffens' brusque manner upset people, but the biggest upset came for him and Verget a few years later, after opening other wineries in the Luberon in southern France in 1997 and in Chablis as a joint-venture with Olivier Leflaive in 2001.

Trouble began just after the new Chablis winery's first harvest, with an unexpected visit from the fraud squad. Having found nothing wrong, they left and Guffens thought no more about it. Six months later, the same officers visited Verget in the Mâconnais "in defence of wine quality". Frustrated and angry that they were under investigation for undisclosed crimes, Guffens threw them out, but the chief inspector continued building a case over the next few years, culminating in a court hearing in June 2009 when all charges were dropped. Guffens telephoned the inspector and left a message with his secretary that he would sue him. Big mistake. A few weeks later, the inspector asked Lyon fraud squad for a commission of inquiry and Mâcon's vice-prosecutor ordered a search warrant and custody.

"They accused me of mixing everything," says Guffens of the morning 20 officers raided his winery and arrested staff. "They said my wine from Burgundy was better because I used wine from the south, and my wine from the south was better because I had added Burgundy. They made accusations that are untrue." So continued an ordeal that pushed him to the limits of endurance: "I was close to killing myself. Having had a life passion for wine and for all I had built, and seeing all that treated like this? Suddenly you find yourself trapped in a war." The inspector told staff that he had indisputable evidence of their producing illegal blends, and that they'd lose their jobs. But when he presented proof it was clear that he had mixed up Verget's 2008 and 2009 declarations of harvest, and there wasn't any discrepancy between yields and production levels.

The case disintegrated in 2011, and the investigation was criticised for several wrong statements, changes to the sequence of the files, and forged reports.

Now, nearly a decade on, here I am with Guffens in the Thames-side office of his UK importers, Farr Vintners, for a retrospective of Guffens-Heynen and Verget wines. Out of the over 600 listings at Noble Rot restaurant, I may have drunk more Guffens wines than any other. It's not that I prefer white wines to reds, or still to sparkling; it's simply because they're world-class Burgundies – my favourite white wines – that you can drink regularly without taking out a second mortgage. I love their tension, textural richness and stony/saline/chalky minerality, and how, as today's tasting attests, they are consistently delicious, no matter how challenging the vintage. The hot temperatures of 2003 were tricky for many in Burgundy, who made wines with too much alcohol and not enough acidity, yet Guffens excelled. His 2003 Pouilly-Fuissé 'Premier Jus des Hautes de Vignes' was just one of several remarkable surprises: a pure and long wine, with lively acidity and freshness balancing the vintage's inherent richness.

That Guffens is in a minority of Burgundian winemakers who consistently produce outstanding wines is no doubt in part because he doesn't adhere to a recipe, always using a different combination of methods. Whether *tri* harvesting grapes from the same vineyard at different ripeness levels to add depth, or improvising *élevage* in an array of different barrels and tanks, he could be Mâconnais wine's answer to Miles Davis – although, as a Pink Floyd devotee, he'd probably opt for Roger Waters instead. Having named his two dogs after the band, he even christened his phenomenal no-sulphur 2002 Saint-Véran Terres Noires 'Atom Heart Mother' after their 1970 album. A rich, buttery, saline ball of energy, it was unanimously voted the cuvée of the tasting. For Guffens, winemaking is an art form for uncompromising expression. As he says himself, "The truth is what you live when you look at yourself in the mirror."

Opposite: Jean-Marie
Guffens and Dan Keeling.

Beaujolais
France

DEEP IN THE BEAUJOLAIS countryside nobody can hear you scream. "Guests have asked if they can stay over after the party, but I told them, 'You're not going to sleep'," says Julien Sunier of his impending birthday celebrations. His isolated Avenas home is, theoretically, just an hour's drive north of Lyon, but it's taken us more than that just to navigate Beaujolais' twisting hillsides, stuck behind tractors and taking wrong turns. Now the thought of finding our way back to civilisation from a raucous symposium of *vignerons* – embittered by recent hailstorms that have decimated this year's crop – is making us sweat. Sure, Noble Rot can party with the best of them, but this sounds intense.

"Man, after all the crazy weather my winemaker friends are due a drink," says Sunier pulling corks from his Beaujolais crus. "I like to make Gamay with freshness, because for me a good wine is an empty bottle." We swirl our glasses of dark ruby Fleurie and its perfume caresses the senses with peonies, cherries, strawberries and earth – it doesn't smell of Gamay so much as a summer walk in the country. Some may lambast Beaujolais for lacking the complexity of neighbouring Burgundy, but that's like using the same criteria to judge Iggy Pop and Beethoven's Symphony No. 5. Fleurie hits fewer notes than Romanée-Conti, but the ones it does it hits with irresistible *joie de vivre*.

Today, Beaujolais – or to be specific, the small percentage of wine produced by top domaines within the ten designated cru appellations (Morgon, Fleurie, Chénas, Moulin-à-Vent, Juliénas, Chiroubles, Régnié, Brouilly, Côte de Brouilly and St Amour) – is a world away from the synthetic banana and bubblegum-flavoured Beaujolais Nouveau that made the region famous in the 1980s. Its renaissance as a region capable of 'serious' wine is complete thanks to a group of *vignerons* christened the 'Gang of Four', who took inspiration from the late Jules Chauvet, a *négociant* and chemist considered the father of 'natural' wine. Led by Marcel Lapierre, and including Jean Foillard, Jean-Paul Thévenet and Guy Breton, the Gang limited sulphur additions and shunned fertilisers, chaptalisation and cultivated yeasts. "Jules Chauvet was a brilliant taster who

Opposite: Moulin-à-Vent.

had memories of what the old wines of Beaujolais used to be like," Jean-Paul Thévenet recalls. "Chauvet said 'Why can't we make wines like that?' People had forgotten a time before fertilisers, but he had done a lot of research and knew how to work the soil. He defined carbonic maceration and other techniques that generations of *vignerons* had been doing by feel." Instead of the heavy, manipulated juice pumped out by the large industrial producers, the friends made bottles for their own drinking pleasure – perfumed, lower alcohol wines where spritz or cloudiness were accepted as part of a 'living' product. "When we all started it was a very exciting time," says Jean Foillard, whose first vintage was 1980. "We were all exchanging ideas and techniques, and it really moved things forward."

Marcel Lapierre passed away in 2010, but he still inspires saint-like reverence among legions of fans. On a recent visit, we met an American wine merchant searching for directions to his grave: later that day the man was spotted next to the headstone in deep contemplation with a glass of one of Lapierre's wines in his hand. Luckily for wine lovers, the family domaine is still going strong, now run by son Mathieu and daughter Camille, who produce three cuvées from 16ha around Morgon. They were also instrumental in helping their friend, and some-time trainee, David Chapel – whose father, legendary chef Alain Chapel, spent a lot of time tasting with Marcel and Jules Chauvet – to begin making wine and set up a winery in Régnié-Durette with his American wife Michele Smith Chapel. For such a relatively new venture, Domaine Chapel is making exceptionally pure, perfumed Beaujolais from Juliénas, Chiroubles,

Left: Julien Sunier.

Fleurie and Beaujolais-Villages vines. "When I was in New York I dreamed of living in Meursault," says Smith Chapel, who previously worked as sommelier and buyer for three-Michelin-star restaurant Brooklyn Fare. "But I'm so happy to live in Beaujolais. It's a different world here – more relaxed and obtainable. If you are starting out from scratch, you can actually buy land and a house."

Granitic rock with sections of sand and clay dominate the Beaujolais crus, which are divided into single vineyard *lieu-dits*. From renowned Fleurie *climats* such as 'La Madone' (The Madonna), 'Grille-Midi' and 'Clos de la Grand'Cour' to Morgon's famous 'Côte du Py' (where *roches pourries*, a.k.a. 'rotten rocks', litter the ground), there's the opportunity here for winemakers to express terroir like their Côte d'Or neighbours, if only they respect the land. "You only recognise terroir when you drink wine that is fermented with yeast from the actual place, and the land is worked properly by plough," says Julien Sunier. "If you make wine from a completely fucked-up herbicide parcel with yeast control and thermovinification – which is a big problem here – you can't talk about terroir. When I go to some of my friends' houses who make the wines this way, you don't see a difference between the crus. You drink the wine and it all tastes the same." Of all appellations, Fleurie and Morgon have the most quality-driven producers working within them, while Moulin-à-Vent is famed for darker, more austere, long-lived wines that gain stylistic similarities to Pinot Noir as they age.

Above, left to right: David Chapel and Michele Smith Chapel, Jean and Agnes Foillard.

Left: Jean-Louis and
Justin Dutraive.

Below: Fleurie.

192

Another winery whose recent vintages have become among the best rated in Beaujolais – and require serious cellar time to fulfil their potential – is Domaine Jules Desjourneys. "My ambition is to make a Gamay that is among the world's 50 best wines," says owner/*vigneron* Fabien Duperray, and his exceptional Fleurie, Morgon and Moulin-à-Vent have claims. A Burgundian who started out as an agent for some of the region's most famous names – Coche-Dury, Domaine de la Romanée-Conti, Arnaud Ente – before moving operations to an old train station in La Chapelle-de-Guinchay, and beginning life as a winemaker at the end of the 2000s, he is perfectly connected to develop his craft. However, another producer whose wines may have already arrived at the apogee of what Gamay can achieve is Jean-Louis Dutraive at Domaine de la Grand'Cour.

Judged on its surroundings, Domaine de la Grand'Cour doesn't live up to its splendiferous name. Decrepit machinery, and a constructor's crane stand outside ramshackle outbuildings, while inside the winery a bowing ceiling is held together by makeshift wooden beams. But from among such environs the humble Jean-Louis Dutraive, with the help of his son Justin, fashions a Brouilly and four Fleurie cuvées headed by the ethereal 'Champagne' – an exceptional wine that balances weight with finesse, and wouldn't taste out of place in Chambolle-Musigny. Justin has also begun making a nascent range of his own wines in part of the domaine's historic cellar, following in his father's footsteps.

Jean-Louis drives down the dirt track that splits his recently decimated 'Clos de la Grand'Cour' vineyard and stops next to the 1.4ha he owns of 'Champagne' – an unremarkable south-westerly slope – and the difference between his well-worked pink granite and his neighbour's drab non-organic vines is obvious. "We lost everything in 'Clos de la Grand'Cour' in 2016, and a lot here in 'Champagne', but at least I was able to buy grapes so we can make some wine," says Jean-Louis. With hailstones the size of golf balls, the weather – a constant threat to a small artisanal domaine such as this – has been horrendous for Beaujolais in recent years. Not that the locals let it get them down, especially if Julien Sunier's birthday celebrations are anything to go by. "The atmosphere in Beaujolais is welcoming," says Julien. "There's less money than other wine regions, so life is simpler. This is a bottle of wine, man! Keep cool!"

Jura

France

IF THE OUTSIDER WINES of the Jura didn't exist, who would invent them?
Even the most creative mind would be stretched to imagine such improbable
specialties. There's Ploussard – a.k.a. Poulsard – a red grape whose pale juice
glows luminous pink that the locals drink before white. Then you have Macvin,
a bizarre, hillbilly moonshine made by fortifying white Savagnin must with
brandy, not to mention Vin Jaune, a Sherry-like 'yellow wine', also made with
Savagnin, aged under a *voile* (veil) of yeast, that transforms into god-like genius
when accompanied by the region's extraordinary Comté cheese. And that's just
for starters. The flavours of the Jura are visceral and alive: naturalistic, raw, sour,
ugly and delicious. Just as rosé belongs to Provence, and Aligoté to the bistros
of Beaune, so these wines are rooted in place and circumstance, as if born
from woodland and alpine pastures. Perhaps some writer would be able create
such characters for a work titled *The Little Curiosity Shop of French Wine*.
But if there's any living winemaker who could do it, it is Jean-François Ganevat,
the Jura's mad professor, who loves experimenting in his low-tech-laboratory-
cum-winery in the hamlet of La Combe de Rotalier.

  A generous man, both in nature and stature, with a gold pirate's hoop
ring through one ear, Ganevat is the superstar who, alongside retired master
vignerons Pierre Overnoy and Jacques Puffeney, has drawn attention to
this obscure constellation in the past decade. "I'm just a peasant," he laughs
at the mention of his naming as *La Revue du Vin de France*'s Winemaker
of the Year in 2018. "It's funny winning awards when I don't like travelling
the world to show my wines. I'm just a normal guy from Rotalier who enjoys
hanging out, drinking wine, and eating cheese and saucisson with his friends."
An influential proponent of biodynamic farming and low/zero-sulphur
additions, Ganevat ferments all five of the Jura's permitted grape varieties,
although it is the noble white grapes Savagnin and Chardonnay, rather than
the delicious but locally less-revered reds Ploussard, Trousseau and Pinot
Noir, with which he particularly excels. Indeed, his Burgundy-like, layered

Opposite: Jean-François
Ganevat, La Combe
de Rotalier.

'Les Grands Teppes Vieilles Vignes', from 100-year-old Chardonnay vines, and his broad, lightly oxidative 'Les Vignes de Mon Père', from Savagnin aged for ten years in old oak barrels, are among France's most exciting wines.

Visits *chez* Ganevat are notorious for lasting a very long time, tasting up to 40 different cuvées that he and his sister Anne produce from 13ha of domaine vineyards, as well as *négociant* wines made from grapes bought from other regions. We taste two such Vins de France from tank: the first a blend of Pinot Noir from Volnay, Gamay from Beaujolais, Grenache from the Ardèche and Pinot Gris from Alsace (successful and delicious); the next a mix of obscurities – Marion, Besson and Galeck – with Gamay and Grenache (file under 'interesting'). "The different grape varieties are fascinating, and I love trying different things," Jean-François says, embodying a typically Jura passion for experimentation, something notably absent from more established wine regions. But although he makes radical cuvées way beyond the prescription

Left: Julien Labet, Rotalier.

Overleaf: Château-Chalon.

of French appellation law, Ganevat is also at the vanguard of a generation that has embraced mainstream Burgundian techniques of *ouillé* winemaking, where wines are rigorously topped up to the eye of the barrel to prevent oxidation, a standard practice almost everywhere else around the world. If the Jura's weird and wonderful outsider styles grabbed wine lovers' attention only a decade ago, this new wave of more conventionally made whites has huge potential for the future.

"Up until about 20 years ago, most people used to leave their wines in barrels without topping up, so they were oxidative to some degree," Ganevat says of the rustic practices behind 'traditional' Jura winemaking. After studying in Beaune before becoming cellar master at Domaine Jean-Marc Morey in Chassagne-Montrachet, he returned home to Rotalier in 1998 to take over the family estate, having learnt techniques such as lees-stirring and rigorously topping up newer oak barrels, much to the chagrin of his oxidative wine-loving, *vigneron* father. Introducing *ouillé* cuvées, as well as converting all his vineyards first to organic, then to biodynamic farming, Ganevat transformed the domaine from one that sold almost all of its wines locally at modest prices to one that now exports 95% of its production to 50 countries. "I learned what to do, and what not to do in Burgundy. After seeing the consequences of industrial farming on the land, I knew I wanted to go completely the other way."

Sandwiched between Burgundy and the Alps, the Jura is France's smallest classic wine region. Producing just 0.2% of national output (roughly 11 million bottles, or a third of the Champagne that Moët & Chandon makes per year), like most European vineyard areas, it was decimated by phylloxera and war, declining from 20,000ha under vine in the mid-1800s to 2,100ha today. Still relatively untouched by outside development, the Jura has no dominant industrial cities and an economy based around wood and cheese production; a bucolic landscape of agricultural crops, forests and pasture for Montbéliarde cows.

"Up until 1974, my grandfather had 2ha of vineyards and 12 dairy cows, which he used for milk to make Comté," says Ganevat's neighbour and fellow ambassador of the topped-up *ouillé* style, Julien Labet. "It was very common to own a farm polyculture; they made everything they needed and sold the rest to buy what they weren't able to produce." Dressed like a rural rock star in floral shirt, flat cap and Adidas trainers, Labet (who runs his domaine with sister Charline and brother Romain) developed his craft at another winery in Chassagne-Montrachet – the legendary Domaine Ramonet – so it's no surprise that his wines have the elegance and precision of high-quality white Burgundy. Saline and sour, with flavours of under-ripe pear and preserved lemons, 'Fleur de Savagnin' is a gloriously wild, warped response to the Côte de Beaune. But, just as Ganevat, Labet and other progressive local winemakers have adopted techniques from their Côte d'Or neighbours, they have also inherited their obsession with terroir.

There are many similarities between the Jura and neighbouring Burgundy, but also many differences. Both have continental climates – hot summers and cold winters – although the Jura is cooler and twice as wet. Both have soils made of limestone, and blue and grey clay marl, too, albeit in opposite proportions. When the two regions were pulled apart millions of years ago, and the Saône Valley formed between them, a top layer of Bajocian limestone was raised upwards to create the east-facing Côte d'Or in Burgundy, while the older, deeper-lying marl clays in the Jura were forced to the surface and violently pushed into the Alps, forming west-facing hills. Today, the Jura's vineyards are 80% clay and 20% limestone (the reverse of Burgundy's 80% limestone and 20% clay), a distinction that manifests itself in the characters of the two regions' wines.

A few hours with Stéphane Tissot is the fast-track to understanding such differences. Another biodynamic *vigneron* with a passion for experimentation, Tissot is a dynamo of enthusiasm who, with 50ha to his name, owns the largest artisanal domaine in the entire region. We begin by tasting his topped-up *ouillé* Chardonnays as he explains how the two soils affect the wines: 'Les Graviers', a racy mineral wine from limestone ("more Burgundy style"); 'En Barberon',

Above, left to right: Loreline Laborde, Les Granges Paquenesses. Stéphane Tissot.

Opposite: La Combe de Rotalier.

fuller-bodied, with bitterness and struck-match aromas from clay ("more Jura style"); and 'Les Bruyères', back to limestone, and a sinewy ringer for a top Meursault. But as the only estate that produces a range of single-vineyard Vin Jaune – the Jura's famous, Sherry-like 'yellow wine' that accounts for just 4% of regional production – it also allows you to see how terroir relates to oxidative cuvées.

"When people speak about Vin Jaune, they normally speak only about power, but when you taste single-vineyard Vin Jaune, there is complexity and delicacy, just like every other fine wine," Tissot says. Often considered a product of process rather than of place – much like the oxidative but fortified Sherry – all Tissot's Vins Jaunes have pronounced characters: 'En Spois' is big and powerful; 'La Vasée' elegant and salty, with a hint of whisky ("very good with oysters"); 'La Mailloche' has bitter, curry notes ("good with Indian food"); 'Les Bruyères', a nutty, powerful "archetypal Vin Jaune"; and 'Château-Chalon', the most delicate, citrusy and bitter, from a prestigious hilltop appellation reserved exclusively for yellow wine.

Bottled in unorthodox stout 62cl clavelins and served alongside local dishes such as *poulet au Vin Jaune et aux morilles*, or at the end of a meal with cheese, if ever there was a wine for thrill-seekers, Vin Jaune is it. Vinified from late-picked Savagnin grapes from very low yields, so as to be ripe and

concentrated enough to withstand the legally required six-and-a-half years' *élevage* in old oak barrels, the wine is left unattended in warm, dry cellars so that a thin veil of *flor* (dead yeast cells) forms on the surface, limiting oxidation and ensuring the development of complex, unusual flavours. The great 20th-century gourmand Curnonsky included Château-Chalon in his list of the five greatest white wines; intense, acidic and bone-dry, it has an outlandish kaleidoscope of flavour, from rancid walnuts, polish and iodine to caramel, fenugreek and curry leaf. Here is the rare wine that has made me laugh out loud in surprise.

As the co-president of Le Nez dans le Vert, an association of 50 local organic domaines, Tissot encourages and mentors many young winemakers in the region, 30 of whom have set up within the last decade alone. "There are no wine consultants in the Jura, and the estates own their vines. The personalities of the producers are in their wines, and there are many differences between each domaine," he says.

One such newbie is Loreline Laborde of Les Granges Paquenesses, who released her first vintage in 2010. Having studied winemaking in Orange and Dijon, before working in the Côtes du Rhône and Burgundy, like many others she was attracted to the Jura by a sense of freedom. "I wanted to come here because of the interesting grape varieties, and the diversity of farming, as I'd done my training in other regions where there's only vines," she says from her tumbledown farmhouse near Tourmont. "I'm really happy to be part of this new generation in the Jura. The solidarity of the Nez dans le Vert grower association has been very welcoming. Everyone helps each other, driving the region forward."

With high-quality vineyards available at affordable prices, it's a good bet that ever-more exciting wines will emerge from the region. "Fifteen years ago, there weren't many new winemakers coming here, because there wasn't a market for the wine," says Labet. "But in the last eight years, the Jura has become very fashionable, and more people have arrived." The most high-profile of these is Guillaume d'Angerville, owner of Volnay's quintessential Domaine Marquis d'Angerville, and his business partner François Duvivier. Starting out in 2012 by buying the 5ha Château de Chavanes in Montigny-lès-Arsures, followed by the 5ha Grand Curoulet from natural winemaker Jean-Marc Brignot, the duo made headlines when they bought the estate of Jacques Puffeney – 'the Pope of Arbois' – and subsumed it into their Domaine du Pélican.

Having been alerted to the potential of Jura wine when he was served 2002 Stéphane Tissot 'Les Graviers' by Parisian sommelier Marco Pelletier, who refused to tell him what it was (he couldn't believe it wasn't from the Côte de Beaune), Guillaume initially set about trying to understand the terroir by employing Burgundian techniques after he and François arrived in the region. But as winemakers usually constrained by three grape varieties

Opposite: Guillaume d'Angerville, Domaine du Pélican.

and a cru hierarchy that stretches back centuries, their attraction to the Jura's varied traditional styles was especially strong. "One of the appealing things about making wine in the Jura was that, for the first time, we were looking at assemblage and grapes that we'd never seen before," says d'Angerville. "Trousseau, Ploussard, Savagnin. Then the oxidative wines. All of those things were attractions, and we liked the challenge." Just as a generation of Jura winemakers learned more mainstream winemaking techniques in Burgundy, so their Burgundian counterparts now drawn here are intrigued by both *ouillé* and outsider styles. "When we struck the deal with Jacques Puffeney, he agreed he'd help us to make Vin Jaune," d'Angerville says, laughing. "A couple of years later, I bumped into him outside the winery and asked, 'What do we do?' He replied, 'Vin Jaune is very easy. You put some wine in a barrel. You wait six-and-a-half years. Then you have Vin Jaune'." Honestly, you couldn't make it up.

Cornas

Northern Rhône Valley, France

"BOOM! It's easy to make a monster wine here, but that's not our goal,"
says Olivier Clape, surveying the scorched stone terraces around him.
Cornas, 'the burnt earth': vast swathes of vines on murderous granite ridges,
soaking up sunlight like happy bathers. "Of course we want our wines to be
big, because that's the character of this terroir, but above all we're looking
for finesse." Finesse isn't a word synonymous with Cornas. Historically,
'hard', 'rustic' or plain-old 'dirty' have been more associated with this most
southerly of Northern Rhône Syrah appellations. But, while in many cases
such opprobrium has been true, a reappraisal of vinous glories from domaines
Auguste Clape, Thierry Allemand and Noël Verset over the past couple
of decades has seen it emerge from the shadows of Hermitage and, latterly,
Côte-Rôtie, to be celebrated among France's most fashionable reds.

Standing with Olivier in 'La Sabarotte', a vertiginous vineyard his family
bought from the late Noël Verset in 2002, it's apparent why great wines can
be made here by those hardy enough to work the land. Above us a panorama
of brutal slopes forms a crucible – providing shelter from the Rhône Valley's
notorious wind, La Bise – which, along with poor granitic soils and intense
sunlight, makes it the perfect place for achieving ripeness while retaining
freshness and character. Farther south, Syrah easily becomes flabby and
uninteresting (Château de Fonsalette, Trévallon and La Grange des Pères make
notable exceptions), although as everywhere, climate change has made a mark.

"I remember tasting 1990 Cornas with Auguste Clape and thinking what
a big wine it was, and trying to guess the alcohol," says Clape and Allemand's
long-time Californian importer Kermit Lynch. "Auguste replied that he'd never
produced such a high-alcohol wine before, but when I asked what it was,
it was only 12.7%. Think about that for a moment! All those years we'd read
about 'the Black Wines of Cornas', these monsters, but in reality they'd never
even been 12.7% until 1990." Almost three decades on, it's hard to find a wine here
– let alone in some more northerly appellations – that's less than 14% alcohol,

Opposite: Golden mouldies,
Domaine Clape, Cornas.

including Clape's future classic 2010. Denser and more tannic than St Joseph, Côte-Rôtie or Hermitage, such traditionally styled Cornas have aromas of blackcurrant, red cherry, olive, herbs, menthol, smoke and hung game, the latter becoming more pronounced with age. It's this wild edge – a character so feral it could have its own chapter in Mötley Crüe biography *The Dirt* – that separates it from its well-mannered neighbours, and conjures gastronomic nirvana when paired with the hedgerow honk of a roast woodcock or grouse. With fine, rounded tannins and a long-building finish, 2010 Clape Cornas – like the now sublime 1990 – is one of the most spellbinding Syrahs I've drunk.

But as much as a visit to the domaine's vineyards is impressive, it's its cellar under the village where time seems to have stood still. A dank underworld of large oak *foudres* between 30 and 50 years old ("used to exchange oxygen through the wood, which gives the wine an edge"), it was here in 1955 that Auguste Clape became among the first in the village to bottle his own production, setting Cornas on course to being marketed as a serious fine wine. "At that time, my grandfather usually sold everything to *négociants*," says Olivier. "They laughed and said, 'Bottle it yourself, but it won't be easy for you!' He started producing a few bottles and, along with Noël Verset and Joseph Michel, began selling directly to tourists and locals in nearby Tain-l'Hermitage." Nobody ever said making a living in Cornas was easy.

First classified as a 50ha appellation in 1938, just before the outbreak of the Second World War, Cornas almost abandoned formal winemaking as soon as it had begun. With scores of local men killed or injured, by the time peace was declared in 1945, it was left largely to widows and wives to manage the vineyards, alongside the traditional local crops of cereals and apricots. The ensuing decades were a continued struggle for survival, with the low price of Cornas wines not enough to cover the high cost of farming, forcing many to find work in the nearby city of Valence (Noël Verset famously went to a night job unloading trains after working his vineyards during the day). Ironically, it would take one of modern artisanal wine culture's greatest taboos – chemical vineyard treatments – to make all the difference to winemakers living on the edge of poverty in the 1970s.

"In one sense herbicide was a miracle," explains Olivier. "Without it, I'm sure there wouldn't be any vineyards left in Cornas, as it was a way for the *vignerons* to save labour and scrape a living. But today, we have the chance to go backwards and be much closer to the soil. Instead of using chemicals, it's very important for us to plough the land." However, whereas tractors or horses can be used on the relatively flat vineyards of Champagne or Bordeaux, the unforgiving Northern Rhône hillsides pose huge challenges – which were characteristically met head on by the first local man to convert back to organic farming, Clape's friend and neighbour, Thierry Allemand.

"The slopes here are very difficult to work, and we can only use winches and ploughs instead of heavy machinery," Allemand says in an almost impenetrable

Opposite, from top: Auguste Clape, John Livingstone-Learmonth and Thierry Allemand, Noël Verset, Olivier Clape.

Ardèche accent. "But Cornas would not be Cornas without these hills. They give it its identity." Now in his sixties, Allemand's no-nonsense demeanour contrasts with that of the laid-back Clape, whom he inspired to return to pre-chemical farming. Producing three cuvées (young vine 'Chaillot', old vine 'Reynard' and an occasional zero-added-sulphur bottling) compared with Clape's five (main blend, young vines 'Renaissance' and 'Vin des Amis', Côtes du Rhône and St Péray blanc), Allemand's wines are often more approachable than the darker, *puissant* Clapes in their youth, blossoming at around 20 years from vintage. Employing semi-carbonic whole-cluster fermentation, minimal sulphur additions and *élevage* in old oak casks, wines such as Allemand's underrated 1994s and extraordinary 1991s channel Cornas' wild side with an elegant Burgundy-esque sensibility.

Given that he began his career as the village postman without any vineyards in the early 1980s ("My family didn't own land and none of the banks would give me credit, so it meant doing double or triple days' work before I acquired my first parcel"), the fact that Allemand has built one of France's great estates alone from scratch is a phenomenal achievement. Today, however, the long days of arduous manual labour have taken their toll, and he's hoping his son Theo will take over the domaine when he shortly retires. Alongside Olivier Clape (with whom he has been doing work experience), Allemand Jnr will join a younger generation of *vignerons* who also include Franck Balthazar, Vincent Paris, Ludovic Izerable (of Domaine Lionnet), Hirotake Ooka and Matthieu Barret, who are continuing to build Cornas' reputation at a time of unprecedented demand. But with such success has also come rising land prices and limited opportunities for fresh blood. Where can young winemakers buy unwanted parcels of land – just as Allemand did all those years ago – in an appellation with finite room for expansion?

One part of the village to which producers are turning their attentions is the high-altitude pastures known as Chaban, named after the stream that rises there and runs through the village into the Rhône. Previously considered too cool to ripen grapes, several large commercial domaines such as Chapoutier and Jean-Luc Colombo have expanded their holdings there, although some question the area's suitability to foster wines with a typically Cornas character. "Chaban is part of Cornas so no changes to the appellation were needed for these new developments," says John Livingstone-Learmonth – author of the definitive book on the region, *The Wines of the Northern Rhône* – as we walk through the high lands later that day. "In the past, the main challenges came from developers wanting to build housing for people working in Valence. In the early 1970s, when Cornas wines were difficult to sell, I was involved in a campaign to stop villas being built on the low-lying vineyards of the village. Now they've become popular enough to encourage people to plant on unsuitable high pastures, which seems something of an irony. Progress or not? That's a good question."

Previous spread: Domaine Clape cellar, Cornas.

Opposite: Cornas vineyards.

As we walk in thick afternoon heat through deserted village streets, Livingstone-Learmonth reflects on a life spent documenting this once almost-forgotten appellation. "Of everywhere I've written about, Cornas is closest to my heart. This village used to inhale and exhale wine, and the hillsides of toil are right in view. It's here where I learned so much from my professor, Auguste Clape, and where dedicated men, some of whom had fought in the war and would work elsewhere to make ends meet, returned to a daunting life of labour. As a young man, it was impossible not to be in awe." Everything and nothing has changed. Cornas' terrain remains as challenging as ever, but its fashionability means the next generation can invest in producing better wine. There may be questions over climate change and rising land prices but, for now at least, there's no turning back. Cornas has left behind the hard wines of old in pursuit of the perfect balance between wildness and finesse.

The Bordeaux First Growths

MICHAEL BROADBENT'S *Vintage Wine* is a rite of passage for many wine lovers. Each page brims with anecdotes and critiques, full of familiarity with distinguished vintages. More than any other tome, it ignited our fascination with the great wines of Bordeaux while also making us ask: who gets to drink such bottles? The answer can be found among the book's numerous vignettes, which include profiles of prolific collectors and accounts of the lavish tastings they have hosted. One such character, Hardy Rodenstock, leaped from the pages of *Vintage Wine* to inspire another book, *The Billionaire's Vinegar* by Benjamin Wallace. Packed with salacious tales, it is another entertaining read (Broadbent filed a defamation lawsuit against Wallace), and there have been rumours of a Hollywood movie ever since. One particular story that captured our imagination was a Rodenstock tasting of 125 different vintages of Château d'Yquem. "Each event must cost Hardy a fortune," wrote Broadbent, "[but] through his generosity I have had the opportunity to taste an enormous range of great and very rare wines." Although Wallace's book accuses Rodenstock of fraud over the notorious 'Thomas Jefferson bottles', a collection sold as having belonged to the American president, and questions the authenticity of other wines, his descriptions of these florid happenings further fuelled our curiosity about this exclusive world.

It could be easy to dismiss such events as bragging contests for the rich, but what about the bottles they're drinking? Wouldn't any wine lover want to taste them? Alas, tickets to such luxurious bacchanalias are in short supply, so it was a surprise when invitations to 'A Festival of First Growths' appeared at Rotter HQ one day. What surprised us most was the line-up, which included 20 of the most celebrated Bordeaux ever produced: Haut-Brion '61, Latour '61, Lafite '53, Mouton '45 and Margaux '28 – the very wines that had enraptured us in *Vintage Wine*. Finally, the time had come for us to drink them ourselves.

Arriving for dinner at the Four Seasons Park Lane, we meet six other tasters – some familiar faces from London, others from the States. We've been

Opposite: 1945 Châteaux Mouton Rothschild, Margaux and Haut-Brion.

guests at numerous interesting, if more modest, events before and have also hosted many of our own, presenting wines from renowned domaines either as 'verticals' (a chronological tasting of different vintages of the same estate or vineyard) or 'horizontals' (a selection of different wines from the same vintage). Over glasses of 1973 Bollinger RD, our host outlines the evening's objective: to gain an insight into the styles of the five different châteaux by tasting each separately as a flight of four eminent vintages. While a simple concept, it's at odds with the more common approach of pitting the châteaux against each other to see which one is 'best' in a given year, which seldom celebrates the unique characteristics each is renowned for.

We begin with Haut-Brion – along with Latour typically our favourite First Growth – and are instantly mesmerised. Savoury, earthy characteristics are balanced against pure cassis fruit, with the château's hallmark gravelly minerality providing tension and focus. Margaux follows: fragrant and floral, with a sensuality conjuring up an understated luxury rather than brash opulence. After that, the four vintages of Lafite are harmonious and serene with silk tannins and flashes of graphite, although two of them are underwhelming in such ebullient company. Next is magisterial Latour: broad-shouldered and powerful but with a sense of control, like being chauffeur-driven in a Bentley at 20mph. Last comes exotic Mouton: infused with cedar, rose petals and spice. All show a distinct house character no matter the vintage.

Rich and sophisticated dishes are paired with the flights, but over five courses they become too distracting for such complex wines. The impeccable condition of the bottles prompts a discussion about provenance, one of the biggest issues facing such events. With several high-profile counterfeiting cases in the news over the past few years, such as the 2013 prosecution of Rudy Kurniawan, anyone buying rare bottles needs to be cautious. However, one of our fellow diners, and world's most experienced critics, Neal Martin, declares many of the bottles to be among the best he's tried. But a tasting like this raises more questions than just provenance, including the morality of spending over £5,000 on a ticket. Of course, the same could be asked about many leisure pursuits, and while we admit to having paused for thought, the truth is that once-in-a-lifetime experiences don't come cheap. But for those who can afford it, was it worth the price? Absolutely. We'll be talking about these wines for the rest of our days.

As the evening wore on, the collection of blue-chip Claret on the table became mind-boggling. All 20 wines were split eight ways, so we were able to drink, rather than just 'taste' them. While it may sound spoiled to question serving so many extraordinary bottles in one sitting – especially as we didn't pay for our tickets – there's no doubt it was quite overwhelming at times. However, 20 wines is a much more manageable prospect than the 100-plus different vintages served at Rodenstock's mega-tastings.

Opposite, above: Preparing the tasting.

Opposite, below: Mark Andrew, Neal Martin and Dan Keeling.

COURSE	WINE	OPEN	DECANT
CÈPE TART 19:35	CHATEAU HAUT-BRION 1945	19:15	BEFORE SERVING
	CHATEAU HAUT-BRION 1959	18:35	19:20 DOUBLE
	CHATEAU HAUT-BRION 1961	18:35	19:20 DOUBLE
	LA MISSION HAUT-BRION 1978	18:35	18:35 ~~XXX~~ DOUBLE
	CHATEAU HAUT-BRION 1989	~~17:35~~	~~17:35~~ ~~XXX~~ ~~DOUBLE~~
RAVIOLI 20:05	CHATEAU MARGAUX 1928	19:55	JUST DECANT
	CHATEAU MARGAUX 1945	19:35	JUST DECANT
	CHATEAU MARGAUX 1959	19:05	19:50
	CHATEAU MARGAUX 1982	18:35	18:35 DOUBLE
PHEASANT 20:35	LAFITE ROTHSCHILD 1953	19:35	20:15
	LAFITE ROTHSCHILD 1959	19:35	20:15
	LAFITE ROTHSCHILD ~~XXX~~ 1966	19:50	19:50
	LAFITE ROTHSCHILD 1986	18:35	~~XXX~~ 18:35 DOUBLE

"I much prefer a crescendo to a strident non-stop blast of trumpets," says Jancis Robinson, about the legendary Château d'Yquem vertical. "The all-day tasting fairly soon turned into a rather trying marathon. I had to swill down an aspirin with 1964 Lanson 'Red Label' between segments two and three." So, is there a danger that regularly attending such events might be too much of a good thing? As Epicurus once wrote: "Be moderate in order to taste the joys of life in abundance". But for those fortunate enough to go, tastings like this are an incredible way to experience the outer reaches of fine wine – especially when the bottles exceed expectations, as these did.

Opposite: Timetable of dreams. 27 October 2017, Four Seasons Park Lane, London.

Flight one: Haut-Brion

The 1989 (★★★★★+) is spectacular, combining intense smoky and savoury
aromatics with pure fruit and the classic Haut-Brion aroma of warm bricks.
The vibrant 1961 (★★★★★+) is cut in a similar style with more autumnal
complexity – cedar, earth and dried spices – and an exceptionally long, building
finish, while the 1959 (★★★★★) has the focused energy that is a hallmark of the
château. The 1945 (★★★★★+) is explosive and open-knit yet elegant and layered,
with the gravelly minerality that characterises the younger wines. Wow!

Flight two: Margaux

A relative baby, the 1982 (★★★★★) has a detailed bouquet of violets, potpourri
and pencil lead, and mellow fruit on the palate. The 1959 (★★★★★) is even more
generous, with sweet fruit, sensual aromatics and a lithe and silken texture.
1945 (★★★) is showing its age, and perhaps not a great bottle, but the 1928
(★★★★★+) is delicate and alluring, with perfect poise and freshness. It smells
like a nosebleed in a Parisian *pâtisserie*: blood, cinnamon and dried fruit.

Flight three: Lafite-Rothschild

The 1986 (★★★) is archetypal Pauillac, full of dark graphite, cloves and cassis,
although it is light and relatively simple. The 1966 (★★★) is charming, if lacking
complexity, whereas the 1959 (★★★★★) is rich and layered with the beautiful

serenity – aptly described as "still as a mill pond" by a fellow taster – typical of Lafite. It is a complete wine with an exceptional perfume of cedar, soy sauce and balsamic vinegar. The 1953 (*****+) is another high watermark for Lafite and does not disappoint. A quintessential Cabernet Sauvignon with bags of graphite minerality and an extended finish that glides along like it's on rails.

Flight four: Latour

The magisterial 1961 (*****+) has monumental structure; rich in mellow perfection and entirely free from the infirmities of age. Although decades away from full maturity, it is still mind-blowing today; the perfect amalgamation of power and elegance, and one of the standouts of the tasting. Unfortunately, the 1959 (***) is showing signs of falling into an iodine-tinged dotage – possibly an off bottle – unlike the rich and stately 1949 (*****+), also remarkably youthful for its age. The 1929 (*****+) is a real charmer too, with a spectacular nose of old spice and blood, and gorgeous richness and length on the palate.

Flight five: Mouton Rothschild

The Mouton flight opens with a 1982 (*****) that's as flamboyant as prime Freddie Mercury, as is the Mouton style. This is one of the best 1982 Bordeaux we've tried, and ready for the long haul. The 1949 (*****+) offers aromatic fireworks, with an exuberant perfume of berries and spice and a silken texture, while the brilliant 1947 (*****+) cranks up the exoticism even further. The final wine is the 1945 (*****+), which lives up to its reputation as an all-time great. It's so young, intense and explosive – and mind-bendingly long.

Pomerol

Bordeaux, France

AT FIRST GLANCE you might be forgiven for not identifying Château L'Eglise-Clinet as the source of one of Bordeaux's top wines. You might describe it as a nondescript workshop or a farm storeroom, but, like most wineries in Pomerol on the right-bank of the River Dordogne, calling it a château requires a suspension of disbelief that would make David Blaine proud. Inside, concrete floors and stark white walls reflect the humble confidence of an estate that could sell its production many times over, the only obvious concession to commercialism an exhibition of paintings by owner Denis Durantou's wife, Marie Reilhac, with handwritten price tags on their frames. Durantou is an intense man with a good sense of humour who, unlike many involved in Bordeaux winemaking, doesn't talk like he's reading from a script. Among flickering shadows in his cellar, we taste several L'Eglise-Clinet vintages while he expresses his displeasure at the flavour that new oak imparts on other wines: "Vanillin is everywhere today – in sausages, in hotel lobbies... It's vulgar!" Overseeing every aspect of the 4.5ha estate (again, something that can't be said of many Bordelais), Durantou produces sensuous Merlot and Cabernet Franc blends that, in superlative vintages such as 1998, combine great density with ethereal lightness – a neat trick that only the most exalted vineyards can achieve.

Once a backwater of smallholders in the shadow of the aristocratic left-bank châteaux, Pomerol only joined the top table of Bordeaux appellations after the Second World War. Today leading châteaux such as Pétrus and Le Pin are as renowned for their eyeball-inflating prices as their spellbinding dimensions, but not all Pomerols are created equal. There is a big variation in wine quality from estates situated on the commune's clay-rich plateau – which helps provide the luxurious velvety texture Pomerol is renowned for – and the less fortunate on the sandier soils surrounding it. One thing that does unite the majority of châteaux, however, is their independent ownership – in contrast to so many top left-bank classed growths, whose owners sold out to financiers

Opposite: Ploughing Château Lafleur vineyards, Pomerol.

and multinationals long ago. Perhaps more by circumstance than design, this commune of family-owned, terroir-focused estates has arguably more in common with Bordeaux's nemesis, Burgundy. After all, where else could you find so many intersecting vineyards owned by *vignerons* more interested in expressing land rather than brand?

"When Jean-Guillaume Prats [LVMH's head of wine] visited he asked me why I use such small tanks and I told him it's because I want to make wines of terroir," says Denis, in a vat room the size of a matchbox. "At the end of the '80s the right-bank estates produced better wines than the left, which was a wake-up call for them. They called us *vins de garage*, but L'Eglise-Clinet has been a family estate since the 18th century and isn't a new creation. Today, many of the big châteaux are more interested in building brands. Did you see the recent advertisement for 'Clarendelle', 'A pink wine inspired by Haut-Brion'? The last thing we are proud of is the terroir, the *lieu-dit*, the local name. And now we're losing this because a First Growth decided to use it as a brand."

The struggle between brand and artisan is a common theme in wine, and nowhere more so than in Pomerol. In the shiny, monogram-embossed tasting room of La Conseillante we meet winemaker Marielle Cazaux and owner Jean-Valmy Nicolas, a banker visiting the estate from Paris for the day. "What's a good wine? For me it's a wine that your father would open for special occasions such as Christmas and birthdays," says Nicolas, and we try not to baulk at the cliché. Later, a few miles north at Château Lafleur, owner Jacques Guinaudeau brings us down to earth extolling the virtues of Pomerol's diverse soils. Our meeting coincides with a visit from the estate's ploughmen,

Above: Denis Durantou, L'Eglise-Clinet.

and the sprightly sexagenarian leads us through Lafleur's 4.5ha 'garden vineyard', pointing out the limitless permutations of sand, clay and gravel. Having bought the estate in 2002 following the death of his aunt Marie Robin, Jacques has kept Château Lafleur family-owned, something that's as much of a coup for future generations of Guinaudeau as it is for Pomerol's independent spirit.

Château Lafleur is atypical Pomerol because of the unusually high proportion of Cabernet Franc in its blend (50%) and requires more time in the cellar to reach its potential than other more Merlot-dominated wines. If Cabernet Franc adds perfume and complexity, Merlot is the power and the colour. "On average there's ten days between when we harvest the two grapes – we're looking for the perfect balance between the aromatic complexity of Cabernet Franc and the charm of Merlot," says Jacques, adding that prior to 1985 they were picked together as a field blend. A few months after visiting Jacques, we meet his son Baptiste, who is taking over the château with his wife Julie, at an extensive tasting of mature vintages in London – a rare privilege that provided many sublime wines. As it is with any extraordinary domaine, trying to put Lafleur into words is a challenge, but the best have a common thread of sensuality, complexity, power and finesse. I'll never forget the magnificent shock of smelling 1989 Lafleur – an unlikely amalgamation of fresh laundry, berries and tar that blew my mind – or the spherical 1950: muscular and dense, but without heaviness, it saturated my taste buds in a similar way to the heavenly left-bank 1945s.

"Merlot can go from being Audrey Hepburn to a real tart in just a few days, so it's important to harvest at the right time," says Fiona Morrison of Le Pin, another premier-league estate, but one that uses a much smaller

percentage of Cabernet Franc. "People think Pomerol is just about Merlot and clay, but Le Pin is actually Merlot and gravel. For us, great terroir is about how water gets fed to the vine." You couldn't hope to meet more eloquent wine lovers than Fiona – who has somehow maintained a proper English accent throughout years living abroad, first in America, now between Belgium and France – and husband Jacques Thienpont. With self-effacing charm, Jacques chalks up his 1979 acquisition of Le Pin to "a happy accident", still somewhat surprised by its rise to almost unparalleled acclaim. As the owners of neighbouring Vieux Château Certan, Jacques' family had considered buying the miniscule Le Pin and merging it into their estate, but thought the deal too rich. Luckily for Jacques, he didn't and, drawing inspiration from the life of his grandfather Georges Thienpont, also a Flemish merchant-turned-*vigneron* who acquired Vieux Château Certan in 1924, reasoned that the time was right to go it alone. With 2018 Le Pin now on the market for £2700 per bottle, the couple talk benevolently about others sharing their success – including chef Heston Blumenthal, who sold a case of the 1989 to make the down payment on The Fat Duck. Originally bought for £330 a case, it changes hands for over £36,000 today. "I didn't imagine Le Pin would end up costing that much – in 1982 we sold it for 15 francs a bottle!" says Jacques.

So, can any wine live up to such princely sums? First, Fiona opens a 2004 Le Pin and a gorgeous roasted perfume of bacon fat, leather and violets brings top Côte-Rôtie to mind. Better still is a youthful 1998 with a velveteen texture and constantly evolving bouquet – so alluring it's almost impossible to wrench your nose from the glass. Could this be Chambertin by another name? "Le Pin often comes across as very Pinot Noir in blind tastings," says Jacques' cousin Alexandre Thienpont of Vieux Château Certan, who farms the vineyards at both estates. "It's very Burgundian in style, but Le Pin is condemned to stay

Opposite: Labelling at Vieux Château Certan.

small because if it were to increase in size, it would have to add more clay to its famous spot of gravel, and thus lose its signature light and aromatic character." But while Vieux Château Certan is a fraction of the cost of Le Pin, and stylistically different as a result of more Cabernet, it is certainly no lesser a wine.

"The fashion for Merlot came after the black frost that decimated the appellation in 1956," says Alexandre in Vieux Château Certan's cellar. "Merlot is more commercial than Cabernet Franc because you don't need as much knowledge to appreciate it. We tasted our 2006 and 2010 with a well-known oenologist, the first a reference for a Cabernet Franc-dominated year, and the second a Merlot one. He described the 2010 as 'a simple wine for barbecues that everyone likes', and the 2006 as 'a more complex wine, like haute cuisine, where you need more knowledge to appreciate it'. For me, a good wine has complexity, and a Merlot-heavy year can sometimes be a bit simple. Of course, 2010 is very good, but doesn't everybody like barbecue?" With cremated sausages and paper cups of warm Pomerol in mind, Alexandre ushers us out of the cellar into the surrounding vineyards. This is one of the few châteaux here whose appearance would pass the Trade Descriptions Act, and we pause and take in the classical architecture. Powerful but understated, elegant yet humble – like the finest wines of Pomerol it's beautiful to behold.

Opposite: Le Pin, Pomerol.

Château d'Yquem & Château Climens

Sauternes/Barsac, France

IT'S NOT EVERY DAY that a First Growth welcomes you to lunch with a "specially created" aperitif, even if it is "a little joke". Made from equal parts Sauternes and crushed ice, given the wine in question didn't make the final blend of Château d'Yquem – arguably, alongside Egon Müller *Trockenbeerenauslese*, the world's finest sweet wine – it's the most extravagant Slush Puppie we've ever tasted. Purists would deem it sacrilege to serve even inferior cuvées from such hallowed terroir 'on the rocks', but one sip and we're hooked. Our taste buds perform cartwheels and we boggle at the gastronomic implications: maybe they're on to something here?

"I like to serve Yquem as an aperitif," says Pierre Lurton, director of Château d'Yquem. "Normally people drink Yquem with foie gras, or at the end of the meal with dessert, but that's not the right time for me – I love to drink it at the start of a meal." Given that we've moved on to glasses of 2013 Château d'Yquem proper, it'd be rude to disagree. Like all good Yquems, it balances freshness and ripeness, and stimulates the synapses in a way that lesser sweet wines can't. But no matter how delicious it is, or how fashionable it once was with Thomas Jefferson or the Russian tsars, like all Sauternes it suffers an image problem today. Because, although people love fizzy drinks, fruit juices and pimped-up lattes, sweetness is a turn-off in wine. No wonder Yquem is coming up with new ideas to engage younger drinkers – and why not serve it as an aperitif, or with Chinese pork, or wasabi-spiked sushi, than with just the traditional pairings?

"Sauternes and Barsac have had a corny image, as something really sweet that you only drink with your auntie at Christmas," says Pierre's cousin, Bérénice Lurton, custodian of Château Climens in nearby Barsac. "Fortunately this image is changing – these wines have such great spirit and fragrance, and are more balanced than people think. Whereas people tend to generalise and say 'I don't like sweet wines' because they had a bad one once, they don't do that so much with reds. That's because a bad sweet wine is really awful,

Opposite: Bérénice Lurton, Château Climens, Barsac.

while a bad red wine is just a bad red wine, and easily forgettable." Paradoxically, not only is Sauternes a harder sell than red Bordeaux, but it's more expensive to make. At Château Haut-Brion in Graves it takes one vine to produce a single bottle of red, whereas here it takes one vine to produce just one glass. Sauternes and Barsac estates are also more at the mercy of the climate, reliant on the emergence of a fungus called *Botrytis cinerea* (a.k.a. 'noble rot') in late summer to make quintessential wines. Triggered by morning mists – from the confluence of the cold local River Ciron meeting the warmer Garonne – alternating with hot afternoons, it shrivels Sémillon and Sauvignon Blanc grapes on the vine, intensifying sugar and acidity, making them ideal for sweet wine. However, *Botrytis* affects bunches in an irregular pattern, progressing through three stages of maturity before becoming 'roasted', the mouldy, nasty-looking stage needed to reach full potential. This means pickers have to meticulously pass through the vineyard multiple times at harvest, and if it becomes too rainy and humid, noble rot can transform into destructive grey rot, turning the crop to mush.

Back at Château d'Yquem, we adjourn to the lavish dining room for a vertical of wines paired with a traditional menu. We begin with salmon tartare and 2014 'Ygrec', a dry Sauvignon Blanc blend made from one bunch

Previous spread: Biodynamic vineyard treatments at Château Climens, Barsac.

NOBLE ROT

of non-botrytised grapes per vine in the château's best plots. Previous owner Marquis Bernard de Lur-Saluces introduced this cuvée in 1959, which was made in an oxidative style until 2000, and it is as elegant and understated as Sauvignon Blanc gets. Next up, 2005 Yquem with guinea fowl, and 1989 Yquem with cheese, the former a surprisingly good match (to be honest, I'd be happy drinking Yquem with a KFC bucket). Just as 'Ygrec' has evolved into a fresher style, Yquem has also had the time it spends in barrel shortened from 30 to 24 months to "improve the fruitiness, and allow the wine to age for a long time in bottle". However, in vintages such as 2012, 1992 and 1972, when the wines haven't met their usual standards, Yquem has been declassified and sold off to merchants, and may even find its way into the generic Sauternes that the estate sometimes uses to make its "little jokes". Who knows, perhaps its Slush Puppie-style cocktail will capture the imagination of a coming generation of young winos? If it needs a suitable name, it has our blessing to call it 'The Rotter'.

Opposite and above:
Château d'Yquem,
Sauternes.

Jurançon
South-West France

LIFE IS GOOD in Jurançon. You can start the day skiing in the Pyrenees, head off for a dip in the Atlantic and still be home for lunch. And what a feast that could be: the region's produce is world renowned and its sweet *moelleux* wines have been famous since the Middle Ages. Surprisingly, though, not everybody is content with this idyllic status quo. "The problem around here is that we don't have any problems," says Lionel Osmin, an influential local wine merchant. "Too many people are comfortable just producing sweet wines for the older generation."

He's right to be concerned. Sweet wine sales are in decline and wineries are over-dependent on local consumption – just 10% of production is exported, compared to a national average of 30%. But if a solution is required, the Jurançonnais are in luck. "The answer is *sec*," says Jamie Hutchinson, referring to the Jurançon Sec appellation that was introduced in 1975, but whose output is rarely taken as seriously as the sweet wines.

Jamie and his wife Jess moved to south-west France to become *vignerons* after years working in London's wine trade; Jamie was co-founder of independent merchant The Sampler and Jess still runs Vindependents from their adoptive home. After struggling with French bureaucracy, the pair have finally planted Syrah on a hillside vineyard in the village of Audaux, while sourcing Petit Manseng grapes from Jurançon for their dry white. "We considered buying vines in Jurançon," recalls Jess, "but some fantastic growers were willing to sell us Petit Manseng from complementary areas. The fruit from Monein is rich and high in alcohol and on its own it makes unbalanced sec, so we blend it with grapes from Lasseube where ripeness is lower but acidity is really high." Their vibrant 2018 Domaine d'Audaux Petit Manseng, labelled IGP Comté Tolosan as the winery is outside the appellation, deftly demonstrates this marriage of freshness and volume.

Such a balancing act is traditionally achieved by blending with Gros Manseng, an underrated variety that contributes salinity and crisp acidity,

Opposite, clockwise from top: Jurançon, Clos Joliette bottles, Damiens Sartori and Lionel Osmin of Clos Joliette.

as well as finesse when vines are sufficiently mature. Appellation rules also permit the lively Petit Courbu, the aromatic Camaralet and the mineral Lauzet; but it's Petit Manseng that has a genuine claim to nobility. Often compared with Chenin Blanc, another grape with excellent texture, sugar and acidity, it remains a niche proposition; so how did the Hutchinsons become so enamoured? Jamie puts an empty wine bottle on the table and gestures towards it. "We tasted Clos Joliette," he says. "They didn't always get it right, but when they did, it was magnificent."

You'd be forgiven for not having heard of Clos Joliette, but the mere mention of its name quickens the pulse of many that have. Yet even to the initiated, it remains an enigma – seldom written about and almost impossible to find. The story begins in 1929, when Maurice Migné cleared some forest to plant 1ha of Petit Manseng. The south-east-facing amphitheatre proved to be a prime spot on clay, iron and limestone-rich soils dotted with *galet* stones (known locally as '*poudingue*'). Migné made the wine and his formidable wife took care of business, selling every bottle for cash and never writing anything down to avoid paying tax. After Migné's death, his widow continued to run the domaine off-the-books, allegedly even paying some employees in sexual favours.

By the 1980s, Clos Joliette had attained cult status. Gérard Depardieu became a regular visitor and tried to buy the domaine in 1989, claiming Migné's widow wanted to sell to him. However, the deal was sabotaged by local authorities who preferred the bid of Michel Renaud, a Parisian *caviste*. After taking over, Renaud excavated terraces and planted another 0.5ha of vines (bringing the total to 1.5ha), maintaining Migné's medieval approach to winemaking and hoarding almost every bottle in the domaine's decrepit cellar.

Since he died in 2015 various succession rumours have circulated, with the uncertainty exacerbated by rival inheritance claims from Renaud's daughter and a son from an 'extracurricular' relationship. If the court settles in favour of his daughter, her choice to take over permanently is Lionel Osmin, whom she installed as estate manager two years ago.

"I'm from the area, so for me Joliette is very special," says Osmin, who introduced organic farming to the vineyard after years of neglect but has no plans to radically alter how the wines are made. "My father had numerous vintages in our cellar", he continues, "and many of them were fantastic, but I believe that great wines were made here in spite, not because, of the previous owners." Based on what Osmin knows of the archaic methods employed by Migné and Renaud, he may well be right. Each barrel was left to ferment at its own pace and, after five years, bottled separately. As a result, the domaine would release bottles from different barrels of the same vintage, labelled identically but with completely different sugar levels. Some had fermented fully and were completely dry; others might be lusciously sweet or somewhere in between.

While Russian roulette was considered part of Joliette's idiosyncratic charm, the extent to which it prevailed became clear when Osmin investigated the contents of the cellar. Twenty vintages of wine were split into *casiers* (bins) of 300 bottles, each representing a different barrel. An experienced team was assembled to taste each bin and rank the wines for quality, before those deemed good enough for sale were analysed for sweetness and divided into three categories: those under 10g/l of residual sugar were sealed with green wax, those between 10g/l and 30g/l with yellow, and those over 30g/l with orange. The results are thrilling and eclectic, veering from razor-sharp, Sercial-like dry wines loaded with dried apricots and roasted nuts, to lusciously exotic stickies that balance ripe mango with searing acidity. The texture and viscosity in the best examples – no doubt a combination of peerless terroir and the inherent quality of Petit Manseng – makes Clos Joliette Jurançon's preeminent wine.

It's ironic, then, that 90% of Joliette bottles should never have been labelled as either Jurançon or Jurançon Sec as most had over 4g/l of residual sugar, the upper limit for sec, and under the 35g/l threshold for *moelleux*. This means library stock has to be released as 'Vin de France' and it's uncertain whether future vintages will be eligible for either AOC. Regardless, Lionel believes Jurançon Sec is the future. "Its enormous potential is the story of our lives", he says, "but the best vineyards have always been used for sweet wines. That needs to change." A handful of local *vignerons* have long been excited by dry wines, such as Charles Hours of Clos Uroulat, where Osmin trained, whose 'Cuvée Marie' is a reference point for the appellation. Likewise, Jean-Bernard Larrieu's dry wines from Clos Lapeyre – particularly 'Vitatge Vielh' – have been stalwarts of Noble Rot's list since we opened.

Elsewhere, high-profile domaines renowned for sweet wines are dedicating increasing energy to Jurançon Sec. At Domaine de Souch, 92-year old Yvonne Hégoburu and her son Jean-René built their reputation on *moelleux* cuvées such as 'Marie Kattalin' but its sec is well worth seeking out. The 2016 is full of the vivid aromas of grapefruit and rock salt, while the elegant 2012 demonstrates how well this wine can age. In nearby Aubertin, Loire legend Didier Dagueneau established 'Les Jardins de Babylone' because of his passion for sweet Jurançon, allegedly staging a midnight raid on Clos Joliette for vineyard cuttings, and his son Louis-Benjamin has continued to improve its exotic *moelleux* wine. The *sec*, made from a tiny parcel of all five permitted varieties, is tense and mineral with succulent lemon fruit. Any region focused on sweet wines ought to have a back-up plan, but Jurançon Sec can be far more than that. Forward-thinking *vignerons* have proven that dry wines deliver on quality and complexity – hopefully it won't be long before others catch on. After all, who's got time for problems in paradise?

Rioja

Spain

CHILDHOOD MEMORIES are powerful things, especially if they are made somewhere like Bodegas López de Heredia. Deep beneath Haro's cobbled streets, the cellars of this most traditional of Rioja houses are the stuff of fairytale – a labyrinth of pungent stone chambers that could convince even Fungus the Bogeyman it was time for a spring clean. Walls cascade with grey, black and green moulds. Cobwebs sparkle like constellations across damp ceilings and every room has a different aroma – a unique blend of old oak, vinegar, mushrooms and decay. For any wine lover fortunate enough to be invited in, it's the sweet smell of anticipation.

"Our father would send us down here when we were children to fetch wines and say, 'You can break your heads but not the bottle,'" says co-owner María José López de Heredia, amid the subterranean gloom. For the past hour we've been trying to keep pace with this warm, unrelenting lady, someone for whom commas and full stops have long since lost practical application. "People ask me about my vocation, but for me it was not about taking over the family business," she says. "I was clear from day one that what I really wanted to do was to help my dad, and the way to help him was to continue with the family business." She pauses, dewy-eyed from the memory of her father Pedro's passing in 2013 at the age of 84. "Did I want to be like him? In many ways, yes. My father was so passionate and such a happy man doing what he did. But in family businesses you go through so many moments when you really want to give up."

Bodegas López de Heredia is nothing if not a family business. Having been handed down through four generations to its present custodians María José, her sister Mercedes and brother Julio, its old-school philosophy and elegant, long-lived wines have remained steadfast through war, fashion and new technologies. Even during the 1980s and 1990s, when it would have been easy to embrace modernisation and ensuing homogeneity like the majority of *bodegas*, it stayed true to the core principles laid down by

Opposite: Bodegas López de Heredia cellars, Haro, Rioja.

María José's great-grandfather, Rafael López de Heredia y Landeta, when he established the winery in 1877. Today Tondonia remains arguably Rioja's greatest estate.

An educated Chilean immigrant, Rafael López de Heredia y Landeta was 21 years old when he set up his eponymous *bodega* during a boom for supplying a French market whose own vineyards had been ravaged by phylloxera. Like his fellow Rioja pioneers, Marqués de Riscal and Marqués de Murrieta (who'd both fought on the opposing side in the Third Carlist War, but later became his friends), Rafael took inspiration from the influential Bordeaux châteaux. "There were no brands like Château Margaux in Spain at the time, so Rafael wanted to create something that could appeal to customers in a similar way," says María José. Seeking guidance from Châteaux Margaux, Haut-Brion, d'Issan and Lafite, Rafael purchased sites around Haro based on their suitability to emulate the regions that his new Gallic clientele base admired most.

Up until 1953, López de Heredia's wines were branded with names such as 'Rioja Cepa Médoc', 'Rioja Cepa Graves', 'Rioja Cepa Borgoña' or 'Blanco Cepa Barsac' before reverting to specific vineyard classifications from 1954 onwards. "He took their advice over what vineyards to buy to make a style that was more Bordeaux, more Burgundy or more Graves," María José explains. Rafael even experimented with plantings of Bordeaux's Cabernet Sauvignon in Rioja, to little success, though his adoption of second-hand French oak barrels, later American due to availability, was of huge importance. Over the next few years, Rioja exports became so successful that it found itself with new, very modern challenges to overcome. "The Rioja appellation was created to fight falsification in 1902," says María José. "Every time something is successful in Spain people want to sell more of it, but because they didn't have enough wine they would fake it. There was even a book published in 1905 that taught people how to make wines in the style of Marqués de Riscal."

López de Heredia's flagship reds are 'Viña Tondonia' (100ha) and 'Viña Bosconia' (from 15ha of vineyard called El Bosque), sold in Bordeaux and Burgundy-shaped bottles, respectively. 'Viña Tondonia' is produced in a "softer, more elegant Médoc style", a blend of Tempranillo, Garnacha, Mazuelo and Graciano grown on limestone and clay. 'Viña Bosconia' is a similar blend (with more Mazuelo and Graciano), from clay-dominant soils, picked over two weeks after Tondonia, producing powerful wines with more colour, body and ripeness. "If it's true about global warming, we need to grow a higher percentage of Mazuelo and Graciano in order to maintain the high acidity and moderate alcohol of traditional Rioja," María José says of the lesser-farmed grapes. Elsewhere in López de Heredia's portfolio is an entry-level 'tapas' red called 'Viña Cubillo', and a fabulous rosado (rosé) that is released to market an unprecedented ten years after vintage. Like Tondonia's white wines (blends of Viura and Malvasia grown in 'Tondonia' and 'Viña Zaconia', a short hop over the River Ebro from the winery), it is unique and delicious.

Above: Barrel cleaning, Bodegas López de Heredia, Haro.

"We would receive congratulations from all over the world for our whites, but it was like Sherry – hardly anyone would drink it," María José says about a time when there was scant demand for López de Heredia's highly sought-after *blancos*. "We had so much stock that we thought it would last 100 years, so we reduced the amount we produced. Now it's the opposite. Everyone wants to buy old vintages and we don't have any to sell." Whether caused by the zeitgeist for consumers demanding authentic products, or by them simply waking up to López de Heredia's outstanding quality-to-price ratio, fashionability isn't an easy fit with María José. "When I go to bed at night I always think, 'Another day, another three thousand emails in my inbox,'" she sighs before recalling a story that perfectly illustrates such unforeseen growth in demand. "Years ago [Basque chef] Juan Mari Arzak called my father and said, 'Pedro, I've got so much 1954 Viña Tondonia in my cellar that my grandfather bought and I can't sell it – please can you replace it?' So my father asked me to go to San Sebastián to see Arzak and tell him that we don't re-buy our wine, we only sell it. So I called my friend [winemaker] Telmo Rodríguez and asked him to come with me for support. We had the most incredible lunch in Arzak's kitchen and left without buying back the wine. Now the sommelier from Arzak always calls me asking for more wine and the whole world has gone crazy. I keep on telling him, 'I regret not buying those old wines back!'"

Left: María José López de Heredia.

Telmo Rodríguez straightens the cuff on his immaculate blue shirt and looks out over the vineyards at Remelluri, his family estate. "I don't want to sound pretentious," he begins, "but our idea is to bring back to life what should have been the most pure and delicate taste of Rioja. I travel a lot and I always ask people what their idea of Rioja is. When they talk about *bodegas* like Faustino or Paterninas I think, 'My god, we're so far from the real taste.'" Once the *enfant terrible* of the Spanish fine wine scene, Rodríguez is now established as one of the country's most successful artisan producers, having set up projects in numerous regions with business partner Pablo Eguzkiza. From Málaga to Toro, Rueda, Cigales, Valdeorras, Cebreros, Alicante and Ribera del Duero, for the last 20 years the duo's strategy has been to begin working with *vignerons* in the most promising areas to produce good low-cost wines, before identifying the finest vineyards available to make high-quality cuvées. "Yesterday I was talking to a few young guys, saying that if they had the sensibility, they can still buy the best vineyards in Spain," says Telmo. "Young people today can still buy the most beautiful vineyards in Rioja because nobody cares about them – we're very lucky." Although Compañía de Vinos Telmo Rodríguez now owns over 80ha of organic vineyards across Spain, he remains especially passionate about pushing what can be achieved in his native Rioja.

A student of local 17th-century viticulture, Telmo blends traditional techniques – such as high-density planting and fermenting field blends – with a Burgundian-style focus on terroir, rather than Rioja's increasingly out

Above: Telmo Rodríguez, Remelluri, Rioja.

of date oak-ageing classification system (Joven, Crianza, Reserva, Gran Reserva). Although Grand and Premier Crus don't technically exist in the DOCa (the region's *Consejo Regulador* laws make it illegal to cite specific place names on labels), village wines such as Telmo's 'Lanzaga', and single vineyard sites such as the future classic 'Las Beatas' are taking Rioja back to the time when wine was – to coin a modern cliché – made in the vineyard rather than the winery. If Rioja wants to retake its rightful place at the top table of the world's wine regions, surely an acknowledgement of origin and terroir is what is required? "The big industrial wineries were the destruction of Rioja," says Telmo. "López de Heredia and Bodegas Bilbaínas used to own their own vineyards, but all the rest weren't interested. They were making wines to send to France because of phylloxera, and they wanted cheap rent – that's why they produce a million bottles today. Those companies are responsible for the loss of the traditional field blends, the bush vines and the great agriculture. I say to people if they want to be part of this [new artisanal] movement, don't sell any more mass-produced brands in your restaurants. Sell growers. Sell places."

'Las Beatas' makes a compelling case for Rodríguez's philosophy. Its ethereal bouquet, lacy texture and ultra-fine tannins are diametrically opposed to the oak-saturated commercial wines pumped out in millions of litres in Rioja today. If, like us, you prize wine's rare ability to combine restrained power with finesse, search out a bottle. Elsewhere in the portfolio Remelluri white is also of particular note, although more experimental for the region. A blend of nine grape varieties aged in oak for 12 months, it doffs its cap to white Northern Rhône and Telmo's apprenticeships with some of southern France's best.

Above: 'The Cemetery', where Bodegas López de Heredia keeps its rarest bottles.

"To work a vineyard in the Médoc is easy, but in Hermitage you have to be a hero to fight for your place," he says of his time with Hermitage's Gérard Chave, who would open vintages dating back to the 1930s to teach Telmo how to make wine. After studying at Bordeaux Wine School, Telmo did stints with Auguste Clape in Cornas, Beaucastel in Châteauneuf-du-Pape, Cos d'Estournel in Bordeaux and his long-term mentor Eloi Dürrbach at Trévallon in Provence.

"López de Heredia is the only bodega that I think has the quality of winemaking of 350 years ago," says Telmo, pouring a glass of 'Altos Lanzaga' over lunch. "I love Tondonia because it represents a very interesting moment in Rioja and is very important. But even today many sommeliers argue it's the original style of Rioja when in fact there was something much purer. In the end the process – the winery – is still very important with Tondonia. The challenge for us was to try to find the amazing old vineyards, and when you see 'Las Beatas' you realise that those terraces were the Grand Crus. Rioja became a wine that is made more in the winery, but the challenge of 'Las Beatas' is to make it in the great places, the Grand Crus of Rioja."

Back in the labyrinth of tunnels under Bodegas López de Heredia, we are en route to a very special room. "Sometimes Telmo wants to be more traditionalist than the traditionalists," María José says of her old friend. "When he talks about recuperating the history of Rioja he doesn't mean the 19th-century history that made Rioja well known, but the previous history – the 17th century. I tell him that we don't know much about how they worked then because there are very few records left. But this is what he wants to do. He's a person who loves the history of the area and he dreams of making great wine." We pass two cellar hands cleaning barrels before rolling them over grooves in the floor, animating them in the half-light like they've taken on a life-force of their own. Employing a full-time cooperage means Tondonia maintains its stocks of used barrels for as long as possible, as the taste of new oak is not welcomed. "Everyone talks about Rioja in terms of oak maturation – Crianza, Reserva – but that's so boring," María José says. "Oak shouldn't give character to the wines. It was originally only a container for stabilising the wine but this has changed through history." We arrive at an iron gate, and María José beckons us in. Despite her great-grandfather's wishes, this otherworldly inner sanctum is known as 'The Cemetery', where Tondonia stores stock of its rarest bottles. "Telmo used to tell me to re-cork the bottles, but the whole point of wine is to be drunk," says María José, selecting a mottled bottle of 1964 Blanco Reserva – "the vintage of the century". She hacks off its crumbling wax seal and pours glasses of golden wine, and as a glorious perfume of roasted hazelnuts and crème brûlée mixes with the room's odour of decay, anticipation turns to wonder.

Comando G

Gredos Mountains, Spain

"THIS IS A CHORD. This is another. This is a third. Now form a band" was how *Sideburns* fanzine famously encapsulated the punk spirit in January 1977. Today, while the medium is different, a similar do-it-yourself attitude pervades Spain's rediscovered wine regions. From the hinterlands of Tenerife and Ribeira Sacra to here, high in the Gredos Mountains west of Madrid, tenacious dreamers such as Daniel Gómez Jiménez-Landi and Fernando García of Comando G have avoided prohibitive set-up costs and revived unwanted parcels of indigenous old vines. Their trajectory may be more "This is a bottle of Château Rayas. This is another. This is a third. Now form a winery," but such democratisation has resulted in some of the freshest vinous finds of recent years.

"Spain has had the potential for great wine since Roman times, but we haven't always had the sensibility or ability to express it," says Daniel at La Fiesta de la Floración, a biennial tasting and live music celebration the duo organise for friends in the Sierra de Gredos. "Now it's developed into a revolution with the focus on local varieties and the landscape. The older generation – people like Álvaro Palacios, Telmo Rodríguez and Peter Sisseck – were the first to open the door in other countries for Spain, and now others with similar philosophies are following them." If not long ago the blueprint for Spanish wine was a one-size-fits-all recipe fetishising new oak, deep colours and high alcohol, things have become more nuanced. "The idea was the more expensive the wine, the more expensive the barrel, but now it's the opposite," says Fernando. "You have to work Garnacha as Garnacha asks, whereas in the past we worked all grape varieties as Tempranillo."

Squint at the vibrant hues of the Sierra de Gredos in spring and you could almost mistake it for the Welsh valleys, broken by a smattering of towns whose best days seem long past. In this impoverished part of central Spain, Garnacha – a.k.a. Grenache – has long been king. Originally a centre for bulk-wine production, the region grows 10% of what it did in its 1950s to '70s heyday, when co-operatives harvested more than a million kilograms

Opposite: Daniel Gómez Jiménez-Landi and Fernando García of Comando G.

of grapes a year. Overproduction, EU laws and high farming costs (due to the steep terrain) eventually made the industry unsustainable, forcing the mass migration of workers into the cities in search of better-paid jobs. Only an hour's drive from Madrid, abundant abandoned bush vines still grow among fig and olive trees at high altitude. With big diurnal day-to-night temperature swings ripening intense, well-balanced fruit, and having missed the chemical abuses of the 1980s, this is a perfect spot for two winemakers citing the world's greatest Grenache – Château Rayas – as their inspiration to set up their own domaine.

"Château Rayas gives you a unique feeling when you drink it," says Fernando. "We fell in love with its finesse and delicate balance. Visiting the estate became a pilgrimage for us," continues Daniel. "We used to go there every year to walk around the vineyards and think about the wine, sleeping in our van in the middle of the fields. After many years of going, we eventually got the opportunity to go inside and meet Emmanuel Reynaud, the owner. As he took us on a tour of the vineyards, he pointed out its features; we kept nodding, thinking: Yes, we know!" Producing seven biodynamic cuvées – six reds from 100% Garnacha and a white, Comando G structures its portfolio around Burgundy's hierarchical cru system. Farmed in obscure granite and sandstone parcels, the range goes from 'village' 'La Bruja de Rozas' to 'Rozas 1er Cru' and four 'Grand Cru' single vineyards: 'Tumba del Rey Moro', 'Las Umbrías', 'El Tamboril' and 'Rumbo al Norte'. What is special about these wines is their balance between generosity and restraint: relatively light in colour, the house style teases delicate perfumes of flowers, rocks and minerals out of pure fruit cores. The silky 'Rozas 1er Cru' is one of my favourite light reds of recent years; at around half the price of the 'Grand Crus', it's the range's sweet spot, lacking none of their deliciousness at this early stage.

Growing up on his family estate in the Gredos Mountains (which he left due to a difference of opinion over cultivating international varietals), Daniel also produces wines under his eponymous Daniel Gómez Jiménez-Landi imprint, while Fernando worked for Telmo Rodríguez, Raúl Pérez and Madrid wine shop Lavinia before setting up Bodega Marañones, where he still makes wine. Launching Comando G in 2008, the estate became the duo's priority in 2013 as it began to garner attention. The name Comando G is a reference to the Spanish title of '80s Japanese cartoon *Battle of the Planets* – a passion for alternative pop culture lies at the heart of what they do.

The Sierra de Gredos is made up of three valleys with different climates: continental in the northern Alto Alberche, and Mediterranean in the southern Alberche and Tiétar. But the Spanish appellation system has not developed to reflect such distinctions, using the generic 'Vinos de Madrid' to define all three zones. Comando G prefers using the unofficial, but more specific 'Sierra de Gredos', printing other vineyard information on its labels outside of the recognised DO and its rules. Elsewhere, interesting local producers such as Bernabeleva, Rubor, Daniel Ramos and Pegaso are helping to draw attention

Opposite: La Fiesta de la Floración, Gredos Mountains, central Spain.

to the region. "We need more wineries here to make the area better known," says Fernando. "We love regions like Burgundy and Rioja, where you smell wine everywhere."

At La Fiesta de la Floración, the morning tasting is winding down for lunch. Everywhere you look are the great and the good of new-wave artisanal wine, from Telmo Rodríguez chatting with Portugal's Dirk Niepoort, to Envínate pouring its new vintage for Meursault's Jean-Marc Roulot and California's Rajat Parr. If everyone here has something in common, it's a love of balanced wines with a sense of place, rather than bombastic concentration. Later in the afternoon, Daniel and his band take to the stage to play Led Zeppelin and Rolling Stones covers, but for now everyone follows the aroma of *pulpo a la Gallega* being served under a canopy of olive trees.

"The reason we're able to make our wines is because Sherry and Rioja have historically done such an amazing job," Fernando says, as bottles are uncorked. "Not long ago, a region with old vineyards and local varieties appeared every year. Suddenly, there were the Canary Islands, or Ribeira Sacra, or Ribera del Duero, or the Gredos Mountains; many different kinds of grape varieties and soils." Spanish wine is undoubtedly in a magical moment. Having weathered the homogenisation of the '80s, when winemakers previously isolated under the Franco regime attempted to play catch-up by planting international varieties, the new generation is able to take advantage of characterful, indigenous vines in regions that time seemingly forgot. With fewer barriers to entry and an irreverent DIY attitude, could that be the whiff of punk spirit in the air? "Spain is like a castle that has been closed for many years," says Daniel. "We're opening the doors and windows, and the world is discovering what treasures the castle has inside."

Penedès

Catalonia, Spain

WINE, IDENTITY, INDEPENDENCE: the sense of struggle is palpable in Penedès, Catalonia. Take Glòria Garriga, for example. Disillusioned by the effects of the vineyard treatments she once sold, she swapped a career as an agricultural engineer for the life of a natural *vigneron* and started Els Jelipins in the hills of Font-rubí. It took almost a decade from her 2003 debut vintage for her wines to begin selling, but they're now listed in some of the world's best restaurants. "I don't have the words to explain how we suffered," she says of the early years when she also had a young daughter to support.

Or Pepe Raventós, the closest thing Catalonia has to vinous royalty, whose lineage stretches back 21 generations and whose ancestor invented Cava in 1872. Having seen how success had corrupted quality at the family's historic winery, Cordoníu (which, alongside La Sagrada Familia, was once among Barcelona's most popular tourist attractions), Pepe's grandfather Josep Maria sold his shares and founded Raventós i Blanc in 1985, only to die from heart failure a year after the first harvest. Pepe and his father Manuel worked tirelessly to avoid bankruptcy, and are now at the vanguard of biodynamic wine in the region.

Forty-five-minutes' drive west of Barcelona, Penedès has long been the centre of Spanish sparkling wine production, yet, like the once-mighty Sherry, its image has been bastardised by oceans of poor-quality renditions. Cava – a blend of Xarel·lo, Parellada and Macabeu, made using the traditional method of secondary fermentation in bottle – first attained international success during the First World War, when much of Champagne was battlefields, and has since become dominated by industrial wineries to service demand. A century on, it is now a method-orientated DO that cares little for terroir expression or sustainable viticulture, something that led Pepe – whose grandfather also established the *Consejo Regulador del Cava* regulatory body – to leave and start the Conca del Riu Anoia appellation for his sparkling wines. Of course, other Cava producers see this as a betrayal, but if you believe in quality farming and

Opposite: Glòria Garriga, Els Jelipins, Penedès.

wines with a sense of place, what should you do? Champagne's largest annual production – Moët & Chandon's 30 million bottles – seems almost artisanal compared with the compromises that Cava's largest producer, Freixenet, must have to make to produce its mind-boggling 200 million.

Aside from the obvious tensions between industrial and traditional organic viticulture, Penedès sparkling wine's most significant struggle comes with such inevitable comparisons with Champagne. Whereas Swartland Chenin Blanc, for example, is rarely judged against Burgundian Chardonnay, Cava operates in the shadow of the greatest drinks marketing success story of all time. Talking with Pepe, a naturally charming advocate for his wines with a deeper, spiritual side – a mix of Dale Carnegie technique and Eckhart Tolle sincerity (the latter is one of his favourite authors) – it's obviously something that's kept him awake at night. I can see what he means when he says Cava is a more mineral wine than Champagne, which he regards as fruitier, but only in the context of Raventós i Blanc's biodynamic bubbles versus standard-issue non-vintage *Grandes Marques*. Juxtaposed against the intense, chalky minerality of, say, Pierre Péters 'Les Chétillons' or other leading Grower Champagnes, only Mas del Serral, from Pepe's top 1ha vineyard, gets close: it's a delicious, saline amalgamation of lemon cream, biscuit and umami to which other Cava producers can only aspire. But, again, why compare apples with oranges?

Pepe's story may be deeply rooted in Cava, but his project making low-intervention still wines – a passion he developed while frequenting natural wine bars such as Diner and Marlow & Sons when living in New York marketing Raventós i Blanc – aspires to elevate the humble into the world class. Back in

Below: Can Sumoi, El Pla de Manlleu, Penedès.

1999, when Raventós i Blanc had to fight to keep afloat, Pepe started producing a still wine called 'Perfum' to increase turnover, while dreaming of one day buying vineyards elsewhere in the region to keep the two styles separate. A keen cyclist, he finally realised this goal in 2016, when he rode past a tumbledown *finca* dating from 1645 in El Pla de Manlleu, west Penedès, and outbid another suitor who wanted to turn it into a chicken farm. Perched on a 600m hill – on a clear day, you can see as far as Mallorca – Can Sumoi has 20ha of old vines out of a 300ha forest estate, a landscape Pepe says he knew would produce outstanding wines the moment he saw it. Although it's only two vintages old, that's exactly how we'd describe the estate's 2018 Xarel·lo: citrusy, pure, precise and long, it leaves a sensation of salt crystals on the tongue and is the perfect foil for the local Palamós prawns.

Of Cava's three grape varietals, the austere, less fruit-driven Xarel·lo (pronounced Sha-rel-oh) is closer in profile to Chenin Blanc than Chardonnay, with excellent potential as a single varietal wine. Part of what makes Can Sumoi such an exciting prospect is not only the renaissance of a long-forgotten heritage – a trend throughout Spanish wine – but the ambition of elevating a grape not conventionally regarded capable of greatness. It's an idea Pepe picked up working for the late Loire Valley iconoclast Didier Dagueneau in 2004. "What inspired me was how he expressed the soil through Sauvignon Blanc," Pepe says. "I thought I must be able to do this with Xarel·lo. The thing I really took away was belief – he was a believer in what he was doing." Taking half the yields of similar producers in Pouilly-Fumé, but with twice as many workers in the vineyards, Dagueneau's meticulous farming practices took Sauvignon Blanc to heights many didn't think possible, an ethos adopted by other *vignerons* today. Pepe takes me to visit Toni Carbó, a local grower from whom he buys

Above: Pepe Raventós.

fruit for Raventós i Blanc, who keeps back 10% of his crop to make his own wine. In Toni's kitchen, we drink his wonderfully tangy Xarel·lo 'La Bufarrella' surrounded by empty bottles of Soldera Brunello di Montalcino and Château Rayas; maverick inspiration abounds.

Over in nearby Font-rubí, there isn't much that's orthodox about how Glòria Garriga taught herself to make wine or, indeed, approaches life in general. Like Pepe and Toni, she uses only organic fruit for the three cuvées she produces at Els Jelipins, but what makes her transition into natural wine so unique is that she has seen agriculture's worst abuses from the inside. "It's very interesting to learn how a multinational chemical company works from within," she says, eyes scanning her basic cellar for memories. "You're forced to forecast

Left: Toni Carbó, La Salada, Les Parellades del Pla del Penedés.

growth in sales, which is crazy, because you have a limited potential market. So you have to convince farmers that they need to use fertilisers, and once they start, they are forced to continue to get the yields they expect. Fertilisers are salt, which makes plants absorb a lot of water, which in turn makes a high production, but it also makes them more sensitive to pests and disease. Then they need to buy pesticides and fungicides to control that. It's like human health: if you eat shit food, you'll get ill and the pharmaceutical companies make more money."

Descended from Argentinian immigrants, Glòria has been coming to the *finca* that houses Els Jelipins' winery since she was a small child as it used to be her parents' place in the mountains. Having never owned vineyards, she has worked hard to build the trust of local growers so she can buy high-quality fruit, while insisting on her own pruning techniques to ensure low yields, and absolutely no fertilisers or pesticides. With fruit harvested from about 1.5ha of vines around the area, her production is tiny, and she has no plans to expand. "Maybe I'm not ambitious enough, but all I ever wanted to do was make enough money to live," she explains, before adding that her early vintages remained unsold until open-minded sommeliers as far afield as the US and Canada began listing her wines in 2012. Which is unsurprising, really, given how different they are from the concentrated, oak-saturated style that dominated the Spanish market for decades.

Of the three cuvées Glòria produces, my picks are her Gravner-esque amber wine, vinified in amphora from Montonega (Parellada) and Sumoll, and a simple but hugely satisfying *rosado*, made exclusively from the latter. The red Sumoll grape is another interesting native that, due to its high acidity, aggressive tannins and capacity for ageing, has been dubbed the Catalan Nebbiolo, although Glòria's *rosado* tames any abrasiveness and ekes out delicate, Pinot-esque aromas. As with many artisanal wine projects started over recent years, it is attention to detail on small-batch productions and meticulous farming that elevate grapes others would consider too mundane to warrant proper consideration to new heights. "It's my dream that one day I'll go to New York or London and see a vertical tasting of Xarel·lo," Pepe tells me. Anything is possible when you believe.

Tenerife

Canary Islands, Spain

"THE MESSAGE TO THE WORLD is that Tenerife wine is nothing new. It has been around for centuries. The thing is the gap of 200 years when it was in decline." So says winemaker Jonatan García Lima of Suertes del Marqués, the Tenerife estate that, alongside a collective of like-minded dreamers known as Envínate, is leading a vinous renaissance on the island. A similar story is playing out across Spain: up-and-coming producers farming unwanted old vines in regions such as Ribeira Sacra in Galicia and the Gredos Mountains near Madrid to make wines that express a unique sense of origin. "That Tenerife didn't export wine for two centuries has benefits," says García Lima. "Merchants couldn't demand indigenous grapes be replanted with international varieties, which helped to prevent phylloxera from ever getting here."

Given that it's located in the Atlantic Ocean due west of the Sahara Desert, it's a wonder fine wine can be grown on Tenerife at all. While numerous flights to the south of the island bring a daily influx of garrulous teenagers, stressed-out families and pensioners for an almost-guaranteed fix of holiday sun, grapes usually struggle to retain freshness at such latitude. Here, around the resorts, the climate is hot and arid; a landscape of palm trees, ravines, candelabra-like cacti and serrated rock formations that recall *A Fistful of Dollars*. But it's on Tenerife's mountainous north coast, where the central Teide mega-volcano traps rain clouds blown south on *alisios* winds and the environment becomes lush and subtropical, that fortune smiles on viticulture. It's also here, several hundred years ago, that merchants made riches by supplying huge quantities of wine to British warships on their way to conquer the globe.

During the 17th century, wine was a necessity rather than a luxury. Poor hygiene rendered most water undrinkable, especially on long ocean voyages, and ports in Tenerife, Madeira, Gibraltar and the Azores were essential provision stops en route from Britain to the Empire. Of course, such strategic importance wasn't lost on the Royal Navy, which tried, unsuccessfully, to wrest Tenerife from Spanish control in 1657, 1706 and 1797 (the latter famously

Opposite: Jonatan García Lima, Suertes del Marqués, Orotava Valley, Tenerife.

resulting in Rear-Admiral Horatio Nelson's right arm getting amputated after the Battle of Santa Cruz), commemorated today by three lions on the capital's crest. But conflict had little effect on the success of British and Irish merchants exporting the island's popular sweet, fortified Malmsey. While sales peaked at 15 million litres in 1600, it would take an American thirst for Madeira to diminish sales significantly by 1700. Later, a dry white known as 'Vidonia' became Tenerife's last significant export, until trade died out in 1830. "If you came to Tenerife 50 years ago, you'd see a landscape of banana plantations," says historian Carlos Cólogan Soriano, the seventh-generation descendant of John Cólogan, one of the island's most successful merchants. "If you came 200 years ago, you'd see only vines."

But enough history. Today, 'Vidonia' has been reimagined by Suertes del Marqués as one of Spain's most exciting white wines. A blend of old vine Listán Blanco from clay and sand soils around the Orotava Valley, a northern appellation where cloud cover moderates temperatures by some 10°C compared to the rest of the island, this is a smoky-fresh, future classic that will appeal to lovers of Jura Chardonnay and Chablis. Unlike the Listán Blanco grown in Sherry country, known there as Palomino, here it has mouthwatering acidity and a signature smokiness from being grown on volcanic clay. Majoring on minerals rather than fruit, if a wine could be described as 'liquid rock', this is it. But the most intriguing thing about 'Vidonia' isn't that it is resurrecting a long-forgotten style, or that the elegant and precise 2017 is one of the most delicious whites I've drunk recently, it's the vineyards where it's grown.

Giants' hair braids, rib cages, spindly spider legs – however your brain processes the ancient vines that line Suertes del Marqués' steep Orotava Valley vineyards when you set eyes on them for the first time, there's nowhere else on the planet quite like it. Trained with a rare technique called *cordón trenzado*, the long vine canes are painstakingly tied back to their sinewy roots after pruning, then propped off the floor with poles. Production is split 25% between white wine (check out their excellent entry-level 'Trenzado') and 75% red, which García Lima has been refining since taking over as winemaker in 2016. Picking grapes early to retain acidity, pressing less, and using long macerations are some of the techniques introduced for 2016 '7 Fuentes', a 'village' red made from Listán Negro and Tintilla (Garnacha) bought from other growers. Fresh and peppery with round, supple tannins, it is a fascinating gateway into a nascent range of single-vineyard cuvées.

Roughly translated, Suertes del Marqués means 'plots of the marquis', although García Lima isn't from aristocratic lineage. His father Francisco began buying vineyards in the Orotava Valley in 1986, selling most of his crop to local domaines, and only decided to begin producing wine commercially in 2006. A seminal moment came two years later when he hired Roberto Santana, a young local winemaker who had just returned to the island after studying oenology in Alicante and working in Jumilla. As they introduced organic,

Opposite: Roberto Santana and Alfonso Torrente of Envínate, 'Margalagua' vineyard, Tenerife.

low-interventionist philosophies, their collaboration was ground zero for a new wave of Tenerife fine wine, bringing centuries in the wilderness to a close. In 2016 Roberto left to focus on Envínate with business partners Alfonso Torrente, Laura Ramos and José Martínez, while Jonatan took control at Suertes del Marqués, creating two island estates that are now the talk of top wine lists around the globe.

Envínate is a unique project that operates like a collective of flying winemakers, who, unlike their 1980s namesakes, prize authenticity above all else. Piecing together fruit from a series of guerrilla-style vineyard purchases, rentals and collaborations with local growers, they produce 14 different cuvées from four different parts of Spain: Almansa, Extremadura, Ribeira Sacra and Tenerife. The last two regions are overseen by Alfonso Torrente and Roberto Santana, whose precipitous vineyards easily top my 'World's Most Dangerous and Hard to Work' chart. Economically and logistically, no large commercial producers would commit to such places: high-altitude mountainsides where grapes must be carried over treacherous pathways, but whose hard-won results deserve to be prized like rare jewels. Gone are the days of young *vignerons* needing hundreds of thousands of pounds in start-up costs for hi-tech wineries, new oak barrels and marketing managers, or to absorb years of waiting for newly planted vines to mature. By thinking creatively, Envínate has become one of the hottest names in European wine.

"We call Táganana 'Jurassic Park' because when we arrived we found a really diverse mix of historic varieties," says Roberto Santana, climbing the 'Margalagua' vineyard. Envínate found this and neighbouring vineyards on Tenerife's north-eastern coast from studying old textbooks; some of the ungrafted vines here are up to 300 years old, sprouting randomly from plots some 200m above the Atlantic. But while Táganana is protected from commercial development by UNESCO accreditation ("Elsewhere on Tenerife people would rather abandon vineyards than sell them, in case someone wants to buy them to build a hotel," says Roberto), many of the region's most historic sites are so inaccessible they will never be regenerated. It's a shame, because this is a sublime place to grow grapes: high vineyards, alive with birdsong and sea air, fostering thrilling, saline wines. Later, back at Mesón Castellano, Roberto's father's restaurant in Santa Cruz, we drink other Envínate cuvées made elsewhere on Tenerife ('Benje' from Santiago del Teide, 'Migan' and 'Palo Blanco' from La Orotava), and indulge in one of the duo's favourite pastimes – blind tasting. Roberto and Alfonso sniff, sip and dissect a succession of unidentified bottles. Where is it from? How old is it? What makes it good? One by one, wines from top French and Italian domaines are revealed, alongside their ambitions. Pitting themselves against the best in the world, the Tenerife new wave has only just begun.

Above: Jonatan García Lima, Suertes del Marqués.

Right: Roberto Santana and Alfonso Torrente, Envínate.

Ribeira Sacra

Galicia, Spain

THERE ARE EASIER WAYS to earn a living than as a winemaker on the edge of the world. "I'm exhausted," says Laura Lorenzo, pressing her weathered hands against her brow. "For the past three years I've worked the vineyards on my own, until last month I could finally afford to hire someone to help. He lasted just a couple of days and then disappeared. Working vines in Ribeira Sacra is hard." Having seen the precipitous drops on the way to her remote winery, Lorenzo is a master of understatement. Relieved to have navigated the roads in this timeless part of Galicia before darkness, we drink her 2015 Daterra Viticultores 'Portela do Vento' – a Mencía blend typical of the light, perfumed reds that have made a name for Ribeira Sacra – and, for a moment, relax. Now, it's only the anticipation of our roller-coaster night-drive back to our hotel that's making us sweat.

The beginnings of viticulture in Ribeira Sacra go far back in time, and it's only in the last 20 years that a handful of *vignerons* have spearheaded a renaissance. The Romans were the first to plant vineyards here some 2,000 years ago, having come to mine gold. Their slaves constructed giant stairways of terraces on three main gorges – the Sil, the Miño and the Bibei. Later, monks farmed the vineyards for centuries until phylloxera, recession and civil war drove scores of locals to leave for new lives elsewhere. The vineyards then laid abandoned for decades until around the millennium when an influx of winemakers, attracted by stocks of old vines and excellent terroir, arrived. Now their challenge is to raise market demand and prices to cover the costs of cultivating such demanding land.

"Many young people feel ashamed to be seen working the vineyards. They want to use a tractor rather than a spade, which isn't possible on this terrain," says Laura. Having bought a winery in the near-ghost town Manzaneda, Laura offsets the expense of farming 5ha in Ribeira Sacra's Bibei Valley with 1ha in the flatter, easier-to-work neighbouring DO Valdeorras. "It's not just that the Bibei vineyards are very old with lots of different grape

varieties, but they've been looked after in many different ways. It's complicated." Having spent ten years as winemaker for the pioneering Dominio do Bibei, if anyone has a chance of deciphering the untold combinations of soil, grape and microclimate, it's Laura and her ex-employer, Javier Domínguez.

Previous spread: 'Camiño Novo' vineyard, Ribeira Sacra.

"In Galicia we don't have the knowledge of other wine regions," says Javier. "The monks didn't write anything down, so we have to learn by making our own mistakes. We're trying to define how to work this land, but it's a 100-year project, for our children." Mencía is the dominant red planting in Ribeira Sacra – a low-acid grape that still has good freshness – which Dominio do Bibei blends with other indigenous varietals, such as Sousón, Mouratón, Alicante Bouschet, Caíño and Brancellao. For whites, Godello and Albariño are most popular, with Doña Branca, Treixadura and Torrontés sometimes included. Soils are a mixture of granite, schist, slate and iron; grapes are de-stemmed and *élevage* takes place in an assortment of vessels, including cement eggs, *foudres* and old oak barrels. "Our wines aren't overly fruity, but they are very expressive – you taste the land, not the grape," says Javier. Having started out by reclaiming dozens of abandoned terraces in 2002, the domaine owns 140ha of land, of which 32ha produce grapes for two reds – 'Lalama', from the lower, warmest part of the valley and 'Lacima' from the peak – and two whites – 'Lapena' ('sorrow') and 'Lapola' ('branch'). Having drunk Dominio do Bibei's debut 2002 'Lalama' at Arzak restaurant in San Sebastían the previous day, we can vouch for their ageing potential. Fresh and perfumed, its bouquet of plums, cherries, minerals and herbs evoke a delicious cross between Cabernet Franc and Pinot Noir.

Joining Laura and Javier, Envínate is also building for the future and making authentic wines in Ribeira Sacra, just as it is in Tenerife (see previous

Left: Javier Domínguez, Dominio do Bibei.

chapter) and elsewhere in Spain. "It's very important to us that our wines age well," says Roberto Santana, one of the four winemakers who make up the company. "To make Ribeira Sacra an important region we have to think long term." Roberto's partner Alfonso Torrente is originally from Ribeira Sacra, where they bottle three red cuvées under the name 'Lousas' ('broken slate'), including one from the formidable terraces of 'Camiño Novo'. A blend of 90-year-old Mencía with Garnacha Tintorera, 'Lousas Parcela Camiño Novo' combines peppery Northern Rhône-style aromatics with rounded tannins akin to Cru Beaujolais. "We love wines with personality, that transport you to the place they were grown," says Roberto. Along with their friends at domaines Guímaro and Fedellos do Couto, as well as Dominio do Bibei and Daterra Viticultores, there is now a community of high-quality winemakers drawing international attention to the region, all facing huge challenges to follow their dreams. "When I left Ribeira Sacra for the first time I thought: people plant vines on flat land too?" laughs Guímaro's Pedro Rodríguez Pérez. There are easier places to make wine than Ribeira Sacra, but we have huge admiration for those who do.

Above: Lunch with Envínate, Guímaro and Fedellos do Couto.

Portugal

IN COLARES you can see surfers riding waves as high as multi-storey buildings and sandy beaches that stretch for miles, but you would be hard-pressed to find a vineyard – strange, considering that in the 1930s it was one of Europe's most prestigious wine regions. Today just 22ha of some 1,000ha of Colares' old, snake-like vines remain on the dunes amid the hotels and restaurants that dominate what was once Lisbon's unkempt backyard. Rising land prices have tempted many locals to sell their vineyards to developers, and the difficulty of growing grapes here has contributed to the shift to tourism. This place is challenging: moderate temperatures with high humidity and strong winds have forced winemakers to develop a unique horizontal viticulture. Not only do Colares' vineyards look different from those anywhere else, they are very hard to work, too.

Francisco Figueiredo, who runs the regional cooperative, calls it "heroic viticulture". Planting young vines means digging 4m-deep trenches and directly placing them in the clay that sits under the sandy topsoil. Over the following years the sand is shovelled bit-by-bit back into the trench by hand, stabilising the vine and preventing phylloxera (the sand-hating aphid never destroyed the vineyards here, unlike the majority of those in Europe). Propped up by short bamboo canes to keep the bunches off the floor, and surrounded by wind breaks made of reeds, these vines are grown with techniques as distinctive as the wines they produce. Robust, velvety textured, high-acidity reds are made from Ramisco, aged for five years in large Brazilian mahogany barrels with another year in used oak *barriques* to tame ferocious tannins. Saline whites with a beeswax and preserved lemon character are made from the local Malvasia de Colares and are just as age-worthy, spending six months in Brazilian wood and a year in steel tank. With 2018 production for the whole appellation down to 6,500l, it's little wonder that the official Colares wine bottle holds just 500ml, instead of the regular 750ml. But awareness of these wines is improving, with new plantings increasing the area under vine.

Opposite: Colares mural and vineyard.

Overleaf: Adega Viúva Gomes, Colares.

MINISTERIO DA AGRICULTURA
COMISSÃO DE VITICULTURA
REGIÃO DE COLARES

Leading winery Adega Viúva Gomes, owned by father and son José and Diogo Baeta, is responsible for some of these new plantings. Historically, the pair have bought wine from Francisco Figueiredo at the cooperative and coaxed extra layers of interest from it through long oak ageing in their cellars, but they soon hope to be vinifying their own wine now they have their own vines (until 1994 a law intended to prevent fraud decreed that only wine produced by the co-op could be called Colares). The duo boast a library of mature vintages that would be the envy of most domaines, with superb wines from the 1930s to the 1960s showing how well Colares can age. "We only have these old wines today because nobody wanted them," Diogo says. "For wines to evolve they need to be made a particular way, and these bottles inspire us to keep those traditional methods alive."

Even closer to Lisbon is Carcavelos, a region that once held such exalted status that its fortified wine launched Christie's debut wine auction in 1769. Back then the land was owned and the wine promoted by the Portuguese prime minister, the Marquês de Pombal, but nowadays you'd be lucky to find a wino who has even heard of the appellation. Like Colares, urban development was a problem, and only averted thanks to Villa Oeiras, a joint-venture between the Ministry of Agriculture and local municipality that has safeguarded 12.5ha of local varieties, out of a total of 25ha left in the region. Ensuring Carcavelos wine has a future, the project, run by Alexandre Lisboa, vinifies its own wines and also makes resources available to other *vignerons* who want to help the region's renaissance.

Vítor Claro, one of Portugal's best winemakers, was the first to take up the offer. His focus had been Portalegre in north-east Alentejo, where he still makes the excellent Dominó wines. But when a friend offered him "two hectares of

Left: José and Diogo Baeta,
Adega Viúva Gomes.

paradise" in a nature reserve in Carcavelos, it was too good to turn down. Although hardly any Carcavelos has been produced in the past few decades, Vítor finds inspiration in old bottles from defunct estates such as Quinta da Bela Vista. Tasting of crème brûlée and flambéed toffee apples, the wines have Madeira-like freshness, though Vítor finds them "softer and more digestible". Old-school Carcavelos was fermented to dryness then fortified, with sweetness adjusted by adding high-sugar must. So far Villa Oeiras has made a conventional Port-style fortification, but Vítor is excited about using traditional techniques in the spirit of the old wines.

The list of Portugal's forgotten wine regions doesn't end there. Setúbal provided wine to the kings of Europe, but the reputation of its sweet Moscatel is far from what it used to be. The Azores Wine Company is doing stellar work reviving endangered varieties in spectacular UNESCO-protected vineyards. Meanwhile, Bucelas was perhaps the most famous of all, name-dropped by Shakespeare and nicknamed 'Portuguese Hock'. Today most of the appellation is owned by industrial producer Sogrape, but in the neighbouring DOC Torres Vedras, Pedro and Manuel Marques of Vale da Capucha farm the same white grapes, Arinto and Fernão Pires.

"The mentality here has always been that big equals good. Someone with 10ha doesn't exist in the eyes of the wine community," says Pedro Marques, whose single-varietal Arinto and Alvarinho whites, and Castelão reds, are redefining this coastal region. The idea of small artisanal domaines has arrived late to Portugal. "When I started in 2008 I had no neighbours working conscientiously," Pedro says, "only farmers selling bad grapes to big companies". Indeed, even though their family has been farming grapes for centuries, Pedro and Manuel are the first generation to commercialise their wine. "Until recently, Portugal never had *vignerons*; almost everybody making artisanal wine here today is first generation."

There are exceptions, of course, such as Filipa Pato crafting red and white 'Nossa Calcário' from Bairrada's limestone vineyards, or António Marques da Cruz of Quinta da Serradinha, who collaborates with Tiago Teles for COZs, a project making natural wines in the Serra de Montejunto. Many such winemakers have spent time working with Dirk Niepoort, who, as well as being the scion of one of Port's foremost families, is one of Portugal's wine innovators. "Dirk is one of a kind – in the north he created a community and encouraged so many people," says Pedro Marques. Niepoort originates from the Douro Valley, but his curiosity has led him to numerous other regions, inspiring his alumni to farm conscientiously and seek freshness and authenticity. "Dirk is fundamental to everything," says Vítor Claro, recalling the time when his oenologist let him down on the eve of his first harvest and he called Niepoort for advice. "He said, 'It's the best thing that could happen to you. You don't need an oenologist – they would only spoil it. Make it simple, make it pure'." Sage advice for the next chapter of Portuguese wine.

Barolo & Barbaresco

Piedmont, Italy

EVEN THE MOST world-weary traveller would find it hard to resist Piedmont's bucolic allure. Negotiating the hairpin roads that wrap around the hillsides of Barolo DOCG and Barbaresco DOCG, the region's two most important appellations, you'll see one magnificent vista of vineyards and castles after another – an enduring landscape that looks as if it has changed little since medieval times. Here, the Nebbiolo grape is king, interspersed with plots of white Moscato and supple red Barbera and Dolcetto – the quotidian drinkers long favoured by locals while their Barolos softened and aged.

Some experienced winos find Nebbiolo's tannins and high acidity a challenge to enjoy. Like Pinot Noir, the grape is very susceptible to terroir and weather conditions and, depending on whether it has time to fully ripen – which takes a while – and is handled correctly, its wines range from rich, fruity and perfumed to brutal and hard. At its very best, it has a delicious bitterness in line with other great Italian drinks and foods, and aromas of roses, tar, liquorice and cherries. You might think of it as the severe Langhe cousin of top red Burgundy – a combination of forcefulness, ethereality and finesse.

Three times the size of Barbaresco, Barolo is historically known for producing the more prestigious wine, with grippier tannins and a denser texture. Barbaresco, north-east of the town of Alba – rather than south-west like Barolo – is slightly warmer, with sandier soils and earlier harvest dates, known for gentler tannins and earlier approachability. But while generalisations apply in some cases, it can be hard to tell the two wines apart, especially as they're grown in so many different sub-plots by producers using diverse techniques and philosophies – as divided as the politics in this part of north-west Italy.

Back in the '80s and '90s, when technological innovations transformed much winemaking, Piedmontese producers polarised into two loose camps. 'Modernists', such as Roberto Voerzio and Luciano Sandrone, made accessible, concentrated wines by lowering yields, sometimes adding international grape varieties, and doing *élevage* in small new oak French *barriques*. 'Traditionalists',

on the other hand, such as the late Bartolo Mascarello and Giacomo Conterno, stuck to making pure, single-varietal wines with long fermentations and ageing in large Slavonian oak *botti* to gracefully express a sense of place and vintage.

Today, Cantina Bartolo Mascarello is owned by Bartolo's daughter Maria Teresa, who still makes wine in the most traditional way. Like Jean-Louis Chave in France's Northern Rhône Valley, who believes the ultimate expression of his prestigious Hermitage AOC is a blend of several different vineyards sited around the hill, Maria Teresa insists that the only way for her to make great Barolo is by blending her four vineyards – Cannubi, San Lorenzo, Rué and Rocche – into one wine, as her dad, his father Giulio, and Giulio's father Bartolomeo, all did in their day.

"The result is greater than the sum of the parts," says Maria Teresa. "I'm honoured to produce Barolo, so I fight to protect its traditional values." Her elegant and silky 2006 is a transcendent amalgamation of pure fruit, minerals and savouriness that rates among my favourite ever Barolos, while the 2012, unusually for a wine famed for its austere structure, is already drinking beautifully. While buying old Italian wine is sometimes problematic – a result of it being undervalued for decades and thus not always appropriately

Above: Serralunga d'Alba.

Opposite: Maria Teresa Mascarello, Barolo.

stored (see 'Out of Order', p104) – when they're on form, mature Barolos made by producers such as Mascarello, G. Conterno, G. Rinaldi, Accomasso and Burlotto can be transportive experiences. Their profiles range from more powerful and sinewy in Serralunga d'Alba, to darker in Monforte d'Alba, lighter and accessible in Verduno, and more sensually perfumed in Castiglione Falletto, with the town of Barolo itself geographically, and stylistically, in the middle.

Over in Barbaresco, traditionalist winemaking is at its apogee at the outstanding Bruno Giacosa and Roagna, while exceptional value is found at Produttori del Barbaresco, one of the best-quality wine co-ops anywhere in the world. But no other producer has done more to raise the reputation and profile of Barbaresco – and perhaps Italian fine wine in general – than Angelo Gaja. A maverick artisan and entrepreneur who raised the quality of his family estate when Barbaresco was considered a lesser Piedmontese wine, then upped the price to match Barolo, Gaja broke with tradition by vinifying individual vineyard plots and using a mixture of French new oak *barriques* and big vats.

Just as controversially, he planted Cabernet Sauvignon in the Bricco vineyard, first releasing it as 'Darmagi' in 1982, and growing an excellent Chardonnay, which he first unveiled as 'Gaia & Rey' in 1983. Tasting this wine at 33 years of age in 2016 was a revelation: it had a complex perfume of toast, smoke, brie and mushrooms with lovely freshness and acidity, a chewy texture, and ripe stone-fruit flavours. 'Sorì San Lorenzo' is Gaja's flagship single vineyard red, which, as in the still tightly woven 1989, can have an almost Burgundian, Gevrey-esque dark-toned profile, while my favourite is the supremely elegant and perfumed 1988 'Sorì Tildìn', which has gorgeous fruit perfectly meshed with savoury elements.

Whether you appreciate Gaja's slick aesthetics or not, it is undoubtedly a winery pushing for ever-greater standards and sustainability. Now run by Angelo's daughters, Gaia and Rossana, the vineyards are all organic ecosystems where wildlife is encouraged through the installation of projects such as beehives. In a return to tradition, the pair have also done away with the 5% Barbera that their father included in the single-vineyard wines, which, for the first time since 1995, are again classified as Barbaresco DOCG. Indeed, the past decade has seen such improvements across Piedmontese farming and winemaking that the 'modernists' and 'traditionalists' have more common ground than ever before.

Joško Gravner

Friuli-Venezia Giulia, Italy

THESE AREN'T EASY WINES to understand. "It's hard to find a drinker interested in this style," says Joško Gravner, slicing a home-made salami on the kitchen table. "The main reason I make them is to express what I'm thinking. Sometimes, when I think about it, I'm drinking my thoughts; there's good and bad in all of them. An angel and a devil." Obviously, this isn't the kind of humdrum sales pitch to be expected from the majority of grape growers. But then there's nothing humdrum about Gravner or his genre-defying wines ("I don't call them 'orange' – I prefer 'amber', which is alive"). Part philosopher, part family man, part farmer, from behind his serene façade he emanates inner strength and conviction in a righteous path – a path he's radically reconsidered several times during a remarkable career.

We're having supper in Gravner's grandmother's old farmhouse in Hum, Slovenia, a village on the border with north-east Italy. Historically, this is no land for the faint-hearted. Dotted with ghostly abandoned border posts – echoes from the days of communism – these verdant hills have been governed by both the Habsburg empire and Napoleon, and witnessed much bloodshed during both world wars. On the table in front of us fish bowl-shaped wine glasses – designed by Joško himself – contain rust-coloured Ribolla, an indigenous white grape that has become his focus. Perhaps meant as a metaphor for his wine's idiosyncrasies – or simply because he likes round glasses – these stemless drinking vessels demand full concentration to avoid swirling the contents everywhere but your mouth.

But, besides colour, what is it about these amber wines that makes them so different? Missing the fresh fruit aromas of conventionally made wine, they almost require a new vocabulary to describe: talking about them feels like trying to discuss music in Japan when you can't speak the language. Eventually, after much cerebral acrobatics, oxidative aromas of over-steeped tea, dried fruit, nuts, orange rind and honey come to mind – a negative imprint of orthodox wine's positive; a yin to its yang. Soaking up tannins over five months

Above: Joško Gravner takes delivery of Georgian *qvevri*, Oslavia, 2004.

Below: Gravner's Dedno vineyard.

NOBLE ROT

of fermentation on the skins in Georgian clay *qvevri* (followed by maturation of six months in *qvevri* and a further six years in large oak barrels), these are complex, full-bodied, textural wines that benefit from being served at room temperature rather than chilled. While technically white wines, they feel more like light reds. "Using maceration helps drinkability," says Joško, citing the centuries-old local tradition of the technique. Indeed, rather than the radical iconoclast as he is often labelled, Gravner could just as easily be described as an arch traditionalist returning to the world's oldest winemaking techniques. And, my, what a journey it's been.

Joško Gravner began working at the family's winery in the 1970s, during a period of unprecedented innovation. Embracing new techniques such as fermentation in temperature-controlled steel tanks and *élevage* in oak *barriques*, he made a name for fresh, fruit-driven Chardonnay, Sauvignon Blanc and Ribolla (and a red made from Merlot, then, from the mid-'90s, Pignolo), referencing his deep love of Burgundy and other French regions. Celebrated by the influential wine guide *Gambero Rosso* and enjoying an expanding customer base, Gravner stood, alongside other young stars such as Barbaresco's Angelo Gaja, at the vanguard of the Italian wine scene throughout the 1980s. But, despite the plaudits, something wasn't right. Having embarked on a research trip to California in 1987, he returned downbeat and disillusioned – not just by the hundreds of highly rated American wines that left him "emotionally cold" – but the realisation that his own wines were just as representative of a generic, 'international' style. Soon, after a period of intense reflection, he set about making the first changes to his practical philosophy: stripping the winery of modern technology and reinstalling large old oak casks and a mechanical basket press.

Other decisive changes followed in 1996, when hail obliterated 95% of his Ribolla crop. Salvaging what grapes he could, Gravner decided to experiment with long maceration on the skins for the first time, and was enthralled by the results. Convinced that this amber, rather than his usual pale wine, was the direction he should take, the following year he performed extended maceration on his entire white production. The only problem was he didn't tell his customers. "Joško Gravner has gone crazy – please come back, Joško," read the headline of one *Gambero Rosso* article that went on to describe his 1997s as oxidised and undrinkable. "The press was really hard at first, because everyone was so used to me making a different style of wine," remembers Joško. "A lot of people thought I was mad, but a couple of years later a few other farmers around the area started trying maceration as well." Following the *Gambero Rosso* furore, over half of the winery's regular stockists returned his 1997s as unsellable. But Gravner dug deep, and continued along his righteous path.

Over time, drinkers began coming around to the new amber style, but Joško was only just getting started. He took his next research trip at the turn

Above: Gravner *qvevri* room.

of the millennium, into the ancient heartlands of winemaking. "When I arrived in Georgia people weren't keen on speaking to strangers," says Gravner. "Because of the political situation they were used to keeping secrets, so I had to learn the way they make wine through silence. It's better to focus on not doing than doing; through silence they didn't need to say much for me to understand what not to do." Reinforcing the low-intervention techniques that he adheres to today – minimal sulphur, indigenous yeasts, no temperature control, organic farming and working to the phases of the moon – perhaps the most profound revelation from his time in Georgia was the use of large earthenware amphorae, which he began importing via Croatia the following year. While many wineries were experimenting with these newly fashionable vessels on small parts of their production, Joško went all in, converting his entire crop to amphora fermentation by 2005. Today, he's aided by his daughters Mateja and Jana, who oversee the business and vineyards, respectively. There's a close bond among the Gravner family, perhaps due in part to the 2009 death in a motorcycle accident of his son Miha, who had one day been expected to take over the estate.

Back in the Hum farmhouse, as we marvel over the fish bowls of amber juice, Gravner discusses the completion of his latest project: the grubbing up of all non-indigenous varietals from his vineyards. "One of the problems with the wine industry is that people don't grow the grapes that already exist in a place, but what they think the market wants," he says. Having discontinued both Bianco 'Breg' (a blend of Chardonnay, Sauvignon Blanc, Italian Riesling and Pinot Grigio) and Pinot Grigio cuvées in 2012, Gravner now focuses on native Ribolla and Pignolo, and has developed a new 8ha vineyard in Dedno, Slovenia. Featuring artificial ponds ("When you put a lake in a vineyard you bring in mosquitos, which bring in birds that feed on the fish; a whole ecosystem that's part of a symbiosis that I want to create") and steep slopes, the space is teeming with adolescent plants offset by very old stocks in Runk (Italy) and Hum. Indeed, such is Gravner's success with the longevity of many of his vines, that Champagne Louis Roederer requested that he train their team in his unique pruning techniques. Quite some compliment, coming from the French.

"It is life itself that I try and put into wines," says Joško, reflecting on the purpose of his career in typically poetic fashion. "Young winemakers shouldn't study oenology, they should study philosophy. With oenology you're able to analyse, but with philosophy you're able to help wine become what it should be. You don't create wine by adding additives, you help it to be what it is." Through triumphs and disasters, disillusionment and reaffirmation, whether or not you like his wines, Gravner's conviction is impressive. "Ninety-five per cent of wines are completely different to mine but they're made for 95 per cent of the population. When God was giving out good taste they weren't paying attention," he says, laughing. Humdrum sales pitches aren't his thing.

Right: Joško Gravner with Georgian *qvevri*, Oslavia, 2004.

Brunello di Montalcino

Tuscany, Italy

"SOLDERA is not interested in talking about other wines. Visitors who do not follow his no-spitting rule get asked to leave. People who don't have their world-view of wine together have been known to burst into tears when he tears the wines they like apart. Believe me, I've seen it." I had been rather looking forward to meeting Gianfranco Soldera, the 82-year-old master winemaker of Brunello di Montalcino, after those comments by a mutual friend, so was dismayed to find out that he'd fallen and fractured a vertebra days before our scheduled meeting. Now he was convalescing in a Milan hospital, and I was mindful that visiting this relatively youthful and often scandal-hit Tuscan DOCG without an audience at his Case Basse estate would be like visiting Buckingham Palace without meeting the Queen. So Soldera agreed that we should instead see his daughter, Monica, who had worked alongside him for years. Sadly, a few weeks after being discharged from hospital he suffered a heart attack and died while inspecting his beloved vineyards in February 2019. Although we never got to meet, just witnessing his uncompromising methods left a profound impression about one of Italy's greatest ever winemakers.

Security at Soldera's Case Basse estate is tighter than the New York Federal Reserve Bank – the consequence of a heinous act of vandalism in December 2012 (more on that anon). Surveillance cameras are everywhere: surrounding the metal entrance gates; lining the driveway, mounted on stakes two metres apart; and guarding every part of vineyard, winery and cellar. Originally from the Veneto, via Milan, where he established a successful first career as an insurance broker, Gianfranco and his wife Graziella saved enough money to buy an abandoned farmhouse with land here in the sub-zone of Tavernelle, south-west of Montalcino town, and in 1972 planted two vineyards ('Intistieti' and 'Case Basse' itself) from scratch. They released their debut Sangiovese *in purezza* – 100% Sangiovese Grosso, as all Brunello di Montalcino is required by law to be – in 1975. Since then, Soldera's wine has developed a reputation not just as the pinnacle of Brunello di Montalcino, but as one

Opposite: Soldera's symbol, Dionysus' dolphin, in the grounds of Case Basse, Montalcino, Tuscany.

Overleaf: Montalcino, Tuscany.

of the greatest reds in the world full stop. "You can tell a great wine by its harmony, elegance, complexity and naturalness," Gianfranco wrote in his book-cum-manifesto *Betwixt Nature and Passion*. "This means balance and proportion, refinement, and manifold sensations of aroma and taste."

This might sound like hyperbole coming from a lesser winemaker, but after drinking his 2004 and 2005 Brunello, I wholeheartedly agree. Effortless and pure, yet taut and dazzlingly complex, these remarkable wines have rewired my idea of Italian reds. Some people compare Sangiovese to Pinot Noir; to me, the major stylistic difference is an extra sweetness to the former's fruit, a reflection, perhaps, of Mediterranean sunbeams, rather than Côte d'Or mists. In any case, such wines make adjectives roll so readily off the tongue – harmonious, natural, original, transparent, layered, delicate, intense – that, under their influence, I never want to drink anything else again, something of a costly and narrow-minded fantasy. At £295 a bottle on release for the current vintage (2015), these are some seriously expensive Sangioveses, even if, once you've seen Soldera's uber-meticulous techniques, you could argue they're still excellent value.

"It might be difficult for many people to understand why we invest so much time, attention and money cultivating grapes to produce just 15,000 bottles, when we could produce 60,000 from the same crop," says Monica. "But, for us, this is the only way to offer the best wine to market. There is no compromise. There is no second choice. We use only the most perfect grapes to make the best wines possible." Indeed, production is the most uncompromising I have ever witnessed: encouraging a wildlife ecosystem in the vineyards with artificial lakes and nests; discarding all irregular-sized berries, including the smallest (almost unheard of at other top domaines, which tend to prize them for having the most intense flavour); not pressing grapes and using only free-run juice; and ageing wines for between 48 and 75 months in large Slavonian oak *botti* – far longer than the minimum 24 months in barrel (followed by another 24 in bottle) prescribed for Brunello by law. While this extended *élevage* gives the wines time to breathe and develop complexity, it also meant "the disaster" of December 2012 – when a disgruntled ex-worker broke in and poured the majority of six vintages' worth of production (2007–2012) down the cellar drains – was more damaging than it might otherwise have been.

The aftermath of such a vindictive act must have been especially disheartening considering the effort that goes into crafting such a limited amount of wine. An outspoken proponent of traditional winemaking, Soldera was instrumental in keeping Brunello and its shorter-aged Rosso di Montalcino sibling restricted to 100% pure Sangiovese (rather than introducing outside international varieties, as proposed by the town's 'modernists') in a 2008 vote by local growers. As a result, he had no shortage of enemies, not least because some also assumed that he was a whistleblower in the same year's 'Brunellogate' scandal, when several large commercial producers were investigated for unlawfully

Above: Monica Soldera, Case Basse, Montalcino.

Opposite: Great wines make most sense in the presence of other wine lovers, such as this 2015 Soldera, served in glasses Gianfranco designed himself.

doctoring their wines (he always denied any involvement). But it was differences in opinion with the Brunello *consorzio* (producers' association) after the wine-attack perpetrator was sent to prison for four years that led to his resignation from the body – and the fact that it later unsuccessfully tried to sue him for libel. Soldera wines are now released outside the official Brunello di Montalcino DOCG. Not that it has done anything to dent demand.

The question is: if Brunello di Montalcino were to permit using Cabernet Sauvignon, Merlot *et al.* – which, according to some modernists, were grown around the town in the 1800s – what would differentiate it from the numerous other red blends of Tuscany? Surely there is enough super-Tuscan, Sant'Antimo and Vino Nobile di Montepulciano to go around without promoting homogenisation? But without the likes of Soldera and his friend and fellow staunch traditionalist Franco Biondi Santi, who died in 2013, to protect it, Brunello di Montalcino is at risk of becoming just another ill-defined DOCG in a country already rife with confusion. Never mind Burgundy being complex: with 350 permitted grape varieties in 20 diverse regions, Italian wine can seem impossibly hard to understand.

"Since I was very young, I've been influenced by my father and grandfather to keep the style of our wines the same," says Tancredi Biondi Santi, Franco's grandson. "What's become fashionable in Montalcino isn't the fancy, modern, full-bodied Brunello, but a style that goes back to the roots, to the traditional style." In many ways, the story of Brunello di Montalcino is the story of Biondi Santi. A short drive from Case Basse, its historic Greppo estate is also ideally positioned for growing Sangiovese Grosso. Dominated by Montalcino's famed galestro rock (among other soils such as limestone, quartz and sand), it is at a high-enough altitude to avoid spring frosts, yet also low enough to enable consistent grape ripening, with good diurnal temperature swings between night and day to develop complexity. It was here in the 1800s that Tancredi's great-great-great-great grandfather Clemente replanted the dominant sweet Moscadello di Montalcino of the day with Sangiovese Grosso, and in doing so invented what would go on to become Brunello di Montalcino.

Clemente first demonstrated Brunello's potential publicly at an agricultural fair in 1869, where he won silver medals for two reds. His triumph set in motion an evolution involving successive generations of his family for the next 150 years. Responsible for innovations such as excluding all grapes other than Sangiovese Grosso, de-stemming, and ageing in large Slavonian oak barrels – as well as establishing a well-stocked wine library to prove Brunello's longevity (an attribute of all the world's finest reds) – Biondi Santi is the only estate to have consistently made wines here since the turn of the 19th century.

Indeed, I have never visited a domaine that's so outwardly obsessed by its wine's ability to age, from proudly exhibiting its last remaining bottles of the 1888 and 1891 vintages to proclaiming that its Riservas all have the ability to last 100 years. Its beautiful 1997 Riserva – a wine Franco identified as among the best of his lifetime – seems likely to live up to that claim: its elegant perfume of dried roses and tobacco leaf leads into a fresh, intense and incredibly youthful palate, followed by a long, building finish. But having sold a majority stake in the estate to French company EPI (which also owns the Charles Heidsieck and Piper-Heidsieck Champagne houses) in 2016, it remains to be seen how Biondi Santi defines its wine over coming vintages. The estate has even introduced selected bacteria to control malolactic fermentations in recent years – not everyone's interpretation of 'tradition' is the same.

So what of the relative newcomers? Of the estates that have swelled the DOCG from around 15 in the 1950s to more than 203 today? Well, if many arrived in the 1980s and 1990s with consultant oenologists, *barriques* and little regard for tradition, there are others, such as Il Paradiso di Manfredi, that fly quietly under the radar and produce Brunello of sublime elegance and harmony. Established in the late 1950s by Manfredi Martini, who had earlier worked for Biondi Santi and was one of the original 25 members of the Brunello *consorzio*, it represents soulful, low-intervention winemaking at its best. "Our philosophy is simple: maximum respect for the soil, maximum respect for the environment, maximum respect for the wine," says Florio Guerrini, a retired maths teacher and Manfredi's son-in-law, who now owns and runs the estate with his wife and two daughters. Their 2012 Brunello is a particular highlight: as perfumed as a summer herb garden, it bristles with youthful energy and flavours of minerals, strawberries and balsamic vinegar. At Castello di Argiano, Elisa Sesti and her astronomer father Giuseppe are also making delicious wines following organic and biodynamic principles, in tune with the pull of the heavens.

But if there is one estate and winemaker that, stylistically at least, seems heir apparent to the exquisite Sangioveses of Gianfranco Soldera, it might be Stella di Campalto at Podere San Giuseppe in Castelnuovo dell'Abate. Shining bright, transparent red in the glass and highly aromatic (dried roses, exotic spices and pure red fruits are again the recurring theme), di Campalto's wines have more in common with those of Vosne-Romanée than super-concentrated and oaked modernist Brunello. "It's like two worlds in Montalcino," she says as Gregorian chants play on a loop in her barrel cellar. "One is like modern Bordeaux – opulent and structured – the other more like Pinot Noir: lighter. For me, Sangiovese is like a difficult Italian man: if you try to control him, he goes away. Instead, I try to listen a lot and not impose my ideas. I'm looking for balance in my wines." With a habit of talking about wines as if they were living people (her 2010 is "full of himself", while one low-lying vineyard is "like a school of nice, happy young children"), it was a series of coincidences, rather than a masterplan, that led di Campalto to produce Brunello di Montalcino.

Originally from Rome and then living in Milan, di Campalto married her former husband in 1992, and his family gifted them the 13.45ha Podere San Giuseppe, a property that had lain abandoned since the Second World War. Not knowing quite what to do with it, and at the time a teetotaller with no

Opposite: Gioia and Florio Guerrini, Il Paradiso di Manfredi, Montalcino.

Opposite: Stella di
Campalto, Montalcino.

Right: Podere San
Giuseppe.

interest in wine, she only moved to Montalcino with her then infant daughters after her "crazy aunt" persuaded her that she should seek an EU grant to plant vineyards there – which she achieved after coincidentally "bumping into the man responsible for funding while he was changing the wheel on his car". Renting a basic house with no heating or television, and only straw mattresses for beds, she planned to establish 4ha of new vineyards over three years with a view to renting them out. Then, just as she was about to sign them over to another producer, she had a change of heart – unsurprising, considering the uncommon natural beauty of the estate overlooking the Ombrone River – and began investigating how to ferment her first harvest instead.

"I bought the most celebrated 100-point *Wine Spectator* Brunello I could find, and drank it with friends alongside bottles from Poggio di Sotto and Soldera over lunch," says di Campalto. "Everyone was really excited about the 100-point wine, but after the meal, that bottle was still full, while the other wines were finished. So I went to see Poggio di Sotto and Soldera, and saw how much importance they put on working the vineyards. For me, the vineyards are everything." Crediting Piero Palmucci, the ex-owner of nearby Poggio di Sotto, as the mentor who helped her improve her winemaking, today di Campalto produces a Brunello that spends more than 45 months in oak barrels and a Rosso that is one of the great-value Italian wines (the only difference between it and its loftier sibling is that it spends around 22 months in barrel). While not yet quite as precise and mesmerising as Soldera, with his uncompromising ethos and techniques, these are the Montalcinos to seek out if you're after the sensual side of Sangiovese at a more attainable price. "Soldera's wines have something that is very difficult to achieve," acknowledges di Campalto. "They are simple and complex at the same time."

Paolo Bea

Montefalco, Umbria, Italy

DO YOU SHY AWAY from high-alcohol Napa Cabernet in the interest of self-preservation? Does the mere mention of Châteauneuf-du-Pape's ABV summon ghosts of hangover anxieties dormant within your bones? Do you pass on Port; avoid Amarone; and would you rather swim an ocean than swallow Aussie Shiraz? If the answer is 'yes' to any of the above, you may be suffering from 'rich-wine neurosis' – a phenomenon defined by Andrew Jefford in *Decanter* magazine, who cites historic terroirs such as Priorat and Maury as examples of how those embracing the zeitgeist for lower-alcohol styles are missing out.

I agree, at least in part. Just because a wine is high in alcohol doesn't mean it isn't harmonious or delicious (Brunello di Montalcino, Vin Jaune and Madeira spring to mind), and with the planet's temperatures rising, balance is one of the most important winemaking challenges of our times. The trouble, however, is that I like drinking wine – and lots of it – which rich styles do not permit. I love copious flavour and manifold aromas and sensations – not feeling as if I've been repeatedly hit over the head with a large rubber truncheon. Indeed, there are few wines I'd like to drink less over a four-course meal than a super-ripe, 15% ABV modern Bordeaux. Whose liver wouldn't thank them for picking its restrained 12–12.5% ABV 1980s predecessors instead? But, of course, there are some vinous heavyweights I'd be happy to go the distance with, then suck up the pain. If, as Jefford suggests, "Those suffering from 'rich-wine neurosis' should seek a cure", then Paolo Bea Sagrantino di Montefalco 'Pagliaro' is the big and beautiful wine I self-prescribe.

Dark and structured, yet graceful and fresh, 'Pagliaro' is the liquid embodiment of "float like a butterfly, sting like a bee". Made from 100% Sagrantino grown in the 400m-altitude 'Pagliaro' vineyard in Montefalco – a 12th-century town midway between Perugia and Spoleto in Umbria – it incorporates aromas of graphite, exotic spices, fruit and flowers with a prickle of balsamic vinegar and a refreshing bitter finish. At circa 15% ABV

Opposite: Giampiero Bea of Paolo Bea, Montefalco.

it is a serious wine that takes no prisoners, and, like old-school reds from Italian greats such as Soldera, Conterno and Quintarelli, demands long ageing in large oak barrels to develop complexity and round its edges; in this case Sagrantino's notoriously fierce tannins. Until 40 years ago, Sagrantino was made only as a sweet *passito* wine, using the *appassimento* technique whereby grapes are dried on rush mats before they're pressed. Today, it has been reinvented as a full-bodied, dry wine with DOCG status by a handful of producers, among them Giampiero Bea, the youthful 60-something visionary behind the Paolo Bea estate.

Bea's family roots go back hundreds of years in Montefalco – one of the few wine towns I've visited where your ears pop on the way in and out because of the high altitude – although grape growing is traditionally only one part of the local polyculture. His father Paolo's principal business has always been farming Chianina cows, the white Tuscan cattle breed used for *bistecca alla Fiorentina*. It was only when Giampiero left to study architecture at Rome University in 1980 that he began lobbying his dad to plant more vineyards and start bottling wine. "Slowly, slowly" – a phrase Giampiero repeatedly uses to convey the winery's gradual development – they refined their Sagrantino wines, alongside smaller plantings of Sangiovese, Montepulciano and Trebbiano Spoletino, although it soon became apparent that they had very different ideas.

"I wanted to produce a dry Sagrantino, but my father wanted to stick to making the traditional sweet style," Giampiero says. "The first time I tried making it, he didn't speak to me for three months!" Because of a lack of experience in producing the dry style, the first vintages oxidised after a few years in bottle, so in 1984 Giampiero started using long maceration to draw

Above: Early morning mists, Montefalco, Umbria.

out more tannin. Today, the wines spend between one and two months on the skins, followed by a year in steel tank, and a further three in large Slavonian oak barrels. "We argued a lot about winemaking at the time," he says, laughing. "Then my American importer introduced me to like-minded producers and I began to absorb ideas. I met Giuseppe Quintarelli in 1993, who was very helpful and became almost like a second father. Then Stanko Radikon, with whom I started ViniVeri, an association of Italian natural wine producers. And I got to know Joško Gravner, who was the first natural wine producer in Italy. It was amazing to be able to speak to such a pioneer."

"Nothing added and nothing taken away" is how Giampiero describes his simple winemaking philosophy – a simplicity that is, in fact, fiendishly difficult to get right. He adds only very minimal sulphur and never filters his wines, as proven by the delicious, jewel-like skins and pips often found at the bottom of his bottles. While other domaines in Montefalco use flavour-manipulating techniques and new oak *barriques*, Giampiero gently tames the small-berried, thick-skinned Sagrantino, resulting in authentic, characterful wines. "Conventional producers get rid of the skin and kill the universe of elements involved in wine. My idea is to use the natural process as a closed circle – this soil, these grapes, these yeasts, which are different in every vineyard." While the annual production of 'Pagliaro' rarely exceeds 20,000 bottles, Bea makes another rarer, even more powerful and monolithic Sagrantino from the 3ha 'Cerrete' vineyard located 50m above ("the Romanée-Conti of Montefalco"). I admire its stylish red-and-white label and ask myself: "Can my head take it?" Never mind 'rich-wine neurosis' – you've got to do what you've got to do.

Emidio Pepe & Valentini

Abruzzo, Italy

THIS IS A TALE of two eccentrics who elevated undistinguished grapes from Abruzzo, in the boondocks of central Italy, into some of the country's most characterful and age-worthy wines. The first, Emidio Pepe, escaped his family's stock-in-trade as poor wheat-field workers by creating an international market for Montepulciano and Trebbiano, speculatively flying to New York City with four bottles in a suitcase in 1967, and touring Italian restaurants around Europe to sell them from the boot of his Alfa Romeo every year. Now in his late 80s, his idiosyncratic winemaking techniques, and distaste for drinking other estate's wares, remain undiminished over 50 years later. The second, Edoardo Valentini, of aristocratic descent, died in 2006 at the age of 72, passing care of Abruzzo's oldest winery – Azienda Agricola Valentini – to his son, Francesco Paolo. An intellectual ex-lawyer influenced by pantheism and ancient philosophy, Edoardo restricted his commercial production to a fraction of its potential, refused nearly all requests for meetings from journalists and importers, and was rumoured to have sent his therapist to wine fairs in his place. 'Conventional' was not a word in either man's vocabulary.

A two-and-a-half-hour drive north-east of Rome on the *autostrada*, through tunnels under snow-capped mountains and past isolated towns, Abruzzo is a hilly agricultural region famed for its tomatoes, wheat and pasta. Travelling to such an ageless landscape makes a city dweller like me feel aeons away from modern life. Pre-Pepe and Valentini, its most important appellations – Trebbiano d'Abruzzo for whites, Montepulciano d'Abruzzo for reds, and Cerasuolo d'Abruzzo, as its own dark-coloured *rosato* made from Montepulciano is known – were only considered capable of producing rustic table wines, simple alcoholic lubricants for washing down the hearty local fare. Often confused with Vino Nobile di Montepulciano, a Chianti-style Sangiovese DOCG in Tuscany, Montepulciano is one of Italy's five most-planted red grapes, and needs time to tame its plentiful tannins and develop finesse. Although there were few other benchmarks when Pepe first set about his

Opposite: Emidio Pepe.

dream of making a fine Montepulciano with the capacity to age – something he regards as the highest respect that can be afforded to a wine – he had no doubt about the grape's potential.

"Before I started making wine in 1964 I used to buy grapes for other people, and Montepulciano was always more expensive than Sangiovese," says Pepe, his voice a low-pitched growl, as if someone has just pulled the choke out on a vintage car. "This gave me an idea of the quality of the grape, as well as its high acidity, which makes it ideal for long-term ageing." An impeccable dresser with a composed, laid-back presence, Pepe has always considered himself a farmer rather than a *vigneron*, with many regular visitors to his Torano Nuovo estate remarking on how often they would find him observing the vineyards rather than in the winery – unsurprising, considering the Abruzzese tradition of *mezzadria* sharecropping, which involved raising animals as well as growing fruit, olives, grains and grapes. Starting with 1ha of vines, today the estate is a healthy 15ha, which Pepe has kept staunchly native and organic, even when the fashion was for Italian wineries to replant with 'international' grapes such as Cabernet Sauvignon, and use labour-saving fertilisers and pesticides. If the joy of travel is about experiencing unique cultures and traditions, I love how Pepe's old-fashioned, low-intervention wines have gone full circle, and are now back in vogue. Even if some of his unusual methods will never be on trend.

I had to check my notes several times to make sure I'd fully understood some of these, because they're so unorthodox. Having learnt from his grandfather, Pepe is perhaps the vinous equivalent of the classic nonna who rubbishes every other nonna's *pomodoro* sauce recipe as inauthentic heresy, utterly convinced that their own method is the one and only true path. For a start, he doesn't use machines in the winery, so grapes are de-stalked by being pushed through a basket, crushed by foot in a wooden trough, then fermented with indigenous yeast in glass-lined concrete tanks (he says old barrels accelerate ageing too much). The wine stays in tank for up to two-and-a-half years before it is bottled without filtration and stacked in a large concrete bunker-cum-cellar that recalls a Champagne house's vault. Then – and this is a very unusual process for still wines – bottles are taken to order to a small side room to be uncorked and decanted into a new bottle by Pepe's wife Rosa, with all spillages drunk by the estate rather than rebottled. Moët et Chandon's high-tech production line this most definitely is not.

"Wine is like a young child, but instead of crying it sends other signals," says Pepe of his methods. "It's the wine that decides what it needs to get rid of – by natural decantation." Every part of the process is done by hand, with different batches of a vintage subject to variations depending on when they will be decanted and released, as well as on their unique natural idiosyncrasies. In the mid-1970s a German merchant unsuccessfully tried to sue Pepe over a parcel of Trebbiano, which undergoes malolactic fermentation in bottle, because it was cloudy. Pepe won the case after a four-hour hearing in Hamburg,

Above: Chiara and Emidio Pepe among 80,000 bottles of Trebbiano and Montepulciano, Torano Nuovo, Abruzzo.

Overleaf: Abruzzo, Italy, with the Gran Sasso mountain range in the background.

during which time a bottle of the wine poured into a decanter as evidence was seen to completely clear up. Like those of Valentini – whose Trebbiano Pepe concedes as finer than his own, but whose Montepulciano he believes his version bests – these wines can sometimes awaken from slumber a little jagged and out of kilter, before righting themselves and evolving finesse and complexity in the glass. But if Pepe prefers a 'reductive' style of anaerobic winemaking, where wine is always protected from oxygen exposure in glass-lined concrete tanks, Valentini's use of large old Slovenian oak *botti* brings something different again.

Perhaps Pepe is right about his marvellous Montepulciano, but Valentini Trebbiano d'Abruzzo is my favourite Italian white wine. Okay, Italy is not, unlike France, famed for its whites per se, but there's something about this one that recalls the elegance and poise of top white Burgundy, though with a slightly different density and textural richness. A recently opened 1990 was fresh and complete almost 30 years after vintage – something few might think possible of the often insipid Trebbiano – while a long and creamy 2012 had the lip-smacking saline minerality and smoky bacon aromas so typical of these wines. Such smokiness comes from the Abruzzo's clay-dominated soils, with the grape's good levels of acidity keeping tension in the hot and often dry climate. By contrast, Pepe's Trebbiano often has a prickle of CO_2 and more of a sense of maceration with some tannins, providing good texture and a bitter, mouthwatering finish. Neither polished nor coarse, these wines are rustic yet very stylish – much like the *vigneron* himself.

While first-hand information about Valentini is hard to come by – this is perhaps the hardest winery in the world to visit – Edoardo Valentini was said to have much preferred his delicate, Pinot-like Cerasuolo *rosato* to his Montepulciano. Given how delicious the latter can be, however, one can but wonder what would have been possible if he had liked it more. I have adored several vintages of Valentini's unique Montepulciano, such as the layered and Port-like 2000, with its Pauillac-esque cigar-box aromas and hit of balsamic vinegar, and the elegant 1985. But Francesco Paolo only produces it sporadically in years when he considers conditions right – perhaps when moderate grape sugar levels permit vinifying a dry wine. He keeps only around 5% of his crop from 65ha of vines, selling the rest to the local co-op Rosciano for *sfuso* 'bulk' wine to be offered to a handful of local restaurants for a few euros a litre. With its love of nature and traditional Abruzzese polyculture, Valentini seems just as happy promoting its olive oil as keeping wine lovers happy.

I wrote a letter to Francesco Paolo Valentini, followed by several telephone messages, to request a visit to his winery in Loreto Aprutino, but having received no answer can only presume that he's upholding his father's long tradition of reclusiveness. However, it is possible to read of the respect he and Edoardo Valentini held for Pepe in the foreword he wrote for his book, *Manteniamoci giovani: vita e vino di Emidio Pepe*, especially considering their different winemaking ideas. "The last time I saw him [Pepe] was in Rome, at a tasting of old Trebbiano," wrote Francesco Paolo. "He had his British cap on, a refined shirt, a distinguished bearing and a serene expression, as if time hadn't marked him. I not only consider him a farmer and an artisan, but a guardian of terroir. Emidio Pepe can wear a jacket and tie or wear work boots, nothing will change, he is authentic." It is this authenticity that makes both estates' wines so lauded today.

Back in Torano Nuovo, Pepe is now in a state of semi-retirement with daughter Sofia overseeing winemaking with granddaughter Chiara. "I'm hoping that grandfather's longevity runs in my genes, although he's still so present with everything it's hard for us to find a role to do," says Chiara. Having recently enrolled at the Beaune winemaking school, she admits to feeling pressure to measure up to such a tenacious patriarch ("Am I good enough? Am I learning enough?"), but the domaine seems in rude health to further its, and Abruzzo's, ascendancy in the minds of foreign wine lovers. With its diverse microclimates and cheap vineyards there is great potential here for a new generation of young *vignerons* to set up their own wineries. However, without Pepe's forward-thinking idea of holding back old vintages to demonstrate Montepulciano and Trebbiano's age-worthiness, or Valentini's uncompromising ethos, this timeless Italian region might still be obscured by the more famous names of Piedmont and Tuscany.

Opposite, left: Valentini Trebbiano d'Abruzzo.

Opposite, right: Emidio Pepe Montepulciano d'Abruzzo.

Frank Cornelissen

Mount Etna, Sicily

HIGH ON THE BLACK SOILS of Mount Etna, among the legions of gnarled, defiant old Nerello Mascalese vines, grows a noxious plant that can be mistaken for fennel. "My horse died from eating that stuff last year," says Frank Cornelissen, bounding between the crooked terraces of his 'Barbabecchi' vineyard. A charismatic former wine broker from Antwerp, Cornelissen is one of a handful of outsiders who have energised a new wave of quality winemaking on the slopes of east Sicily's active volcano since the turn of the millennium. "The local vet wanted to know what had killed the horse, so he cut its stomach open and found that eating the plant – ferula – had caused internal bleeding," he continues. "It's a bit *rustic* up here sometimes," he deadpans, and a grin spreads across his face.

'Rustic' is probably how any estate agent worth their percentage would describe the horseshoe-shaped DOC wine-growing area around the slopes of Mount Etna. With its approach to road planning seemingly owing more to chance than design, and scores of buildings half-built or half falling down, what Etna lacks in northern Italy's verdant sophistication it makes up for in charm. After a few minutes climbing the steep, 910m-high 'Barbabecchi' (where Cornelissen produces 'Magma', his top cuvée), we pause next to an old stone *palmento* and watch workers from one of Sicily's largest commercial producers, Planeta, levelling an adjacent vineyard. "That's not a good evolution for Etna – how can land treated like that represent terroir?" says Frank, a dreamer whose first ambition on Etna was to produce wines that tasted like "liquid rock".

This sense of 'somewhereness' lies at the heart of what he's striving to achieve. "My ultimate goal is to demonstrate the different territories of Etna," Frank says later, pouring out the entry-level 2014 'Contadino' (now known as 'Susucaru') back at his Solicchiata winery. He picks up a cane that, combined with his white hair, lends him the air of a prophet, and begins pointing out the 22ha of different vineyards he owns on a map. From 'Chiusa Spagnolo' ("one of the Grand Crus") to 'Malpasso' ("sometimes top-heavy"), and back once more to

Opposite: Frank Cornelissen, Mount Etna.

Overleaf: Close to the summit of 'Barbabecchi' vineyard, Mount Etna.

his favoured 'Barbabecchi' ("the wines have a beautiful elegance"), we take a trip Below: Frank Cornelissen.
through the volcano's limitless nuance of altitudes and subsoils, where old lava
flows need between 300 and 400 years of decomposition to become suitable
for viticulture. If understanding the Côte d'Or's long-established vineyard
classification system is complicated, defining Etna's microclimates is an even
more daunting task. And besides: growing vines *on cooled lava flows?*

We sink our noses into the 2014 'Contadino', the most rated vintage
for Sicilian wine in a decade, and alongside the stony minerality that is a
Cornelissen trademark, are taken aback by a waft of ripe black cherries. If we've
long been an admirer of these unique wines – intrigued by what looked like tiny
lumps of lava floating in the luminous early cuvées – more recent years have
upgraded the deliciousness, with synthetic bottle closures and gross filtration
improving consistency. "Today, I think a little fruit is pleasurable," he says,
laughing. "Until 2011 my wines were a representation of Frank Cornelissen,
but since 2011 they're much more a representation of Etna."

Right: Amphorae in the
Cornelissen winery.

Cornelissen's passion for wine started at 14 years old, drinking benchmark classics from Domaine de la Romanée-Conti and Haut-Brion with his father, before becoming disillusioned by the mid-'90s trend for super-concentration. "I was disappointed and angry with what was going on in the wine world, when some Barolo became oak soup, and Australian wine tasted like fermented marmalade," he says. "The fatter and the thicker the wines, the better people thought they were." So, after considering buying vineyards in southern Portugal ("another interesting wine-growing area because of its microclimates, and the transparency and intensity of light"), he left behind a life broking wines in Belgium and set about defining his own style using low-intervention techniques. "I don't have shit to do with the natural wine movement," says Frank, citing a general lack of respect towards classical wine culture in the natural wine bars of the early noughties as a turn-off. "But I like things in a natural way, and don't want to feel guilty when I drink something. I like things clean, healthy and tasty."

His early vintages on Etna were made around the time when he met fellow new wave pioneers Andrea Franchetti of Passopisciaro, and Marco de Grazia of Tenuta delle Terre Nere. All three men have reputations for being larger-than-life personalities. Franchetti is a former restaurateur, wine importer and producer based between Etna and his Tenuta di Trinoro estate in Tuscany, while de Grazia, also a successful American wine exporter, now lives full time on the volcano. "I started out with a bit of a strange idea, but everything made logical sense," says Frank. "But I had to start somewhere. If you take Franchetti's first few vintages, they taste like oak soup, and after that he improved. The same with Marco de Grazia. My errors were in over-oxidising wines because I didn't want any fruit, I wanted liquid rock, because that was my idea of wine. But that has gradually evolved, and as you go on you start understanding the different terroirs better."

All three men have been central to developing the region to a point where its top wines can now stand comparison to Old World classics in terms of their quality and authenticity. Although wine has been made on Sicily for thousands of years (it's Italy's largest grape producer, responsible for lakes of low-quality whites and reds), Etna's high-altitude, un-grafted vines, long-growing cycle, and sandy, phylloxera-resistant soils set it apart. "There was no scene when I set up here in 2000," says Frank. "When I first met Andrea in 2003 I thought he was some kind of Bordeaux cocktail maker [Franchetti controversially uses Petit Verdot in his top wine], and he thought I made fucked-up, no sulphur natural wines. But it was great – he's a fantastic person. I also met Marco de Grazia, who was responsible for modernising a lot of the modern Barolo scene, which I profoundly fucking hated. But we all had a ball together at the beginning." Since then "the meals at Marco's place have got a bit more normal" and the revelry has mellowed. But the fact that people with such different philosophies get along so well is perhaps testament to a shared pioneering spirit.

Opposite: Cooled lava flow from 1981 near the Franchetti winery.

While well-respected wineries such as Benanti and Calabretta have been in production on Etna for decades, these outsiders, alongside a new generation of well-travelled locals such as Alberto Graci, Giuseppe Russo and Tenuta di Fessina's Silvia Maestrelli, are setting new standards for what can be achieved. Two other Etna estates that particularly impress are Vino di Anna, owned and run by Anna Martens and Eric Narioo of UK importers Les Caves de Pyrene, and the locally owned Pietradolce, whose vineyards in Contrada Rampante are idyllic. Most impressive is its 'Barbagalli' site, a horseshoe-shaped amphitheatre that produces fruit for a velvet-textured, multi-layered wine with a sensuality akin to red Burgundy. Côte d'Or-lovers should seek out Pietradolce's evocatively perfumed, mineral Etna Rossos rather than many of the fruit-driven New World Pinots sometimes recommended as alternatives.

Close to the summit of 'Barbabecchi', above the crooked terraces, we follow Cornelissen into a cleared section of vineyard that he has earmarked to replant with Riesling vines. "People think that it's all about vineyard height on Etna, but that's bullshit, it's about subsoil," he says, scooping up a handful of black volcanic earth and letting it seep through his fingers. Around here locals have to buy special car insurance, and clean their vehicles' air filters on a daily basis, removing detritus from clouds of rock and dust spewed periodically from the volcano. So is it a passion for German wine that is responsible for him choosing Riesling over Etna's widely planted indigenous white, Carricante? "No way! I hate boring German Riesling!" he snaps, adding that anyone questioning planting non-indigenous varieties can "Fuck off, it's my choice". Then the next minute he's extolling the virtues of the "stunning" German Riesling of Peter Jakob Kühn and Koehler-Ruprecht, before launching into a diatribe about people, grapes and, you guessed it, terroir. A farmer with the temperament of an artist, Cornelissen is one of wine's most contrary stars.

Right: Daily news,
Castiglione di Sicilia.

Below: Lock up your
daughters. And sons,
wives, cats, dogs, etc.

Germany

SWEETNESS is a word that strikes fear into wine lovers' hearts. Not only that, but unless you've been stuck at the restaurant at the end of the universe for the past few years, it can't have escaped your attention that sugar generally has become public enemy number one. Coca-Cola, Kellogg's Corn Flakes, even Mr Kipling's Cherry Bakewells are under the spotlight, and with good reason. For the first time in history, the world has more overweight than underweight people and, according to many, sugar consumption is to blame. So, where does that leave German Riesling – which many presume always to be sweet – on a health-conscious fat planet?

I feel sorry for winemakers in Germany's Mosel Valley, truly I do. Their lives are not easy: long hours spent tending vines on treacherous slate hillsides; relatively low prices that barely cover high production costs; and precise, yet complicated, label definitions that baffle all but the savviest customers. *Kabinett, Spätlese, Auslese, Trockenbeerenauslese:* we all have limited attention spans, and angular foreign words describing ripeness levels don't make them longer. Today, most people's idea of Mosel Riesling is as saccharine as Roseanne Barr gone AWOL in the pick 'n' mix aisle, yet in its early heyday between 1860 and 1890 it was predominantly a dry wine, to be drunk young. From Munich to Manhattan, Mosel's *hochgewächs* ('exalted growth') wines even supplanted Bordeaux, Burgundy and sweeter Rhine wines, which need long maturation in bottle, at the top of luxury restaurants' wine lists.

Fast-forward 50 years to just after the Second World War, and sweet wines began to grow in popularity. After years of food rationing, the luscious *Spätlesen* and *Auslesen* that estates such as Joh Jos Prüm had been mastering for decades tasted heavenly to sugar-deprived drinkers. Developing strong export markets in Britain and the US, this sweet wave of Riesling was phenomenally successful and inspired masses of low-quality imitations. Sugary abominations marketed as Liebfraumilch, many of which contained no Riesling, flooded the market during the 1980s, cheapening the grape's image.

Opposite: Egon Müller's gnome, Scharzhof manor house, Saar.

Coinciding with the lighter cooking trend *nouvelle cuisine*, as well as 1985's Austrian wine scandal, which saw producers prosecuted for sweetening wines with toxic diethylene glycol, Mosel Riesling's reputation went into decline. But just as every action has a reaction, so in the 1980s another wave of winemakers harking back to mid-19th-century styles emerged, and the cycle was complete. So, what is the authentic face of Mosel Riesling today: dry or sweet? Well, it all depends on your perspective...

There are few domaines in Germany as celebrated, or in their own way as traditional, as Wiltingen's Egon Müller-Scharzhof. Located near the Saar – a cool tributary of the Mosel where vines mostly grow away from the warming influence of the river – the Scharzhof manor house sits resplendent among acres of rolling woodland at the foot of the imposing Scharzhofberg. Now in the hands of Egon Müller IV, the latest in a long bloodline to bear the same name, the estate produces a *Trockenbeerenauslese* (the rarest and highest grape-ripeness level under German *Prädikat* wine law, typically with *Botrytis cinerea*) that is both the zenith of sweet Riesling and the world's most expensive white. Recently sold for £13,802 inc VAT per bottle on UK release, it's no use describing 2017 Egon Müller 'Scharzhofberger' Trockenbeerenauslese on the 100-point system beloved of many critics. Here only the *Spinal Tap* scale will do. With sugar and ripeness levels cranked up to 11 balanced against super-fine acidity also at 11, like Nigel Tufnell's modified Marshall amps, this wine has an extra notch. But while extraordinarily concentrated and intense, it is also sensuous and controlled: an extreme exemplar of the sugar/acid equilibrium that makes sweet Mosel Riesling unique.

Left: Egon Müller 'Scharzhofberger', Heymann-Löwenstein 'Rottgën'.

That Egon Müller only produces off-dry to sweet styles is influenced by Scharzhofberg's marginal climate. Here in Europe's coolest vineyards, grapes have struggled to fully ripen as recently as the 1980s. Historically this has stopped them from developing enough sugar to ferment to a fully dry wine circa 12% ABV, but was perfect for preserving the tartaric acidity needed to balance residual sugar. Like 'sweetness', 'acidity' is a word that many find unattractive (no one particularly appreciates 'acid attacks' or 'acid indigestion' either), yet it's essential for clarity and tension in wine. Indeed, it's the idiosyncratic harmony of high acidity and sugar with low alcohol – between 7% and 8% ABV for *Kabinett*, *Spätlese* and *Auslese*, and around 5.5% ABV for *Trockenbeerenauslese* – that sets sweet Mosel Riesling apart from other regions, enabling it to evolve for decades. Bottling his wines less than six months after harvest (compared to around 18 months for many fine white Burgundies), Müller prefers to bring "full concentration into the bottle as fast as possible", even at the expense of youthful charm. These wines require years for terroir characteristics to emerge, and that he opts for such short *élevage* is fascinating considering how many customers don't have the means to cellar wines today. If 19th-century Mosel was dry and consumed young, these are anything but.

"We focus entirely on off-dry to sweet styles because no other region in the world can make wines like these," says Katharina Prüm, scion of the Joh Jos Prüm estate in Bernkastel-Wehlen, 60km north-east of Egon Müller. Like the delicate high-acidity wines of the Saar and nearby Ruwer Valleys, those of this iconic estate on the Middle Mosel aim for elegance rather than power. But how, in a world dominated by white wines routinely fermented to dryness, is sweet Mosel made? By harvesting late for the ripest possible grapes, when temperatures drop during the cold German winter many yeasts stop fermenting naturally, while others are manually arrested by chilling in temperature-controlled steel tanks.

"It is like a puzzle every year, and impossible to predict which ferments will stop," Prüm says. "Sometimes we have two tanks of what we think will be a *Spätlese*, and one ferments fast and then stops, so it might be medium-dry, and then the other stops early and we blend the two. The first part of the puzzle is the harvest period and fermentation, and the second is in the spring after harvest when we blend the wines." Of all *Prädikat* designations, *Trockenbeerenauslese* is by far the hardest to produce. As well as inconsistent botrytis infection and high-labour costs due to the amount of times labourers have to pass through the vineyards in order to pick suitable fruit, the fermentations are affected by massive sugar levels that mean yeasts often struggle to reach the 5.5% ABV required by law. Both Prüm and Müller are among the top tier Mosel estates producing sweet and off-dry Rieslings of ethereal lightness. On their day, such wines are incomparably delicious: a 2002 *Spätlese* served with a strawberry mille-feuille at Le Manoir aux Quat'Saisons in midsummer is one of the best wine and food combinations I have ever tasted – as vivid and perfumed as a walk through the restaurant's bucolic gardens. "Other parts of the region, like the Terrassenmosel, are more about power," says Prüm. "Producers there have more alcohol and less acidity, so they couldn't produce our style and we couldn't produce theirs."

We're hundreds of metres up the Uhlen terraces in the Terrassenmosel (a.k.a. the Lower Mosel), where Reinhard Löwenstein and wife Cornelia Heymann helped revolutionise winemaking in the 1980s. "The first time my family made sweet wine was 1961 – before that we'd made dry wines for 500 years," says Löwenstein, looking down at the river below. "When we started Heymann-Löwenstein it was clear nobody was waiting for a new producer making *Kabinett* and *Spätlese*, so we decided not to make them. It wasn't about whether they were good or bad, but the Germans and French never drank them, and many customers didn't cellar wines like before. I'm a big fan of Egon Müller, but I'm drinking his 2001s at the moment now the sweetness has gone. People used to say that the best dry wine is a 20- or 30-year-old *Auslese*."

With no local estates making accomplished dry Riesling at the time, Löwenstein took inspiration from Emmerich Knoll and Franz Hirtzberger in Austria, improving quality by focusing on old vines, picking late, limiting yields and introducing some shorter macerations. Soon, critics began saying Heymann-Löwenstein had created a new style of Mosel Riesling. With a signature salinity, gleaned from blue and red quartzite slate vineyards, these are powerful, aromatically complex wines whose rock, flower, smoke and stone fruit aromas slowly unfurl in the glass. Some question dry winemaking in the Terrassenmosel – that its relatively full body and alcohol levels can just as easily be found in Alsace or Austria – but why quibble when there's so much pleasure to be had? All three Uhlen single vineyards are a masterful combination of ripeness and tension, as well as the earlier approachable 'Rottgën', which smells of wet slate and tropical fruit, and grips the palate like Velcro. However, when you witness the monorails built to shuttle grapes down the vertiginous terraces, and crumbling stone walls needing constant repair, the economics that have forced many wineries here to shut become obvious. "People are always discussing how they can cut production costs, but I'm the only one saying we have to increase them to make a wine that's so amazing that people will pay what we need," says Löwenstein. "If you make something in the middle – a cheap wine – you're dead before you've started."

Swimming against the tide of local closures, Weingut Keller – the Rheinhessen estate that has risen to international superstar status over the past decade – made a foray into the Mosel in 2018, buying the 0.8ha 'Schubertslay' vineyard in Piesport. "It's like coming home for us," says Klaus Peter Keller, whose mother is from the region. Having studied at Geisenheim wine school before beginning work at his parents' winery in 2001, Keller talks with excitement about his métier: you don't have to be a wine lover to be

Opposite: Uhlen terraces, Terrassenmosel, Germany.

a winemaker, but it is so obviously integral to his success. "Wine isn't just our job, it's our biggest hobby," says Keller, pouring glasses of 2017 'Kirchspiel' Grosse Gewächs. Since writing about 2007 'Kirchspiel' GG (his debut solo vintage) in the first issue of *Noble Rot*, I've held deep affection for this powerful-yet-precise wine: a bolt of pure energy among the top tier of dry modern German wine.

Taking control of his family winery in 2006, Keller and his wife Julia have reduced residual sugar levels across their range of sublime *Grosse Gewächs* (a prestigious VDP vineyard categorisation for dry, relatively full-bodied Riesling) from around 6g to under 2g over the past decade, informed by their love for low-dosage Champagne and racier modern styles of white Burgundy. That they have held tastings of their top cuvée, 'G-Max', alongside Coche-Dury Corton-Charlemagne with Jean-François and Raphaël Coche shows the esteem in which their wines are held. "I try to make Rieslings that are really, really dry," says Keller. "When I compare a Riesling with 6g to 8g to top white Burgundy, which normally doesn't have any residual sugar at all, they're too sweet for my palate. For me a drier style has more precision and energy for ageing over the long term." Whether or not Keller will apply this philosophy to his 'Schubertslay' holdings remains to be seen (he also professes an appreciaton of *Kabinett*), but for another star German estate whose Rieslings are equally celebrated across all styles, we travel east from the Middle Mosel to the Nahe.

"We're good at making both dry and off-dry Riesling," says Cornelius Dönnhoff in Oberhausen an der Nahe, a town in the middle of the region sometimes known as 'the tasting room of Germany' on account of its diverse soils and styles. "We have cool nights, similar to the Mosel, which, combined with slopes, gives us the high acidity needed to balance sweetness; and, on the other hand, we have very warm days, similar to the Rheingau, which we need to achieve the ripeness to make dry wines." Fermenting 20 cuvées across various sugar levels, although around 60% of their production is dry, Dönnhoff is an example of a German estate able to make all styles at the top level. "We see the demand for dry wines becoming greater every year, but that doesn't mean we don't want to make the off-dry styles," continues Dönnhoff. "We don't produce wines to fit the market; we produce wines that fit specific vineyards best. We have some where the grapes have lots of acidity, so it's better to produce off-dry wines, and others where the fruit gets too ripe, so it's much better to produce dry wines. We make a reflection of the landscape."

Expressing the slate and volcanic soils that dominate this part of the Nahe, Dönnhoff's range provides a long and enjoyable tasting experience. While the off-dry Rieslings don't quite match the ethereal raciness of those from the Saar, Ruwer and Middle Mosel, the region's greatest asset is being good across the board, particularly the powerful *Grosse Gewächs* and *trocken* wines. "I make wines a little bit drier than my father did, but that's my personal taste. In all the great wine estates around the world, the winemakers aren't making the wine for

Opposite: Klaus Peter Keller, Rheinhessen.

other people, they're making the wines they enjoy drinking." Just like opinions on whether dry or off-dry is the most authentic Mosel style, a preference for either is subjective. I'm drawn to drier wines for their versatility with different foods and occasions, but no matter how much the sweet styles fall out of fashion nowhere else on the planet can produce such scintillating lightness.

Northern Greece

AS SON OF ZEUS and god of wine, Dionysus arrived on Mount Olympus to take his place in the pantheon and turn the fruit grown on Greece's highest peak into the mythical 'nectar'. Today it may be mortals who tend the grapes, but the vineyards retain a mystical atmosphere, bathed in sunshine during the summer and shrouded in cloud throughout winter. Reminiscent of those on Mount Etna in Sicily, their gnarled old bush vines sit in amphitheatric crevices carved into mountainsides, or sprawl over hillocks like oversized tarantulas. The appellation of Rapsani in the southern foothills of Olympus is visually beautiful and as yet unsung. How appropriate, then, that it has proven an ideal place for Greece's finest red grape, Xinomavro, a variety just as anonymous on the international stage.

Xinomavro is as difficult to grow as it is to pronounce (stress the second syllable: ksi-NO-mav-ro), and has fierce tannins and cherry fruit similar to Italy's Nebbiolo. But to think of it just as a Barolo-alike would be to do it a disservice. Notes of dried herbs, tomato and olive unfurl with age, which contemporary *vignerons* balance by emphasising the primary fruit characters and taming its jagged tannins. Great Xinomavros are complex, evocative wines with a distinctive Greek accent. The grape is a widely planted native of Macedonia in northern Greece, although in anything other than ideal conditions it is capricious – another similarity to Nebbiolo. Poor, calcareous soils, meticulous farming and low yields are prerequisites for growing Xinomavro to full ripeness, and not many winemakers manage it.

There are four official appellations, referred to as PDOs, that focus on Xinomavro in Greece: Naoussa, the best known and most interesting; Amyndeon, a cool climate area made famous by Alpha Estate, but showing promise for sparkling wines at Domaine Karanika; Goumenissa, a warmer region where producers such as Tatsis, Chloi Chatzivaryti and Ligas, a few miles beyond the appellation border in Pella, are attracting attention for their natural wines. And then there's Rapsani. The 20th century was devastating for

Opposite: Kostis Dalamaras, Domaine Dalamára, Naoussa.

this rural community, who had to contend with phylloxera and a series of wars. During the 1960s a co-operative winery was founded, and in 1971 Rapsani became one of the first Greek appellations to be granted PDO status. Although its future seemed bright, by the late 1980s the co-op had been repossessed by the bank and the local wine industry faced oblivion. Then, Tsantali – a large commercial winery with interests across northern Greece – stepped in, taking over the winery and buying the production of Rapsani's growers. Since then the region has been rejuvenated.

"Xinomavro performs very well here, but it takes time to reveal its complexity," says Thanos Dougos, one of the handful of local growers farming own-rooted old vines on precarious slopes of up to 800m elevation. But he is less than enthusiastic about the stipulation that PDO wines must be a blend of Xinomavro with two other local grapes. "We managed to change the rule that forced wineries to blend equal amounts of the three grapes, so now we can focus more on Xinomavro," Dougos says. The obvious potential of Rapsani has attracted the attention of wineries in Naoussa, two hours' drive to the north, in a similar way to how Burgundian domaines have launched projects in Beaujolais and the Jura. One of the most gifted outsiders to arrive is Apostolos Thymiopoulos, who could be the catalyst for a new era of quality, small-production wine on Mount Olympus. His foray into Rapsani won't be the first time that he has broken new ground. When in 2003 he released 'Earth & Sky' Naoussa (labelled 'Uranos' in the US) it redefined Xinomavro, its plush berry fruit and silken texture a stylistic counterpoint to the dried-out, tannic monsters that were the norm. Over the years, Apostolos has continued to hone his craft by farming biodynamically, moving to larger-format barrels that leave less of an oak imprint, and pursuing a more elegant style.

"Apostolos showed that there was another side to Naoussa," says Markos Markovitis, another winemaker with a contemporary approach. "My father used to say that when they were first bottled the wines were undrinkable," says Markos, laughing, as he opens a vertical of wines, spanning from the 'Château Pegasus' era of his father and grandfather through to post-2011 bottles produced after he took over and started using the family name on the label. The '84, '86, '97 and '99 have all aged superbly, but more recent vintages highlight an evolution in style. "I'm curious to see how the younger wines will develop," he says. "Today, yields are half what they used to be and the wines have much more balance and density." This pursuit of balance is an objective shared by nearby Domaine Dalamára, where a generational shift has also taken place. Kostis Dalamaras cut his teeth in France at domaines Trapet, Giboulot and Clos du Rouge Gorge before converting his own estate to organic farming and spontaneous fermentations, as well as significantly reducing the use of sulphur dioxide, when he returned to Greece. Kostis' flagship is the single-vineyard 'Paliokalias', from sandy-clay soils over limestone bedrock, one of Greece's most elegant and delicious reds. A tiny parcel of 100-year-old own-rooted vines in the heart of the slope is used to make my favourite Naoussa, the impossibly rare Dalamára 'Vieilles Vignes' (2015 production was 328 bottles!)

Naoussa has come a long way since 2010, when sales of the region's wines declined so much that large commercial producers lobbied to have international varieties such as Merlot, Syrah and Barbera admitted into the PDO. Happily, that never happened, and the appellation kept its authenticity intact. Since then, moves have been made to officially delineate the various crus that make up the PDO zone, and Naoussa is now established as the benchmark for quality Xinomavro.

But if Naoussa is the frontrunner for Xinomavro production today, then what of Siatista, a place renowned during the 1800s for producing some of Greece's finest wines? This isolated region has spectacular mountainous terroir and geriatric vineyards, but its wines are now almost unknown. Dimitrios Diamantis is one *vigneron* focusing on protecting Siatista's heritage, by making wines that showcase its potential. "First we had to save the vines, but now we need to take the winemaking forward, by focusing only on quality," says Dimitrios in 'Magoutes', a mountain pass full of old vineyards on Mount Siniatsiko. Clambering down beautiful hillsides, past centenarian bush vines protruding from rocky limestone soils, it's easy to understand why Dimitrios wants to emulate his grandfather, who was one of Siatista's top growers. "The Xinomavro is different on this side of Macedonia – it ripens earlier and gives softer, more elegant tannins," he says. "We have the opportunity to do something really special, but we need more people to come here and understand what we have." The similarities between Siatista and Rapsani are striking.

Back on Mount Olympus, Apostolos Thymiopoulos is revelling in the opportunities presented by being first in. "The stony terroir in the higher elevation zones of Rapsani is ideal for Xinomavro, and the weather is very dry, so we get lovely aromatics, fantastic structure and purity of fruit," he says, at the bar of the local taverna. "The grapes are more tannic and yields are about a third lower in Rapsani compared with Naoussa, so I think the wine will need longer to mature. It's going to be exciting to see what happens." But how does it compare to his home turf? Could Rapsani have even greater potential than Naoussa? "I'm here to find out, and that's why so many other winemakers are looking for vineyards," he says, with a smile.

Santorini

Greece

"THIS WAS A BEAUTIFUL 100-year-old vineyard, but the municipality gave permission for it to be turned into a bike track for tourists," says winemaker Haridimos Hatzidakis. Minutes before we'd stood breathing the salty sea air in his 'Mylos' vineyard, discussing the unique Santorinian terroir and vines so ancient that no one knows how old they are. Now, here we were, faced with proof that this heritage is under threat from relentless development. Had we not spent the rest of the afternoon tasting his brilliant wines, it would have been harder to forget that track; the sight of every new luxury hotel and supermarket a reminder of how Santorini's vineyards have shrunk by over 75% in the past 100 years. Tragically, Haridimos died a few weeks after our meeting, leaving his daughter Stella to continue his legacy. But spending even a short time with this great man was an insight into a culture that desperately needs protecting.

Thankfully, the world is waking up to the vinous treasures that this crumb of volcanic rock is capable of producing. The combination of high-quality indigenous grape varieties, unique terroir, and numerous small, quality-focused domaines has alerted wine lovers to the rewards that can be found off the beaten track. But while two million tourists a year make Santorini one of the most-visited places in the Mediterranean, there is some way to go when it comes to a better understanding of its wines. Assyrtiko is 75% of plantings here and has begun to get the international recognition it deserves, even if it will prove difficult for other regions to match the acidity, ripeness and energy it achieves here. In old vineyards co-planting alongside other white varieties, such as the aromatic Aidani or fruity Athiri, is commonplace, as it is with red grapes such as the structured, high-acid Mandilaria and juicy Mavrotragano. Santorini is home to several unique varieties that can't be found elsewhere, although Assyrtiko is by far the best known.

Then there's the island's history – few places on earth rival 3500 years of winemaking. There have been plenty of catastophes along the way: invaders,

Opposite: Oía, Santorini.

earthquakes and masses of volcanic activity, which includes one of the largest recorded eruptions in history. An explosion around 1500 BC caused a tsunami so big that it wiped out the Minoan civilisation on Crete, and is believed to be behind the legend of Atlantis. Yet while it was apocalyptic for the islanders, it gave Santorini its completely unique terroir. "The main thing that helps to distinguish Santorini's wine is the earth," says winemaker Paris Sigalas, referring to the mix of pumice stone, volcanic ash, sand and rock called *aspa*. The soil is so hostile to organic matter that little beyond tomatoes, fava beans and vines can grow, and phylloxera – the aphid scourge of vineyards across the world – never stood a chance. This makes Santorini one of few regions where all plants are own-rooted, and centenarian vines almost come as standard (there are stories that some here are 500 years old).

Another peculiarity about Santorini is that it is technically a desert, and the only water available to vines comes from humidity and moisture in the morning mist. But it's not just thirst they have to contend with – the fierce Meltemi wind whips throughout the Aegean in the summer, and can render common vine-training methods obsolete. For millennia, the locals have combated the elements by using a system of basket vines called *kouloura* to shield grapes from the wind and trap as much moisture as possible. All of these factors lead to a maximum yield of 25hl/ha – so modest that it would make the Champenois (who routinely harvest triple that) sob. But the pay-off for the best wines here is concentration and detail, marrying saltiness and minerality with the energy of volcanic soil.

Hatzidakis' wines capture the essence of Santorini, particularly the uncompromising 'Nykteri' and lush and oak-accented 'Louros'. Not everybody appreciates such a distinctive style, but Haridimos attracted a well deserved cult following. The wines, like the man, have big personalities ("Assyrtiko needs a certain level of alcohol to release its aromatic characteristics," he once told me). 'Louros', in particular, is among the best whites of the Mediterranean.

Those looking for a more 'classic' take on Santorini can also find plenty to excite. At Gaia, Yiannis Paraskevopoulos and Leon Karatsalos define the chiselled, mineral style with 'Thalassitis', while the 'Estate' Assyrtiko by Argyros and the PDO Santorini bottling from Sigalas deliver a saline hit of volcanic rock and preserved lemon. Although these four are the most-talked-about wineries on Santorini, a handful of more recent projects has brought new blood. Apostolos Thymiopoulos, for instance, is best known for working with Xinomavro in northern Greece (see previous chapter), but his Santorini wines under the Acroterra label have made a big impact. Just as interesting is Vassaltis, where Yiannis Valambous produces elegant Assyrtikos. As well as classic and 'Barrel Aged' cuvées, he now makes a *pét nat* and boundary-pushing wine aged under flor that prove this is *the* Santorini address to watch. Likewise, Mikra Thira, a project backed by Biblia Chora, a renowned winery from the Greek mainland, is full of promise. "The thing I love most

Opposite, middle: *Kouloura* basket vine.

Opposite, right: Paris Sigalas.

NOBLE ROT

about drinking Santorini is that you can really connect the wines with the terroir," says winemaker Ioanna Vamvakouri, who is focusing on the vineyards of Thirassia, a small island adjacent to Santorini that falls under the same PDO. "Understanding the distinctive character of the different sub-zones is the next step for the island's wines."

Ioanna is not the only person fascinated by single-village/vineyard wines. Hatzidakis makes 'Louros' exclusively from vineyards in Pyrgos, and Sigalas makes a single-vineyard wine from 'Kavalieros' in Imerovigli. He also recently released the first vintage of his '7 Villages' project, a set of wines from the island's most distinctive terroirs all made in an identical way, fermented and matured in steel tanks to minimise winemaking influence. The results are fascinating, from the richer 'Akrotiri' (a hot area in the south) to the more perfumed 'Pyrgos' (the island's highest vineyard zone) and elegant, salty tang of 'Megalochori' (a well-exposed coastal site). Still, not everyone is convinced. Stefanos Georgas, former winemaker at Argyros, believes more is achieved by blending terroirs. "Single-village wines only show one face of Santorini," he says. "Pyrgos gives you something great, but what am I missing? Whatever it is, I get it from Imerovigli or Episkopi."

This tradition of blending can also be seen in Argyros' Vinsanto, a luscious sweet dessert wine from which the Vinsanto name originates (despite the Italians co-opting it). Lots of wineries produce Vinsanto, but Argyros' 12-and 20-year-old bottlings are brilliant, complex wines that have the quality of others that sell for ten times the price. Owner Matthew Argyros is rightly proud of this "very old tradition of Santorini", but is apprehensive about the future. "Real estate is the big enemy of the local vineyards," he says. "We need to find a balance between development and respect for the natural landscape." With talk of an application to UNESCO to get World Heritage status bestowed on the vineyards, moves are afoot. Home to the oldest continuously farmed vineyards anywhere in the world, Santorini's heritage should be cherished.

Above: The caldera, Santorini.

English Sparkling Wine

IT'S AUGUST and the sky is thick with black clouds as we drive south from London. By the time we get to Hampshire, the rain is beating down so hard that driving conditions, let alone grape-growing conditions, are treacherous. So far, so English. But after we park and make a dash through the downpour to Hambledon Vineyards, stereotypes are left behind. English sparkling wine has come of age, and the Champenois could soon have a fight on their hands.

It's not news that English fizz has kicked-on immeasurably, but there seems to be an increased confidence in the air. At Hambledon, owner Ian Kellet exudes the self-assurance of someone who made a fortune in the City before embarking on a dream to "make the pre-eminent English wine, bar none". Kellet arrived in the village known as the 'cradle of cricket' in 1999, purchasing England's oldest commercial vineyard – planted in 1952 – and building a gravity-fed winery (one that eschews pumps to allow gravity to naturally move wine through phases of production). At the time he studied oenology at Plumpton College and planted a ten-acre test bed to conduct trials on various variety, clone and rootstock combinations with the help of Champagne Pol Roger. Grapes from the first harvests were sold off to other English sparkling producers, before Hambledon released its inaugural 'Classic Cuvée' (2014) and 'Première Cuvée' (2015). Both wines are impressive, with good tension and minerality – something Kellet attributes to the terroir. "Chalk matters," he says. "It's not a lie that England has the same soils as Champagne, it's just that many English estates haven't chosen them and stand on green sandstone." Limestone bedrock forms an arch that cuts through parts of Dorset, Hampshire, Sussex and Kent, diving under the English Channel and re-emerging in northern France.

The importance of soils is shared by winemaker Dermot Sugrue, an affable Irishman making Wiston Estate wines 30 miles east of Hambledon. "The terroir discussion is going to be really important over the next ten to 20 years, and I'm very excited about it," he says, convinced that expressing

Opposite: Hampshire, southern England.

differences between the southern counties and their vineyards is key to
unlocking England's potential. Wiston Estate is a bucolic, 6,000-acre estate
in the South Downs National Park, with 16 acres of chalk planted with
Chardonnay, Pinot Noir and Pinot Meunier, although the winery is housed
in the less-salubrious confines of an old turkey slaughterhouse. Sugrue was
tempted away from his old job making wine for Nyetimber to plant vineyards
here in 2006, and uses a rare traditional Coquard press – the efficacy of which
he became convinced of while working in Champagne. "I love Champagne,
particularly the Growers – they are making the most interesting wines
over there. I also like *Grandes Marques* such as Pol Roger and Jacquesson,"
he says.

Back at Hambledon, many of the big French houses come in for criticism
from Kellet: "The quality of *Grande Marque* Champagne is, broadly speaking,
awful. Provenance is now very important, but to a large extent the main houses
don't even grow their own grapes." He can smell Champenois blood, even if
they remain oblivious. "At the moment they're not interested, because English
sparkling wine is tiny, but within ten years it's going to be all over the front
pages of the newspapers. There's going to be a war. They're going to be livid."
Kellet predicts that English sparkling wine could take 25% of Champagne's

Above: Dermot Sugrue,
Wiston Estate, West Sussex.

UK market share – its biggest export market – over the next decade, and is convinced that a lack of supply is one of the only things holding back the industry's development.

But while he and others bemoan the shortage of English wine, a surge in plantings over recent years has taken the total area under vine in the UK up to an estimated 3500 ha. With the public starting to be proud of English fizz, and potential in major export markets such as the USA, producers are seeing additional plantings as an opportunity for growth. Of course, high-quality is essential for its reputation, and it is here that the naysayers have plenty to say. Some critics say that some famous names are commercialising their wines before they are ready, without them having spent enough time on their lees. "Ageing is fundamental – you must be patient with the wine," says Sugrue.

There are other quality-related factors, such as the plantings of Seyval Blanc, Müller-Thurgau and various hybrid grape varieties that have been loyally defended by hobbyists and farmers for years. Now, the influx of expertise and money over recent years has not only shifted focus to better tasting Chardonnay, Pinot Noir and Pinot Meunier, but also on to the clones and rootstocks best suited to this rain-sodden climate. And then there is the chalk. Like Kellet says, "chalk matters", and there is only so much to go around. The Champenois figured out long ago that the soils of the Côte des Blancs should be reserved for Chardonnay, while the sandier and more clay-rich soils were better suited to the Pinots. Harnessing the potential of different terroirs and understanding what should be planted where will be crucial in delivering English quality long term, and is what makes Grower Champagne so compelling today. Over the Welsh border in Monmouthshire, Ancre Hill uses biodynamic farming for a very good Blanc de Noirs, and there is growing interest in the wines of Ben Walgate at Tillingham and Adrian Pike at Westwell. Both are experimenting with ageing Ortega in amphora and making delicious lightly sparkling *pét nat*. With climate change and improvements in viticulture and winemaking, are we witnessing the roots of our own growers' scene? Whatever the case, it's clear that English sparkling wine is now a genuine alternative to Champagne.

Rot 100

Here's a few of the vinous madeleines that we cherish most.

Dan

1862	TTC Lomelino Verdelho
1945	Château Haut-Brion
1950	Château Lafleur
1971	Salon Champagne 'Le Mesnil'
1978	Jacques Puffenay Arbois Vin Jaune
1978	Domaine de Montille Volnay 1er Cru 'Les Taillepieds'
1985	Domaine Ponsot Clos de la Roche 'Vieilles Vignes'
1988	Krug Champagne Vintage
1988	Robert Jasmin Côte-Rôtie
1989	Clos Rougeard Saumur Champigny 'Le Bourg'
1990	Charles Joguet Chinon 'Clos de la Dioterie'
1990	Jean-Louis Chave Hermitage
1991	Noël Verset Cornas
1996	Coche-Dury Meursault 'Les Rougeots'
1996	Domaine Roulot Meursault 1er Cru 'Les Perrières'
1999	Domaine de la Romanée-Conti La Tâche
2000	Raveneau Chablis Grand Cru 'Les Clos'
2002	Comte Liger-Belair La Romanée
2003	Château Rayas 'Pignan'
2005	Soldera Brunello di Montalcino Riserva
2006	Bartolo Mascarello Barolo
2007	Weingut Keller Riesling 'Kirchspiel' GG
2008	Jacques-Frédéric Mugnier Chambolle-Musigny 1er Cru 'Les Amoureuses'
2010	Houillon-Overnoy Arbois Pupillin Poulsard
NV	Jacques Selosse Brut Rosé

Mark

1945	Château Mouton Rothschild
1955	Giacomo Conterno Barolo Riserva 'Monfortino'
1961	Château Haut-Brion
1964	R López de Heredia Rioja Gran Reserva
1982	Château Pichon Longueville Comtesse de Lalande
1989	Raveneau Chablis Grand Cru 'Valmur'
1990	Coche-Dury Meursault
1990	Denis Bachelet Charmes-Chambertin
1990	Armand Rousseau Gevrey-Chambertin 1er Cru 'Clos St Jacques'
1991	Noël Verset Cornas
1994	Château Haut-Brion Blanc
1995	Château Rayas
1995	Domaine Gramenon Côtes du Rhône 'A Pascal S'
1996	Coche-Dury Meursault 'Les Rougeots'
1996	Domaine Roulot Meursault 1er Cru 'Les Perrières'
1998	Grange des Pères
2000	Sylvain Cathiard Romanée-St-Vivant
2002	Comte Liger-Belair La Romanée
2002	Ramonet Chassagne-Montrachet
2002	Armand Rousseau Chambertin
2007	Coche-Dury Corton-Charlemagne
2010	Domaine des Comtes Lafon Montrachet
2010	Auguste Clape Cornas
2011	Sandhi Chardonnay 'Sanford & Benedict'
2015	Hatzidakis Santorini 'Assyrtiko de Mylos'

Rotter HQ Favourite Regular Drinkers

Domaine Roulot Bourgogne Blanc

E & E Vocoret Chablis 'Le Bas de Chapelot'

Ulysse Collin 'Les Maillons'

Domaine Tissot Arbois Chardonnay 'Les Bruyères'

Guffens-Heynen Mâcon-Pierreclos
'1er Jus de Chavigne'

Jules Desjourneys Pouilly-Fuissé 'Vignes Blanches'

Thibaud Boudignon Savennières 'Clos de la Hutte'

Michel Gonet Extra Brut 'Mesnil Grand Cru'

Schafer Fröhlich Riesling 'Vulkangestein'

Château des Tours Côte du Rhône Blanc

André Perret Condrieu 'Coteau du Chery'

Sylvain Pataille Marsannay 'Clos du Roy'

Domaine de la Grand'Cour Fleurie
'Le Clos Cuvée Vieilles Vignes'

Maison MC Thiriet Côte de Nuits-Villages 'Aux

Montagnes'

Philippe Alliet Chinon 'Coteau de Noiré'

Stella di Campalto Rosso di Montalcino

Paolo Bea Sagrantino di Montefalco 'Pagliaro'

Montevertine Toscana IGT

Envínate Ribeira Sacra 'Lousas Parcela
Camiño Novo'

Dalamára Naoussa 'Paliokalias'

Ten Beautiful Wine Regions to Visit

Côte d'Or, Burgundy

Beaujolais

Anjou-Saumur, Loire

Barolo, Piedmont

Montalcino, Tuscany

Mount Etna, Sicily

Ribeira Sacra, Galicia

Mosel Valley, Germany

Santorini, Greece

Santa Barbara, California

Ten Exciting and Unusual Wines

Les Vignes de Paradis Chasselas 'Sous Voile'

Domaine Bizot 'Les Violettes'

Selosse 'Substance'

Suertes del Marques 'Vidonia'

Els Jelipins Rosado

R López de Heredia Rioja Rosado

Cota 45 'Ube Miraflores'

Armand Rousseau Bourgogne Blanc

Gravner Ribolla

Scholium Project 'The Prince in His Caves'

Ten Most Mouth-Watering Wine Lists

Tour d'Argent, Paris

Vantre, Paris

Les Bouteilles, Nantes

Le Bout du Monde, Beaune

Laredo, Madrid

Villa Más, Catalonia

Rekondo, San Sebastián

Kaia-Kaipe, Basque Country

Pasquale Jones, New York

The Modern, New York

Glossary

Appellation
In France an AOC (*appellation d'origine contrôlée*) or AOP (*appellation d'origine protégée*) is the district where a wine is certified to have come from. See also DO, DOCa (Spain), DOCG (Italy), VDP (Germany) and PDO (Greece).

Barrique
A relatively small wooden barrel used for fermenting and/or ageing wine, the most commonly used of which are the Bordeaux *barrique* (which holds 225 litres) and the Burgundy *barrique* (228 litres).

Biodynamic viticulture
A form of farming and vineyard management based on the teachings of Rudolph Steiner.

Blanc de Blancs
Champagne made exclusively from white grapes, typically Chardonnay.

Blanc de Noirs
Champagne made exclusively from red grapes, typically Pinot Noir and Pinot Meunier.

Botti
Large Italian wood casks for fermenting and/or ageing wine. Typically made of Slavonian oak.

Col fondo
Traditional style of artisanal Prosecco made using the ancestral method.

Crémant
French term for sparkling wines made outside of Champagne using the same 'traditional method' of production.

Cru
French word for a vineyard, or 'growth'. A 'Cru Classé' is one that has been classified. 'Premier Cru' and 'Grand Cru' have specific meanings, depending on the region where they are used.

Cuvée
A specific batch of wine.

Dosage
A sugary final addition to sparkling wine that determines sweetness.

Élevage
The process of ageing, or 'raising', a wine between fermentation and bottling.

Field blend
A mixture of different grape varieties planted within the same vineyard.

First Growth
The top five châteaux in the Haut-Médoc, Bordeaux: Latour, Lafite, Margaux, Haut-Brion and Mouton Rothschild.

Foudre
Large French wood casks for fermenting and/or ageing wine. Typically made of French oak.

Grande Marque
Large producer, typically a *négociant*, in Champagne. Translates as 'great brand'.

Grosses Gewächs
Superior category for German dry wines launched by VDP in 2002.

Joven, Crianza, Reserva, Gran Reserva
Classifications relating to the duration of *élevage* of Spanish wines in some DOs.

Kabinett / Spätlese / Auslese
Three common *Prädikat* categories of German Rieslings relating to grape ripeness at harvest.

Lieu-dit
The given name of a specific plot of land within a larger appellation (although not an appellation itself).

Monopole
French term for a vineyard that belongs to a single owner.

Négociant
A producer who buys grapes or wine from third parties to sell under their own label.

Noble rot
A.k.a. *Botrytis cinerea*, a fungus that, given the right conditions, shrivels ripe white grapes on the vine, concentrating their sugars and making them ideal for producing the world's finest sweet wines.

NV
Non-vintage wine made by blending the production of different years.

Ouillé
French term for a wine that has been regularly topped up while ageing in barrel to produce a fresh, orthodox style. Used in the Jura to differentiate it from non-topped-up, *'sous-voile'* and oxidative styles.

Own-rooted vine
A vine that has not been grafted on to an American rootstock to protect against phylloxera.

Passito
Italian term for a wine made from dried grapes.

Pétillant naturel (pét nat)
Lightly sparkling wines made by the ancestral method of stoppering a wine while still fermenting in bottle so that carbon dioxide can't escape and is absorbed into the wine.

Phylloxera
Aphid that attacks the roots of vines and gained notoriety by devastating vast swathes of European vineyards in the late 19th century.

Premature oxidation
A.k.a. Premox, a problem famously affecting white Burgundy, as well as other wine regions, where seemingly random bottles oxidise at an unusually rapid rate and become out of condition long before their time.

Solera
A system of barrel-ageing and fractional blending commonly used for consistency in Sherry.

Sous-voile
Term used in Jura for wines made 'under a veil' of yeast cells, producing a style reminiscent of some Sherries (where the veil is called 'flor').

Terroir
French definition of a vineyard's total natural environment. Wines of 'terroir' have a unique sense of 'somewhereness'.

Traditional method
A technique to produce high-quality sparkling wine through a secondary fermentation inside bottle. Previously known as the *méthode Champenoise*.

Trockenbeerenauslese
Official category (in Germany and Austria) of rare and costly-to-produce sweet wine, made from grapes affected by noble rot that are selected berry by berry.

Vigneron
Grower-winemaker with weathered hands and dirt under their nails.

Village wine
Burgundian term for a wine made from grapes grown in vineyards assigned a village-level appellation, eg Vosne-Romanée.

Vintage
Can mean either the year that a wine was made, or the physical process of the harvest.

Volatile acidity
A wine fault at high levels, when it can smell like nail-polish remover and/or vinegar. In smaller doses it can add complexity and lift.

Wine Bore
Relax – try not to be one...

Index

Picture credits

All photography by Benjamin McMahon apart from:

Tom Cockram, pages 19, 21 (top row) centre, 24–25, 111,
233, 267-270, 318–27, 329, 332–7;

Juan Trujillo Andrades, page 20 (top row) left (4th row)
left (5th row) right; 21 (top row) right, (2nd row) centre & right,
(5th row) centre left; 26, 40–5, 54–5, 60–1, 87 above right & left;
89, 159–165, 189–92, 205, 206 above right & below, 208–11,
226–31, 236–42, 245, 247, 260–65, 272–6, 279 below, 282, 309–17;

Alex Lockett, page 20 (top row) far right;

Tom Sheehan, page 20 (3rd row) far left;

Dan Medhurst, page 21 (top row) far left;

Elena Heatherwick, pages 21 (3rd row) far left; 30 & 108;

London Metropolitan Archives, City of London
(Collage: the London Picture Archive, ref. 73094), page 28 above;

London Metropolitan Archives, City of London
(Collage: the London Picture Archive, ref. 133802), page 31;

Rick Pushinsky, pages 169 & 173;

Jon Wyand, pages 179–80;

Gail Skoff, pages 206 above left & centre;

Gravner archive - photo Maurizio Frullani, pages 279 above & 283;

Gravner archive - photo Alvise Barsanti, pages 280–1;

Robert Billington, pages 339–40;

Artworks by:

Dan Keeling, inner front & back covers;

Egle Zvirblyte, page 1;

Jose Mendez, pages 2, 46, 68, 71;

weloveyoyo, page 6;

Matthieu Bessudo, page 15;

Bob Johnson, Johnson Design, Healdsburg, CA,
www.behance.net/9trebor9, pages 20, 51 & 53;

Adam Batchelor, page 29;

Michael de Forge, pages 56, 64;

Mark Long, pages 94, 104–7;

Lilli Gärtner / www.lilligaertner.de, page 122;

Nancy Keeling, page 124;

New Order *Blue Monday* Album Artwork,
Licensed courtesy of Warner Music UK Ltd, page 128;

Pixies *Doolittle* (P) 1989 Licenced Courtesy of 4AD Ltd
By arrangement with Beggars Group Media Ltd, page 129

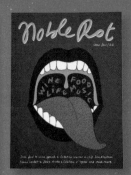

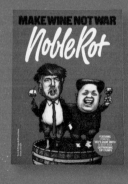

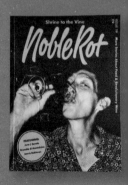
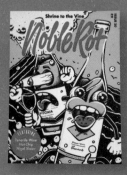

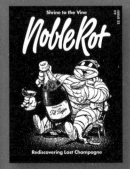

Publishing Director and Editor: Sarah Lavelle
Art Direction: Dan Keeling and David Tanguy
Design: Praline
Cover Design: Kellenberger–White
Copy Editor: Nick Funnell
Head of Design, Quadrille: Claire Rochford
Picture Research: Samantha Rolfe-Hoang
Head of Production: Stephen Lang
Production Controller: Nikolaus Ginelli

First published in 2020 by Quadrille,
an imprint of Hardie Grant Publishing

Quadrille
52–54 Southwark Street
London SE1 1UN
quadrille.com

Cataloguing in Publication Data: a catalogue record for this book
is available from the British Library.

ISBN 978 1 78713 271 9

Reprinted in 2020 (twice), 2021
10 9 8 7 6 5 4

Printed in China

FSC
www.fsc.org
MIX
Paper from
responsible sources
FSC™ C020056

ACKNOWLEDGEMENTS

Noble Rot is a magazine and two restaurants, but it is also an idea connecting wine, food and creative arts lovers. We've been helped by so many like-minded souls that it is almost impossible to name everyone here. Writers, illustrators, photographers, graphic designers, sub-editors, proofreaders, printers, distributors, stockists, chefs, waiters and waitresses, winemakers, interviewees, cleaners, crowdfunding supporters, lawyers, accountants, investors, readers, diners and imbibers: thank you all – you know who you are.

Wine from Another Galaxy would not have been possible without the love and support of our wives, Naomi Keeling and Magdalena Andrew, and families. Special thanks must also go to Tim Bates at Peters Fraser + Dunlop, who tenaciously pursued the idea of a *Noble Rot* book, Sarah Lavelle and the team at Quadrille, Marina O'Loughlin, Stephen Harris, Paul Weaver, Oliver McSwiney and Remus Brett.

We've been fortunate enough to have worked with some hugely talented creatives on this book, especially photographers Benjamin McMahon, Juan Trujillo Andrades and Tom Cockram; David Tanguy and Michael Curia at Praline design studio; Kellenberger-White; Emily McBean; Rachel Dalton, who designs Noble Rot magazine and added extra layout ideas; Nick Funnell, who corrected our gramma, and Zeren Wilson for additional words. Lastly, a big shout to Jeremy Leslie at magCulture and Alex Bond for picking up the phone and lending their magazine design advice whenever we've called. Chin-chin.

Dan Keeling and Mark Andrew co-founded Noble Rot magazine in 2013, and restaurants of the same name in Bloomsbury in 2015 and Soho in 2020. Dan has won three Louis Roederer Awards and a Fortnum & Mason Award for his writing about wine and food. In his previous career in music he was managing director of Island Records and head of A&R at Parlophone Records, where he signed Coldplay and Bombay Bicycle Club, among others. Mark Andrew is a Master of Wine who previously worked as head buyer at a renowned London merchant. Dan and Mark founded wine merchant and importer Keeling Andrew & Co in 2017.